AFTER AUGUST

After August

BLUES, AUGUST WILSON, AND AMERICAN DRAMA

Patrick Maley

UNIVERSITY OF VIRGINIA PRESS
Charlottesville and London

University of Virginia Press
© 2019 by the Rector and Visitors of the University of Virginia
All rights reserved
Printed in the United States of America on acid-free paper

First published 2019

9 8 7 6 5 4 3 2 1

Library of Congress Cataloging-in-Publication Data
Names: Maley, Patrick, 1981– author.
Title: After August : blues, August Wilson, and American drama / Patrick Maley.
Description: Charlottesville : University of Virginia Press, 2019. | Includes bibliographical references and index.
Identifiers: LCCN 2018055530 (print) | LCCN 2018059205 (ebook) | ISBN 9780813943022 (ebook) | ISBN 9780813942995 (cloth : alk. paper) | ISBN 9780813943008 (pbk. : alk. paper)
Subjects: LCHS: Wilson, August—Criticism and interpretation. | Historical drama, American—History and criticism. | African Americans in literature. | Blues (Music) in literature. | Identity (Psychology) in literature. | American drama—20th century—History and criticism.
Classification: LCC PS3573.I45677 (ebook) | LCC PS 3573.I45677 Z77 2019 (print) | DDC 812/.54—dc23
LC record available at https://lccn.loc.gov/2018055530

Cover photo: Used by permission of the estate of August Wilson

For Jackie

Contents

Acknowledgments ix

Introduction: Identity, Performance,
and the American Dramatic Tradition 1

Part I. Blues Dramaturgy

1. Blues and the Social Human 17
2. "I Am the Blues": August Wilson as Bluesman 42
3. August Wilson's Blues 63

Part II. Performance, Identity, and Reimagining American Drama

4. "God A'mighty, I Be Lonesomer'n Ever!":
   Eugene O'Neill's Aesthetic of Whiteness 111
5. "Laws of Silence Don't Work": Tennessee Williams
   and the Problem of Sexualized Masculinity 141

6. August Wilson's Legacy and Its Limits:
   Worrying the Line in Katori Hall and Tarell Alvin McCraney   169

   Notes   203
   Bibliography   219
   Index   229

Acknowledgments

IDEAS FOR THIS BOOK emerged in the contemplative wake of theater. I saw Eugene O'Neill's *Beyond the Horizon* at the Irish Repertory Theatre in New York, and then August Wilson's *Jitney* several days later at Two River Theater in Red Bank, NJ. The heaviness of O'Neill's tragedy, rendered with full destructive force by director Ciarán O'Reilly and brought wrenchingly to life by Wrenn Schmidt's Ruth, sat with me for days and accompanied me to Red Bank. Ruben Santiago-Hudson's production of *Jitney* made unmistakable the compassion that Wilson offers his characters, and revealed O'Neill's reticence to do the same. After *Jitney, Beyond the Horizon* became a play about characters suffering under the unrelenting force of a pitiless tragedian, and Wilson's world emerged as one more understanding of human flaws. After seeing both plays on stage, neither was the same.

My first gratitude for this book must therefore go to theaters and artists who are committed to vibrant productions of challenging drama. Along with Two River and the Irish Rep, I thank specifically (though not exclusively) the theaters that have stimulated my thinking by allowing me to see productions of plays under discussion in the following pages: Signature Theatre Company, McCarter Theatre, Luna Stage, Howard University Department of Theatre Arts, Brooklyn Academy of Music, Manhattan Theatre

Club, Goodman Theatre, Target Margin Theater, Roundabout Theatre Company, American Repertory Theater, and The Greene Space. Many of the ideas in this book and elsewhere in my scholarship owe a great debt to the American theater, which continues to shape me intellectually and emotionally.

Much of my access to theater has been afforded by work as a critic. I am grateful to Patricia Bradford at *STAGE Magazine* for welcoming me into the critical fold, and to Richard Patterson and Molly Grogan at *Exeunt Theatre Magazine,* and Christopher Kelly at *NJ Advanced Media* for opportunities to share my thoughts, delights, and occasional misgivings about live theater. I (and my students) have also benefited from the generosity of theater artists Brandon Dirden, Crystal Dickinson, Ruben Santiago-Hudson, Stephen McKinley Henderson, and other members of the August Wilson community who have been willing to share their passion.

I wrote this book while a faculty member at Centenary University, work that could not have been accomplished without the vision and support of Barbara Lewthwaite and Jim Patterson. I thank both for their dedication to fostering a culture of research. I extend special gratitude to Sharon Decker, whose tireless support and encouragement have had a deep impact on this book and my career. Colleagues Robert Battistini and Richard Sévère made valuable contributions to my thinking about and writing of this project, and my research benefited consistently from the work of the team at the Taylor Memorial Library, especially Tim Domick and Steve Macmillan. I am grateful for the opportunity to work through the ideas of this book in collaboration with some extraordinary Centenary students: Angela Chiu, Nicole Fisher, Michael Fortino, Michelle Graf, Joseph Marra, Taylor Ruszczyk, Deanna Ryan, Leora Shahay, Jonathan Steinberg, Tyler Thurgood, Kiersten Toye, and Alexandra Wechsler. For financial support, I thank Centenary's Faculty Research and Development fund and the Office of Academic Affairs.

The exchange of ideas with colleagues beyond Centenary has also been immeasurably fruitful. Andy Oler, Kevin Riordan, Patricia Schroeder, and Shane Vogel read portions of this manuscript and improved it through their feedback. Annika Mann, Jenny Mann, Jennifer Smith, Maura Smyth, Stephen Watt, and Adam Gussow were very helpful at various points in the research, writing, and publishing process. Adam Gussow's modernbluesharmonica.com and David Barrett's bluesharmonica.com have been particularly influential to my thinking about blues music and its history. My appreciation for the generosity of Shane Vogel and Stephen Watt cannot be understated.

Eric Brandt and Helen Chandler at the University of Virginia Press have been invaluable guides through the uncertain terrain of publishing a first book, and the feedback of my anonymous peer reviewers improved the book drastically.

Much of this work benefited from the engagement of colleagues at the Comparative Drama Conference, the Northeast MLA Convention, the August Wilson Society, the American Studies Association Annual Meeting, the Transforming Contagion Symposium, Centenary's Faculty Research Forum, and the Louisville Conference on Literature and Culture since 1900.

I offer warm thanks to Dad, Susan, Melissa, Susie, and Richard for the support, encouragement, and patience of family.

Like all my undertakings, this book has benefited enormously from the staggering love and generosity of my wonderful wife, Jackie, to whom I offer my humblest gratitude, appreciation, and love, and the promise of a lifetime full of overly long hugs.

AFTER AUGUST

INTRODUCTION

Identity, Performance, and the American Dramatic Tradition

FROM LATE AUGUST THROUGH the end of September in 2013, New York City radio stations WNYC and WQXR curated dramatic readings of all ten plays from August Wilson's *American Century Cycle*. Under the artistic direction of Ruben Santiago-Hudson and Stephen McKinley Henderson, the series assembled contemporary theater's most preeminent Wilsonian actors and directors at New York's Greene Space to perform and preserve audio recordings of the plays. The event also featured six editions of an "August Wilson Talk Series," panel discussions on topics such as "Religion, Spirituality, and Africa," "Bringing Black Works to Broadway," and "The Women of the *American Century Cycle*." For a little over a month, Wilson's work and spirit held court in lower Manhattan. "Over the next five weeks," announced Santiago-Hudson on the evening the series opened, "we plan to set this city on fire with the spirit, passion, integrity, and truth of August Wilson."

The series did much to stress the complexity and logic internal to the *Cycle*. When *Radio Golf*'s Harmond Wilks announced that his grandfather was Caesar Wilks, for example, a knowing sigh came from the audience at The Greene Space, many of whom had met the infamous Caesar only four days earlier in the performance of *Gem of the Ocean*. Similar complexity became clear in *Seven Guitars* and *King Hedley II*, which occupied The Greene

Space only eight days apart. The first featured the vibrant Canewell and vivacious Ruby of 1946, and the latter presented Stool Pigeon, the mystic into whom Canewell ages by 1985, potentially unhinged by the psychological effects of his actions in the time between plays, and Ruby after a rough adulthood full of challenges and their repercussions. Similarly, the obstinate defiance of Troy Maxson in *Fences* grew more poignant and tragic when considered in comparison with Levee's same attitude in *Ma Rainey's Black Bottom*, performed only two days earlier.

These connections and others are evident in the play's scripts, but the performance series rendered them more vivid and essential. Over the course of the event, the plays melded more clearly and cohesively into the sort of unified whole that they only became more than twenty years after Wilson began writing them. It was not until the completion of his final play, *Radio Golf*, that something called the *American Century Cycle* could tenably be said to exist rather than be in progress. Thus, a performance series like the one at The Greene Space concentrates the experiences of thinking about individual *Cycle* plays in reference to the unified whole, perhaps allowing audiences to reassess the influence of Aunt Ester in 1990's *Two Trains Running*, for example, after finally meeting her in *Gem of the Ocean*, from 2001. That she never appears in *Two Trains* calls into question Holloway's faith and the strength of his character, but her work in *Gem* provides greater understanding of Holloway's spiritual journey. Performance of more contemporary work, that is, allows for more thorough reflection on its antecedent, encouraging fresh new thought about what has come before.

The series at The Greene Space helpfully demonstrates some of the methodology and goals of *After August*. Through performance, the series was able to engender a reassessment of the past through the lens of the present. The juxtaposition of contentious fatherhood in *Fences*, *Jitney*, and *King Hedley II*, for example, reveals the *Cycle*'s concern with the tension of generational inheritance. That theme emerges in 1987's *Fences*, reappears in 1996's *Jitney*, and does so again in 1999's *King Hedley*, each time repeating, revising, and directing audiences' gazes backward in history to look with fresh eyes at already familiar plays. *Fences*, that is, becomes a newer and richer play after the two later plays.[1] Regardless of their date of composition, each *Cycle* play relies on the nine others and the unified whole in order to unlock its greatest import, a condition made vivid through performance.[2]

This book argues that the same is true for the perpetually growing body of American drama, and that Wilson's work is an especially evocative interlocutor with modern and contemporary American plays. Eugene O'Neill's 1920 play *The Emperor Jones,* for example, becomes richer through the specific lens of *Gem of the Ocean,* which premiered over eighty years later. In O'Neill's play, the physical journey of an African American man quickly turns mystical, as the play's title character encounters ghostly visions of his past while wandering desperately through the jungle. Terrified by apparitions of men he's killed and others that have abused him or his ancestors, he reacts defensively, trying to shoot them. In *Gem,* Citizen Barlow takes a mystical journey to the City of Bones, a spiritual land under the Atlantic Ocean created and populated by the remains of African slaves killed during the Middle Passage. His trip is at once enlightening and healing: wracked by guilt, the character gains communion with his African ancestors, gives himself over to their influence, and emerges from the vision a more fully developed person. The process and result of Citizen Barlow's journey cast that of Brutus Jones in new light, showing Jones's missed opportunities for self-discovery while encountering experiences from his past. Jones violently resists the chance to work through the experiences and challenges presented to him in his visions, suggesting that he is perhaps not doomed from the outset but rather that he fails to undergo reparative self-discovery. Considering *The Emperor Jones* in light of the later *Gem of the Ocean,* that is, allows for a reconsideration of O'Neill's protagonist as on a potentially edifying journey thwarted by his own obstinate defensiveness. Citizen Barlow thrives because he allows himself to be vulnerable, revealing Brutus Jones's refusal of that condition.

In this way, contemporary audiences of American drama have the benefit of contextualizing the form's history within a broad historical landscape, reevaluating forebears through the lens of their successors. *After August* suggests that Wilson is particularly valuable in that regard, especially in light of his concern with the harrowing task of crafting a clear identity for one's self that is sustainable within a certain social sphere. The challenges of this process are paramount themes in Wilson's work, as they are throughout American drama. This theme exists in American plays throughout the twentieth and twenty-first centuries, but reexamining the field through the lens of Wilson opens productive new avenues for understanding how the search for sustainable identity lies at the very heart of the American dramatic tradition.

In the spring of 2017, for example, New York's Irish Repertory Theatre staged a production of *The Emperor Jones* whose excellence is only enhanced by allowing for the influence of Wilson. Director Ciarán O'Reilly created an expressionist world full of haunting masks and disquieting puppets, while Obi Abili's Brutus Jones grew more and more disturbed and ethereal as his torturous descent toward death hastened over the play's eighty minutes. With the help of evocative lights, setting, and sound, the play enveloped the Irish Rep's small space, transforming the theater into the jungle that swallows Jones and conscripting audience members into the environment of trees, shadows, and terrors. A revival, the production evoked memories of the theater's acclaimed 2009 *Emperor*, starring John Douglas Thompson and also directed by O'Reilly; in its stagecraft, it pointed back to the Provincetown Players' original 1920 production; and in its presentation of a black actor speaking the stilted dialect that O'Neill crafts for Jones, it recalled the many controversies and charges of racism that have attended the play's history. But in its mysticism, the production also evoked the voyage Citizen Barlow makes to the City of Bones accompanied by a small group of supporters, recontextualizing Jones's struggle. Allowing for this Wilsonian influence on O'Neill redefines the performative conditions at the Irish Rep by aligning audience members with Citizen's supportive community, offering the bodies sharing space with Abili's Emperor as potential but rejected support for his journey of self-discovery. Wilson, that is, allows for an enriched understanding of the Emperor's individualist obstinacy, revealing that Jones alienates not only the black island community but also the broader spiritual community. Wilson deepens an understanding of O'Neill's Jones as self-destructive in his stalwart individualism (a trend that chapter 4 demonstrates is pervasive throughout O'Neill's work).

The key that unlocks Wilson's influence for rethinking American drama is what *After August* calls his blues dramaturgy. In blues, Wilson found not simply a musical genre, but rather a performative mode of joining with community in a shared project of understanding the self and others vis-à-vis history, ancestry, art, spirituality, politics, pain, and joy. This became the foundation of his dramaturgy. The playwright made many claims about the social, spiritual, and historical importance of blues, but said very little about blues as music. Certainly blues entered his consciousness first as music—he cites a chance encounter with a Bessie Smith record as a moment of awakening—but although he says he knew the music spoke to and for him, his artistic drives would never lead him to music. "I don't play an instrument," he wrote, "I don't know any musical terms. And I don't know anything about music."[3] Still, he did not shy from making large claims about blues' significance, calling it "the book of black people ... an entire philosophical system at work," "the best literature we have as black Americans," and perhaps most significantly, "the wellspring of my art."[4] This juxtaposition between his lack of musical pursuits and his attribution of great influence to blues reveals that there is something other than blues' musicality that Wilson finds so significant. This book argues that the playwright identifies an ethos of performative, social self-crafting underpinning blues musicality and molds that ethos into a dramaturgy.

A blues ethos guided Wilson to use drama to examine personal and racial identity, developing a series of plays deeply concerned with their characters' attempts to craft and establish identities within limited social spheres. His plays take place in one space—a recording studio, a diner, a backyard, a taxi station—and his characters' efforts are directed almost entirely at establishing themselves within that space, convincing the other characters to recognize them as the person they would like to be, and freeing themselves from what Paul Carter Harrison calls "a constant psychic and spiritual liminality as they struggle for existential definition."[5] The struggle to escape this liminality is a process that *After August* calls social identity crafting, and the various degrees of success achieved by Wilson's characters depend in large part on how willing they are to recognize the necessary involvement of their audience in the antiphonal process—the call-and-response so typical of blues—of crafting a recognizable self. Troy Maxson, for example, tries to overpower his limited community into respecting him, and pays a great price for his hubris, while Citizen Barlow, on the other hand, eventually learns to receive the productive input of his community and incorporate it into his own performance of self. In both cases, and in many others throughout Wilson's *Cycle*, characters' identities rely on collaboration with their community, and the central conflict of the play hinges on the success of various projects of social identity crafting.

On the one hand, this dramatic method is influential because it paved the way for a generation of Wilson's successors to respond to questions of identity, particularly revolving around African American experience. Wilson's blues is a dramaturgy concerned with initiating and cultivating call-and-response dialogue, first with a small, potentially like-minded community, and then incrementally with broader social spheres. Antiphony about questions of identity lies at the heart of Wilson's blues dramaturgy, and twenty-first-century playwrights have regularly adopted the strategy in ways that bear clear markers of Wilson's influence. Particularly compelling successors to Wilson, like Katori Hall and Tarell Alvin McCraney, who are the focus of chapter 6, find room for their own methodology by repeating Wilson with a difference, building off his example into something distinctively their own, but it remains nonetheless clear that Wilson's unique approach to the question of black identity provided his successors with new dramaturgical tools.

In other important ways, attention to Wilson's blues dramaturgy is revelatory of concerns and strategies pervading the American dramatic tradition that includes work of playwrights preceding his career. The challenge of social identity crafting is a powerful trend in plays by Eugene O'Neill and Tennessee Williams in particular, both of whom wrestle constantly with the tension between self and other with a view to crafting a recognizable, sustainable self. Many American dramatists foreground the challenge of developing a clear sense of self, but Wilson's dramaturgy is especially enlightening with regard to O'Neill and Williams, whose influential work treats the challenge of self-actualization as a master theme. Reexamination of how these writers treat their characters' daunting existential challenges can yield productive new insights throughout the long, sinewy paths of their influence. The responses of Wilson's characters to uncertainty about and threats to their social identities elucidate the great difficulty Williams's men often face responding to restrictive social demands for masculinity, and the woeful repercussions that many of O'Neill's characters endure for feeling entitled to avoid the sociality of identity crafting. In short, thinking through Wilson's dramaturgy opens fresh avenues into the plays of O'Neill and Williams, and reveals American drama's obsession with performing the conflicted self within uncertain social terrain.

Of course, to approach the work of O'Neill and Williams through the lens of Wilson presents certain obvious challenges. The first is history. O'Neill and Williams significantly predate Wilson, and claims of influence usually run along neat chronological lines so that the predecessor influences the successor. This familiar approach guides the discussions of Katori Hall and Tarell Alvin McCraney in chapter 6, but the chapters on O'Neill and Williams presume that valuable precepts from Wilson can enrich understanding of his predecessors. Certainly *After August* does not claim that O'Neill or Williams were influenced as writers by a dramatist whose career flourished after their deaths, but the book does insist that audiences and critics of American drama can and should subvert historical stricture to allow for greater intertextual flow. As experiences in the present can help one recontextualize and better understand experiences in the past, encounters with contemporary art do the same for art that preceded it. Rarely does anybody think about the work of Aeschylus independently of his successor Sophocles; few consider Christopher Marlowe outside the lens of his successor Shakespeare. Harold Bloom argues that this is because the power of Shakespeare's work subsumes Marlowe's, but a more pedestrian approach suggests that Shakespeare changed the game of early modern English drama in ways that shine new light on what Marlowe was doing earlier. *After August* argues that Wilson similarly offers audiences new tools with which to examine his predecessors. "August Wilson shook the American theater until it finally began to part its eyes and see all of its invisible men and women," suggests Marion McClinton, a frequent director of Wilson's work.[6] This unsettling of the American dramatic tradition in the late twentieth and early twenty-first century offers a productive opportunity to rethink the tradition with new perspective. Emerging there are not only invisible men and women but also the harrowing performative process by which these characters attempt to make themselves visible.

The other challenge with putting Wilson and his blues dramaturgy in conversation with O'Neill and Williams is race. Despite the spread of blues music into white audiences and performers, blues remains a distinctively African American aesthetic that arose out of social conditions of blackness in the early twentieth century; Amiri Baraka in fact calls blues "autonomous black music."[7] Art forms will almost always break the bounds of their origin (and the history of popular music shows how white artists are particularly eager to appropriate black styles), but blues remains always in reference to blackness. In similar terms, Wilson's work clings to the black experience in America. "Without the characteristic schizophrenia of Du Boisian double consciousness," points out Sandra G. Shannon, "Wilson depicts an African American cultural identity that can and must naturally and unapologetically exist both separate from and apart from American society."[8] As Shannon and others recognize, Wilson's primary goal as a dramatist was to understand black life in America, and his strategy for doing so was to home in on elements like dignity, family, community, and ritual that prove particularly consistent concerns throughout black history. To take this material into the terrain of white drama risks evacuating its power of specificity.

It would therefore be inaccurate to claim that O'Neill and Williams deploy blues techniques, and this book does not make such a claim. But it is productive to allow the blues techniques of Wilson to reveal central concerns in the earlier playwrights. Attention to how Wilson responds to the black American experience, that is, illuminates O'Neill's and Williams's particular methods of crafting their own characters' crises of identity, allowing for new questions of O'Neill and Williams, producing fruitful new understandings of their plays. At the core of Wilson's project is an examination of identity, and it is here that his plays provide useful tools for rethinking many contributors to the American dramatic tradition. Fundamental to Wilson's blues dramaturgy is the tentative performance of self before what one hopes is a like-minded and empathetic audience willing to respond to that performance with recognition. This social process is the thread that leads from Wilson throughout American drama. The plays of Williams and O'Neill in particular prove consistently to hinge on the process of social identity crafting, concerned especially with how their characters negotiate the complicated nexus of self, other, and social conditions. Wilson's dynamic and complex portrait of black Americans embroiled in this process throws a penetrating light on the struggles of Williams's sexualized men and O'Neill's destructively lonely characters.

Wilson is particularly important in this vein because, as Harry J. Elam has shown, the playwright's work concerns itself with revisiting, recontextualizing, and ultimately redrafting history. For Wilson, the present, which is merely the most current manifestation of timeless conditions and tensions, exists in constant dialogue with the past; history evolves and changes its shape as the present unfurls. This is why Wilson's *American Century Cycle*, although written over the course of about twenty years, is best considered as a breathing, dynamic, unified whole. With each new play in the *Cycle*, Wilson's existing work and identity as a playwright changed shape, and when the *Cycle* reached its conclusion it demanded a reevaluation of its constituent parts as well as its wholeness. Examining that wholeness underscores the importance of thinking backward through aesthetic history, allowing successors to affect an examination of their predecessors.

This is of course possible only by accepting the invitation of latter-day works to revisit earlier plays. Hans-Georg Gadamer's notion of the aesthetic qualities of art relying upon lived experience is helpful in enabling such an approach. "The experience of art," he says, "should not be falsified by being turned into a possession of aesthetic culture, thus neutralizing its special claim." Such an aesthetic culture can be time-bound and historical, as if to say that O'Neill's plays belong strictly to early twentieth-century American culture. Rather, Gadamer continues, "*all encounter with the language of art is an encounter with an unfinished event and is itself part of this event*" (emphasis in original).⁹ As Gadamer suggests, the encounter of audience or critic or reader with a play contributes actively and constantly to the aesthetic development of that play; the unfinished event never concludes. Thus, audiences who encountered *The Iceman Cometh* in 2015 at the Brooklyn Academy of Music, for example, contributed to the unfinished event that is O'Neill's play as actively as did audiences at its 1946 premiere or at any time between the two productions. But a 2015 audience potentially brings with it experience gleaned from any number of plays written and performed after 1946, and so *Iceman* finds itself in conversation with and influenced by O'Neill's successors.

Drama does not therefore develop as a series of stolid, time-stamped artifacts that progress forward in an orderly fashion, but is rather always in productive conversation with predecessors and successors. Every time a play appears on stage it presents itself anew, initiating a fresh dialogue with the dramatic tradition. In her work on contemporary drama, Soyica Diggs Colbert rightly rejects "the idea of influence as a one-way street," arguing instead for conceptualizing influence "as a feedback loop that infuses dramatic works with fragments that disrupt a linear formulation of influence."¹⁰ That feedback results from a long and continued history of performance and production, and Colbert's notion of the loop speaks to the musical practice of harnessing and deploying the sounds of feedback. Ruben Santiago-Hudson's 2012 production of *The Piano Lesson,* for example, feeds back through landmarks like Lloyd Richards's premiere 1987 staging, and the 1995 television adaptation, all of which feed back through earlier dramatizations of African American family like Lorraine Hansberry's *A Raisin in the Sun,* itself making a fresh statement with the Kenny Leon's 2014 Broadway production. At each step along the way, performance invites audiences to reinvestigate and rethink earlier plays. "Performance," says Colbert, "enables an active engagement with the past that transforms not only what will be but also what was."¹¹ Indeed, performance insists that not even long-ago-written monuments of the stage are immune to fresh influence, as the dramatic tradition remains consistently dynamic and evolving.

The Greene Space series made this concept vivid in the work of August Wilson, but *After August* suggests that backward-looking influence is a fundamental notion for conceptualizing aesthetic intertextuality, and particularly enlightening for American drama. American drama, that is, need not be the case of playwrights like Susan Glaspell, Eugene O'Neill, Arthur Miller,

August Wilson, Suzan-Lori Parks, and Annie Baker making chronologically successive contributions to a progressing field; rather, each of these artists and any number of others force a reassessment of the field in its entirety, including the work of earlier artists. Rather than operating as a one-way timeline, American drama operates in the rhizomatic model of aesthetics offered by Deleuze and Guattari or, to employ a blues concept, in the mode of Houston A. Baker's notion of a matrix: "a point of ceaseless input and output, a web of intersecting, crisscrossing impulses always in productive transit." Baker points to the railway juncture as an example of this matrix, a place "marked by transience. Its inhabitants are always travelers—a multifarious assembly in transit."[12] Conceiving of American drama as a matrix puts playwrights and their work in the position of travelers, stopping repeatedly at the juncture while in transit in order to contribute to its dynamic, evolving shape.

This matrix exists most clearly and tenably in the complex web of reception woven by audience, critics, scholars, and others. It is here, for example, that playwrights like Aeschylus and Annie Baker can exist side by side, and that contemporary plays and events can re-situate thinking about even the earliest drama. Genre and the social operation of art, after all, find purchase for the most part in responses of audience and critics. Aristotle was no playwright, and he lived two hundred years after the height of Attic tragedy, but he has had at least as much influence on the history of tragedy as Sophocles. Concentrating on how responses shape the reception of art begins to reveal an aesthetic matrix in operation. Such responses—writing, discussing, and debating about the production of art—form the engine driving that matrix.

It is in this productively amorphous space that influence can flow outside the restrictions of chronology. Responses to a provocative 1987 play like *Fences,* for example, could reshape thinking about *Death of a Salesman,* from 1949. Wilson's Troy Maxson struggles just like Willy Loman to maintain a level of personal and domestic dignity; both commit infidelity and, in part as a result, find themselves in violent Oedipal struggles with their sons. Certainly Miller's play helps contextualize Wilson's, but thinking in the other direction is also productive. Recognizing that Troy Maxson is a 1950s African American garbage man living in a ramshackle home elucidates the privilege underscoring Miller's play. Willy Loman might not have the life of which he dreams, but his white-collar job has earned him a car, a house, and the ability to free himself from debt, if only belatedly. Miller's critique of the American dream gains greater depth as Troy's struggles to stay afloat cast Willy's eagerness to get ahead in a more disparaging light.

In similar ways, *After August* suggests that the work of Wilson can productively exist side by side with the plays of Williams and O'Neill in the mind of audiences well versed in American drama. Certainly there is no requirement to consider the drunks of *The Iceman Cometh* in Harry Hope's saloon prior to considering the largely sedentary denizens of Memphis's diner in *Two Trains Running*, for example, but Wilson's play points intriguingly back to O'Neill's, encouraging reexamination of the dramatic and social forces running throughout Hope's back room. *After August* posits this approach as an important and valuable method of responding to American drama, one that embraces the complexity and inherent untidiness of the aesthetic matrix in the interest of examining productive and unobvious connections between plays. Treating the American dramatic tradition as an inherently sloppy creation of audiences and critics turns out to reveal powerful trends of social critique running throughout plays from across the twentieth and twenty-first centuries.

Blues and Everything After

Part 1 of *After August* argues that the social operation of blues reveals a deep investment in social identity crafting giving shape to Wilson's work. Chapter 1 combines studies of social history, music, and critical theory to examine blues as a performative expression of self. After emancipation and the failure of Reconstruction, the southern black experience in the early part of the twentieth century was marked by community, oppression, disenfranchisement, and a determined effort to construct and sustain identity. For many southern blacks, blues was an important component of this effort, in part as a rebuttal to the dehumanizing precepts of Jim Crow. The graphic history of spectacle lynching in the post-Reconstruction South exposes the purposeful efforts of the white power structure to strip personhood from black bodies. Because juridical systems of terror intimidated vocal resistance, some southern blacks turned to blues communities, where between the lines of blues performance they could make claims of humanity to their audience in the uncertain hope of receiving a ratifying response. "I am human, despite Jim Crow's claims to the contrary," was one important implication of a blues performance, expressed in the hope of receiving an implied response of "Yes, we the community recognize and support your humanity." Chapter 1 examines this complex performative ritual in detail in order to demonstrate how a blues ethos precedes and exists independently of music, in fact permeating blues expression in literature, art, and elsewhere.

Chapter 2 argues that Wilson conducted himself as a bluesman, using drama as a means of expressing, exploring, and crafting black identity for himself and his characters. Wilson's blues ethos becomes clear in an important constellation of the playwright's work beyond the *American Century Cycle:* his large body of interviews, his polemic speech "The Ground on Which I Stand," and his monologue memoir play, *How I Learned What I Learned.* This work reveals that Wilson turned to theater guided by a blues impulse, seeking to use performance as a means of social identity crafting. The playwright's collection of interviews shows him actively self-crafting as a bluesman; his fiery 1996 speech demonstrates that he considers American theater an essential mode of developing and cultivating racial identity; and his memoir play puts theory into practice, as he turns to theatrical performance with the explicit purpose of performing the self before an audience.

Chapter 3 reads the *American Century Cycle* and its social project within the framework of blues dramaturgy, demonstrating how Wilson's characters work to develop sustainable identities within challenging social terrain. Believing that present conditions are best understood through communion with one's cultural ancestors, the playwright sought a clear sense of African American identity by fostering cultural and historical community through performance. Wilson's *Cycle* cultivates black community through a dramaturgy guided by blues principles like call-and-response, blues humor, linguistic stylization, and the soothing of sorrow through performance. Rather than focusing exclusively on blues music within plays, this chapter shows a blues aesthetic animating the dramaturgy of the entire *Cycle,* revealing Wilson's investment in humanizing his characters.

Chapter 4 opens the book's second part, which suggests that rethinking Wilson in the way part 1 suggests allows for a reinvestigation of the social operation of American drama. Chapter 4 examines the force of privileged whiteness in the work of Eugene O'Neill, arguing that much of the playwright's tragic gloom is rooted in his characters' avoidance of the type of social identity crafting found in Wilson. Many of O'Neill's characters are obsessed with who they are and how they are perceived, but the drive for individualism infused in them by their playwright's whiteness causes them to balk at productive engagement with other people. The result is a litany of plays brimming with isolation, alienation, loneliness, and, in turn, dire destruction. Ultimately, Wilson's blues techniques throw into relief the overbearing and corrosive force of whiteness short-circuiting the process of social identity crafting in O'Neill. His characters demonstrate a presumption of aloof isolation from the community, an attitude that bars them from productive self-crafting.

Chapter 5 argues that Wilson's dramaturgy of social identity crafting helps reveal Tennessee Williams's biting critique of midcentury American expectations of masculinity. Williams's queer and hyperphallic men, rarely fitting normative midcentury expectations of masculinity, seek better understanding of themselves, but their calls for self-examination result in dissonance when returned by the community with oppressive regulatory responses. Tom Wingfield lacks a functional linguistic social sphere, while Brick Pollitt has so internalized regulatory demands of masculinity that he repeatedly and angrily refuses offers to discuss his conflicted sexuality. In these and other men throughout his work, Williams critiques harshly the regulatory force of midcentury American masculinity. August Wilson's dramaturgy reveals that many of Williams's characters suffer because of their existence in dysfunctional antiphonal communities.

The book's final chapter focuses on the work of two important successors to Wilson: Katori Hall and Tarell Alvin McCraney, both of whom repeat and revise Wilson's techniques. As Wilson focuses on Pittsburgh as a microcosm of black America, Hall sets several plays in Memphis over the course of several generations, and McCraney's trilogy *The Brother/Sister Plays* examines the development of a community in one fictional Louisiana town. Both playwrights use space productively in ways similar to Wilson, and both concentrate on their characters' complex and fraught performances of self. But they depart from their predecessor by exploring people and spaces in the black community that the *American Century Cycle* only touches on or ignores completely. For Hall, that is women; for McCraney, queer black men. Both playwrights are guided by Wilson's dramaturgy, but both uniquely extend those strategies in order to add complexity to their black societies by bringing to center stage groups of people frequently left on the periphery.

Ultimately, *After August* suggests that Wilson's blues dramaturgy highlights American drama's obsession with the complicated process of defining a sustainable self through performance. Wilson's work reshaped how theater treats black characters, and in the process his plays were gradually and incrementally contributing to a reshaping of black American identity. This was and still is done in collaboration with audiences, and the *Cycle*'s contribution is only one of many components of that identity. But the *Cycle*'s social consciousness nonetheless shows that theatrical performance enters into a dialogue of identity, and that the desire for sustainable identity cuts to the core of American drama. The kind of contested humanity evident throughout the history of black America emerges similarly in the history of wide variety of communities and individuals scorned for racial, ethnic, bodily, sexual, and religious identities. Wilson's work shows how theater can be a universal tool of self-crafting, enabling the examination, assertion, and cultivation of humanity through antiphonal performance. Wilson dedicated his career to doing so for black Americans, but theater proves to be a broadly capacious vehicle toward the development of selfhood.

PART I
Blues Dramaturgy

1
Blues and the Social Human

Also always absolutely inseparable from all such predicaments and requirements is the most fundamental of all existential imperatives: affirmation, which is to say, reaffirmation and continuity in the face of adversity. Indeed, what with the blues (whether known by that or any other name) always somewhere either in the foreground or the background, reaffirmation is precisely the contingency upon which the very survival of man as human being, however normally unsatisfied and abnormally wretched, is predicated.
—Albert Murray, *Stomping the Blues* (1976)

AUGUST WILSON ASSERTED THAT "the blues are without question the wellspring of my art" but explained neither how the African American tradition of blues flows as if a spring into his plays, nor how he understood the nature of blues in the well from which his art takes such profound inspiration.[1] His assertion that blues contains "a philosophical system at work" does little to clarify.[2] He got a bit more specific when he called blues "a flag-bearer of self-definition" and suggested that blues is "the cultural responses of blacks in America to the situation that they find themselves in."[3] Wilson indicates here that he considered blues not simply a particular style of music but rather a cultural, historical, and spiritual expression of black selfhood in response to social circumstances. He found in blues the concept of using performative art to contribute to the development of black American identity. Understanding Wilson's blues therefore requires more than unpacking musical aspects of his plays; the task first demands a reckoning of salient characteristics of a blues aesthetic particularly attuned to both the artistic qualities and the social investments of blues.

Wilson discovered blues as music but engaged with it as an ethos that precedes and underwrites any specific mode of expression. Behind the music of Bessie Smith, he heard a particular attitude of black life, finding what Sandra G. Shannon calls "a nonverbal means of understanding the gamut of emotions locked up inside him," as well as the urge to express that attitude performatively.[4] This ethos guided him as he shaped his drama. In the same way, Langston Hughes engaged aesthetically with a blues ethos in much of his poetry, Romare Bearden did in his collage art, Zora Neal Hurston did in her prose, and Robert Johnson did in his songs. By so doing, each of these artists created blues. Kalamu ya Salaam argues that "the blues aesthetic is an ethos of blues people that manifests itself in everything done, not just in the music," insisting that "the mere thought that the blues is mainly music is a grossly euro-centric misconception."[5] Although music is the most prominent expression of a blues ethos, it is neither the only nor the principal blues form. Instead, blues proves first to be a mindset about life that breeds methods of aesthetic and performative engagement with the world. For Wilson as for many others, music opened the door to the performative and aesthetic resources of blues, and so this chapter follows his trajectory through blues music and its social history toward more broadly applicable characteristics of a blues aesthetic. The key components of blues articulated below underpin the blues art of Wilson and other nonmusicians as much as they do that of blues musicians like Son House. The playwright's work does not emulate or replicate blues music, but expresses a blues ethos that informed his dramaturgy in the same way it informed the music of Muddy Waters.

Blues, Community, and Resistance

In blues, Wilson found expressions of the manifold black experience in America, performed with a view to the development of personal and communal identity. This quality grows out of blues' historical roots in the post-Reconstruction American South when black identity was particularly in crisis; as Salaam succinctly states, blues people "didn't become blue until after Reconstruction, after freedom day and the dashing of all hopes of receiving/attaining our promised 40acres&1mule."[6] Angela Davis calls blues "the predominant postslavery African-American musical form" that is connected directly to "a new valuation of individual emotional needs and desires." Davis argues that blues is of a piece with newly freed slaves and the first few generations of their descendants wrestling with fresh challenges in this era: "The birth of the blues was aesthetic evidence of new psychosocial realities within the black population."[7] Reconstruction posited support for black personhood and dignity, but worked most often to disenfranchise blacks and reinforce white power with the dawn of Jim Crow. The combination of freedom and oppression forced blacks to scramble to adjust to new, radically redefined social conditions. As Davis demonstrates, the particular expression of selfhood in blues emerges out of an era that occasioned what Amiri Baraka calls "the amazing, albeit agonizing, transformation that produced the contemporary black American from such a people as were first bound and brought to this country."[8] This is an era when notions of black American identity were opaque, in flux, and regularly challenged.

The development of blues was particularly pronounced, for example, in the Mississippi Delta, a region rife with racial tension and violence.[9] The Delta is a fertile tract of land between the Mississippi and Yazoo Rivers, abundant in cotton fields, extending roughly from Vicksburg in the south to the Tennessee border in the north; around the turn of the twentieth century, the region's exceeding fertility precipitated rapid expansion of farmland and, as Edward P. Comentale has shown, precipitous industrialization. Dubbing the Delta a "rural factory," Comentale asserts that "of all the regions of the South, [the Delta] most violently and extensively suffered the processes of *modernization*" (emphasis in original). The region, says Comentale, "soon came to be known as a great cosmopolitan hub, a rural city of sorts."[10] This industrial boom and the relatively high wages it promised in the early decades of the twentieth century attracted large populations of newly or first-generation freed slaves to the region and in turn fomented tension between conservative traditionalists and the evolving forces of modernization. Any promises of an honest living for Delta blacks quickly faded into the sham system of sharecropping as the differences between slavery and post-Emancipation labor blurred. "The master, overseer, slave-catcher, and patroller of an earlier time had been supplanted, in the post-Reconstruction period, by the bossman, prison-farm captain, and sheriff," points out Adam Gussow; "whips and chains had been redeployed in the context of a reconfigured prison-agricultural complex that coexisted with a putative freedom."[11] Blacks were free, but they were disenfranchised, oppressed, and dehumanized at every turn by white institutional power. As Comentale suggests, black identity, "poor as it already was, was liquidated, made fungible, reduced to its productive minimum and then channeled through the abstract forms of the economy."[12] As the socioeconomic forces of modernity progressed under the guise of Reconstruction, advancement opportunities dissolved for black workers across the South, and the powerful white minority pounced on the opportunity for further oppression.

Blues developed among and to a certain extent in response to this social system. It is not a coincidence that the Delta could be both what James C. Cobb calls "the most southern place on earth" and, according to Clyde Woods, "one of the world's most prolific cultural centers."[13] Early blues evinces a complex trove of responses to the black American experience, expressing feelings of longing, joy, community, family, spirituality, shared suffering, affirmation, desire, and identity, among others, and one prominent aspect of this menagerie is a rebuttal to the dehumanizing oppression of Jim Crow. Salaam and others suggest a direct connection between the social order and the development of blues. Salaam calls blues "the cultural manifestation" of all the suffering and anger attendant upon the broken promises of Reconstruction; Gussow goes a step further, claiming that "blues was a mode of resistance" to the harsh policies of Jim Crow, and R. A. Lawson argues that "blues musicians created, told, and retold stories that were culturally oppositional—opposed to white supremacy, Christian forbearance, and bourgeois pragmatism and propriety."[14] These critics and others indicate that part of what Wilson heard in blues was social and political resistance to objectionable conditions of black life.

But Wilson's plays are not agitprop, and blues rarely sounds like protest music. Paul Carter Harrison's claim that "Wilson is concerned with the significations of ontology rather than the objective documentation of casually related responses to oppression formulated as direct protest" applies as accurately to blues music as it does to the *American Century Cycle*.[15] Wilson said that his awakening to blues came from listening to Bessie Smith's "Nobody in Town Can Bake a Sweet Jelly Roll Like Mine," for example, a playful, bawdy song more concerned with sex than politics. There in fact exist few examples of activism in the music or its social history, and little evidence suggests that blues engendered any great political uprisings or momentous social change. For these reasons among others, critics like Elijah Wald argue against trying to identify social consciousness in music whose history runs so directly through good-time tent shows, jook joints, and house parties. Decrying what he calls "romantic foolishness" in blues criticism, Wald insists that early Delta blues was "notable for its professionalism and humor," full of "up-to-date power and promise," and not the genre of "folkloric melancholy" that he argues is a retrograde creation of latter-day critics and theorists. For Wald, the term *blues* "has always been, first and foremost, a marketing term" invented by record companies to categorize black popular music.[16] Wald's argument not only denies that Delta blues contained a sociopolitical response to systematic oppression but suggests that its earliest practitioners were able to avoid such oppression through the unique avenue of economic uplift offered by the music.

This argument is not without merit. Certainly the folkloric image of a raggedly dressed black man moaning out his pain on a porch while strumming a rustic guitar in the company of a weary old hound dog has become misleadingly pervasive. As Paige A. McGinley has demonstrated, the early blues tradition functioned similarly to popular theater, with skilled professionals—most notably flamboyant women like Ma Rainey and Bessie Smith—working a circuit of venues stretching across the South. Later, performers' professionalism frustrated the primitivist desires of blues revivalists, as in the case McGinley highlights of Huddie Ledbetter, whom John Lomax promoted as "the instinctive, untutored Lead Belly," but who showed himself on stage and in the studio to be "learned, professional, and sophisticated."[17] Also, as Karl Hagstrom Miller shows, most early twentieth-century musicians in the South were simply playing the music they knew, not necessarily some specific genre that would only later be dubbed *blues*. Miller points out how "a variety of people—scholars and artists, industrialists and consumers—came to compartmentalize southern music according to race," which underscores Wald's larger point that the people eventually dubbed "Delta bluesmen" were entertainers trying to make a living through music.[18]

Often, early bluesmen and blueswomen had more in common with modern matinee idols than they did with poverty-ridden sharecroppers.

And yet, in Wald's polemic eagerness to subvert the trend of "romantic foolishness" he identifies in blues criticism, he overcorrects, casting blues as a method of lucrative entertainment akin to modern pop music and ignoring the form's social responsiveness. Certainly blues artists have been "intelligent professionals" from the beginning; Baraka points out that as blues developed stylistically, "classic blues took on a certain degree of professionalism," allowing for the emergence of an "artisan, a professional blues singer." But professionalism and emotive expression are far from mutually exclusive. Baraka suggests that blues developed into "the first Negro music that appeared in a formal context as entertainment, though it still contained the harsh, uncompromising reality of the earlier blues forms. It was, in effect, the perfect balance between the two worlds."[19] In plying their trade with the goal of making a living, black musicians across the South in the early twentieth century were nonetheless important components of a community—what McGinley calls "a black southern public"—gradually stitching itself together around the shared search for sustainable identity fostered by blues expressiveness.[20] Wald's book, however, remains an invaluable contemporary example of a key component of the social operation of early blues: because trickster blues people have duped Wald. At the heart of what Gussow calls the "freedom needs and trickster sensibilities" of blues artists is the instinct to conceal from community outsiders any defiantly expressive claims to feeling and emotion.[21] If believing that blues was just black entertainment kept the dangerous gaze of white folks away from their black community, then certainly blues artists would have been happy to support such a myth. But as Wilson recognized, Delta blues trafficked in far more social criticism than revealed by a surface reading of its songs and prominent artists.

Still, despite Cornel West's insight that blues is "on intimate terms with the catastrophic" and "a coming to grips with catastrophe expressed lyrically," passionate protest and stalwart political resistance are rare in blues.[22] The antilynching anthem "Strange Fruit," made most popular by Billie Holiday, is a notable exception to the general rule of black music in the first several decades of the twentieth century. Protest blues certainly exists—McGinley highlights examples of activism performed by Brownie McGhee, Sister Rosetta Tharpe, and Huddie Ledbetter, among others—but most song lyrics from the era are full of sorrow, sardonic jokes, desire, joy, sexual innuendo, longing, bravado, and any number of other feelings that are not overt, impassioned protests against social oppression. But as Gussow, Lawson, and others argue, and as Wilson recognized, the social operation of blues is far more complex than the semantic content of its lyrics. Indeed, Ralph Ellison argues that "the blues are not primarily concerned with civil rights or obvious political protest; they are an art form and thus a transcendence of those conditions created within the Negro community by the denial of social justice. As such they are one of the techniques through which Negroes have survived and kept their courage during that long period when many whites assumed, as some still assume, they were afraid."[23] As discussed above in the introduction, Houston A. Baker argues that blues is best "conceived as a matrix . . . a point of ceaseless input and output, a web of intersecting, crisscrossing impulses always in productive transit." Baker insists that "the task of adequately describing the blues is equivalent to the labor of describing a world class athlete's awesome gymnastics. Adequate appreciation demands comprehensive attention."[24] The social critique and personal expressiveness that Ellison and others highlight in blues lie deeply within a matrix founded upon indeterminacy and misdirection, expertly concealing from certain audiences its personal expressiveness and social consciousness while simultaneously seeking specific audiences within the matrix to hear and respond to that which is concealed.

Blues in fact contains vast amounts of expressiveness through which Delta blues people performed their humanity among a potentially supportive, developing community, often contra an oppressive white hegemony that sought to deny humanity to black bodies. Arguments about the connection between blues and human subjectivity are firmly grounded in the blues critical tradition: Albert Murray argues the connection in this chapter's epigraph; Gussow suggests that what he calls a "blues subject" emerges out of early blues; James H. Cone insists that "blues affirm the somebodiness of black people"; Comentale argues that blues performs "an ultimately open-ended process of self-creation and self-revision"; and as quoted above, Wilson calls the genre "a flag-bearer of self-definition."[25] Perhaps most explicitly, Jon Michael Spencer argues that "those who created and sang the blues were constantly trying to affirm their personhood in the face of abject racist bombardment and 'head-bashing' by the overculture."[26] The heart of Jim Crow was a dehumanization of black people, and blues offered a retort to this notion. In the interest of better understanding how Wilson entered his drama into this socio-aesthetic tradition, therefore, the current chapter examines the precise performative strategies through which blues artists fostered communities of shared strength and identity by expressing their humanity within a society so suppressive of any such expression. The trickster sensibilities of blues people, it turns out, begin with language and performance.

Blues in the Lion's Den

The socially responsive component of early blues finds provocation in the oppressive power structures of Jim Crow. Although Wald is quick to minimize the impact of systematic violence in the Mississippi Delta on the birth of blues, he does report that "though it makes up less than a sixth of the state's area, the Delta accounted for over a third of the lynchings reported between 1900 and 1930, and was legendary for towns with signposts warning black people not to be caught within their borders after sundown."[27] Blues historian Giles Oakley considers racist oppression so central to the music that he opens his seminal study of blues with an examination of the social conditions of the Delta, insisting that "the dominance of the white minority was absolute, economically, educationally, politically and socially," and pointing out that "Mississippi has a reputation for racism and bigotry from the earliest days of Emancipation; its record of lynching, reaching a bloody peak in the early days of the Jim Crow laws, was appalling." Oakley goes on to quote a gruesome 1904 newspaper report describing the torturous conditions through which Luther Holbert, a black man accused of murdering his white boss, was lynched along with his wife. The man and woman were tied to trees as their fingers, toes, and ears were cut off and sold as souvenirs to the mob of over a thousand people; Holbert's beaten skull was cracked and his eye dangled out by a strand; "quivering" flesh was bored out of both victims by large corkscrews. Equally terrifying is that report that "two blacks had already been killed by a posse in mistake for Holbert."[28]

From the many reports like these of what Gussow dubs "disciplinary violence" in the Mississippi Delta, two crucial preconditions of blues' social consciousness emerge.[29] First, the evidence of such extreme violence against black bodies suggests that the torturers had deemed the people inhabiting those bodies valueless, stripped not only of democratic rights or basic human dignity, but more so of any claim to humanity within a society. The existence that many whites were attempting to impose on their black neighbors recalls Giorgio Agamben's conception of "the state of exception," whereby the law "radically erases any legal status of the individual, thus producing a legally unnamable and unclassifiable being." For both Agamben and Judith Butler, the post-9/11 American practice of indefinite detention at Guantanamo Bay—whereby detainees are deemed legally unclassifiable as "neither prisoners nor persons accused"—is where "bare life reaches its maximum indeterminacy."[30] Agamben helpfully provides a conceptual framework in which to understand more clearly the method of terrorism underlying Jim Crow in the Delta. Ex-slaves and their descendants had certain rights which, though limited, extended to protection from murder. But Jim Crow worked systematically to strip blacks of those rights and cast them into the state of exception. If the life of a black body had no rights or protection under the law, then it could be exploited and killed at will. "If [a black man] killed a black," says bluesman Honeyboy Edwards of this era, "generally wouldn't nothing much happen to you," because the powerful white farmers needed black bodies to work their fields and so there was little sense in sending a murderer to jail and wasting two viable workers.[31] In this case, both the dead black man and the black murderer exist in a de facto state of exception, outside the rule of law and entirely beholden to the whim of political power structures. But crimes did not need to be nearly as capital as murder: a black man looking at a white woman in a way that could be misconstrued as lecherous, for example, or simply being in certain towns after sundown was grounds for dehumanizing violence. The precarious social situation of the Delta reveals that blacks could face terrible retribution for attempting to embody their humanity while under a constant white gaze.

Of course, they often faced the same violence for little justification, which reveals the second crucial precondition of blues' social consciousness: in the Jim Crow South, white violence on black bodies was easily provoked and often arbitrary. The story related by Oakley of Luther Holbert's lynching makes this point clear: the horrific torture came only after two other men were killed by a mob who mistook them for Holbert. These two victims were guilty of little more than bearing something of a resemblance to Holbert, and one suspects that there is little justification for the torture and execution of Holbert's wife other than simply being married to an accused murderer. As Davis demonstrates, black women under Jim Crow not only risked lynching but were also targets of "white racists for whom rape was a weapon of terror."[32] This is a terrifying social order in which to live. Gussow relates the story of a firsthand account of a middle-class black man in the

1930s asked about entering the South: "'He said it was like walking into a lion's den; the lions are chained; but if they should become enraged, it is doubtful whether the chains would hold them; hence it is better to walk very carefully. . . . Every Negro in the South knows that he is under a kind of sentence of death; he does not know when his turn will come, it may never come, but it may also be at any time.'"[33] The violence of a wild animal can hardly be predicted and is certainly not predicated on justice or law: it arbitrarily treats its victims as disposable.

Faced with the terrible reality of a social order that dehumanized them and was constantly at the ready to exact arbitrary violence against them, many southern blacks found the performative expression of self through art a useful means of developing individual and community strength. As Koritha Mitchell has shown, for instance, a number of dramatists portrayed black humanity through normative domesticity in lynching plays, defined by the theater historians Kathy A. Perkins and Judith L. Stephens as *"a play in which the threat or occurrence of a lynching, past or present, has a major impact on the dramatic action"* (emphasis in original).[34] Mitchell writes that "dramatists who lived and wrote in the midst of lynching often refused to feature physical violence; their scripts spotlight instead the black home and the impact that the mob's outdoor activities have on the family. Indeed, the dramas most commonly depict exactly what mainstream discourse denied existed: loving black homes."[35] This is the sort of work that Alain Locke calls "the folk play," praising it as "the drama of free self-expression and imaginative release, [that] has no objective but to express beautifully and colorfully the folk life of the race" and suggesting that it is a stronger form of resistance than direct propaganda: "There is more strength in a confident camp than in a threatened enemy."[36] Although the context of production for lynching plays differs from blues in important ways—writers of lynching plays lived primarily in the Washington DC area, were educated and literate, and had the support of the NAACP and influential people like W. E. B. Du Bois—the model of these plays illuminates the social operation of blues. For these plays are not heated agitprop; they are instead implicit performances of black humanity. By writing lynching plays, encouraging black families to dramatize them in their homes, and staging them in public, black communities made a dramaturgical claim to domesticity, as well as an implicit claim to the humanity necessary to cultivate that domesticity. The savage rapists and whores of white propaganda do not have the human complexity of characters in lynching plays.

Like lynching plays, early blues songs sought to express and cultivate the complexity of black humanity, but they did so more covertly and subtly. To examine just one of myriad examples, Son House's 1930 recording of "Walkin' Blues" abounds with the lyrical and stylistic tropes so familiar of Delta blues, but nonetheless proves Davis's claim that "blues contain many layers of meanings that are often astounding in their complexity and profundity."[37] The lyrics are full of loss, wanderlust, downheartedness, disillusionment, and ultimately dark humor: "I got the blues so bad until it hurt my tongue to talk / if I had the walking blues, oh it'd hurt my feet to walk," begins House, before explaining in a later verse that the source of this particular bout of blues is the loss of a lover: "I got up this morning just about the break of day / I was hugging the pillow where my good gal used to lay." House professes feelings of abandonment and sorrow, but although he may be wracked by loneliness, he is not going to lie in bed all day and cry; he is going to go out and search for some way to assuage these blues: "When I start to walking, I'm gonna walk from sun to sun / I ain't gonna quit walking until my turn is done." Accepting the fact that this feeling is not going to be easily remedied, House closes his song with a sardonic nod to the fickleness of blues:

> Oh, good morning blues
> blues how do you do?
> Says I just come here momma
> to have a few words with you.

"Walkin' Blues" evinces a rebuttal to the Jim Crow pretext that ex-slaves and their descendants are subhuman primitive creatures. House's act of hugging the inanimate pillow reveals the desperation of the heartbroken, searching for some token of his love, however symbolic or fleeting. He firms up his resolution, however, and puts on his shoes to head out the door and look for some answers, ultimately traveling along a range of emotional registers, from loss and wallowing to determination, however desperate that determination may seem. As challenges piteously mount, House turns to gallows humor, shaking his fist at the blues he personifies as the cruel mistress, "momma." These are all common moves in the blues of Son House and others, and more importantly, they are recognizable human emotions, attesting by their very presence to the human subjectivity of their possessor. The song's final verse asking "blues, how do you do" is a conventional trope, showing up in many songs by House and others; by adding it to this song, House invokes and places himself among all the other performers who have sung the lines and audiences who have heard them. House performs not simply loneliness and longing but also the humanity necessary to feel those emotions, and he does so by entering into and utilizing the forces of the blues community.

A paradox emerges here. On the one hand, "Walkin' Blues" stands as a representative example of Gussow's claim of blues' character as "a social response to the grievous spiritual pressures exerted on working-class black southerners," and "a cultural form that enabled black people to salve their wounded spirits and assert their embattled individuality."[38] On the other hand, stories of lynching and terror related by Oakley, Gussow, and others attest to the horrible danger connected with any sense of expressive black dignity, subjectivity, or personhood. One must therefore wonder how black people could express their humanity in rebuttal of the dominant white hegemony in this dangerous lion's den and escape lynching. If white society is working so very hard to cast the black body into a state of exception and keep it there through oppressive biopolitics, where is there room for the black body to claim a socially viable voice?

Blues and the Signifyin(g) Human Voice

Amid an array of emotions and community investments, early blues was particularly creative at expressing the human self covertly within a social environment eager to shut down any such expression. Part of the performers' goals was—like Elegba, the Yoruba trickster orisha of their African ancestors—to get one over on their antagonists. As Lawson points out, southern blacks who were backed into dangerous corners by violent white supremacists but remained insistent on finding a mode of resistance "were forced to protest in ways that were unrecognizable to whites."[39] Doing so would require black blues artists to embody the subjectivity necessary to express their humanity while eluding the spiteful gaze of a disciplinary panopticon. This was a dangerous endeavor, but the performative mode of blues facilitated the defiant assertion of black humanity through covert expression intended solely for the initiated black audience.

Often the coded language of blues is tied up with sexuality—"Nobody in town can bake a sweet jelly roll like mine," claims Bessie Smith; "I'm a crawling king snake baby," insists John Lee Hooker; neither is particularly subtle—but even here songs offer social protest layered within lyrics. Davis argues that "blues registered sexuality as a tangible expression of freedom," and she demonstrates how lyrics that might seem simply bawdy in fact make defiant claims to complex humanity.[40] Similarly, Gussow has shown that the apparent silence in the blues lyric tradition about the ubiquitous fear of lynching is subverted by close inspection of allusions and innuendo pervading the tradition. In many blues lyrics, Gussow finds evidence of coded expressions of performers' fears and anxieties, expressed covertly because lynching was a taboo among those subject to its caprice: the danger whose name one dare not speak. By unpacking the blues lyrical tradition, Davis and Gussow underscore the urge of early blues performers to express performatively their own feelings, fears, joys, and desires. A central subject of blues, that is, is the artist's selfhood.

Delta blues artists could perform that selfhood within suppressive environments by communicating within the subversive linguistic structure of "Signifyin(g)." Calling Signifyin(g) "black double-voicedness" and "the trope of tropes, the figure of figures," Henry Louis Gates theorizes this mode of language as a covert means of expression through misdirection. Signifyin(g) is "not engaged in the game of information-giving," he says, but is instead "the language of trickery."[41] To signify is on a certain level to pun, parody, trick, or insult, but more specifically it is to pun the trope of punning, parody the trope of parodying, and not be concerned with everybody understanding the punch line. Instead, the signifier, like a coy trickster, is quite certain that many will not get his or her meaning, but that those for whom the covert expression is meant will understand. As Saidiya Hartman has shown, Signifyin(g) has roots in slavery, when slaves who were made to perform songs and dances in the master's house enacted their defiance covertly through nonsense and misdirection; "work songs," points out Angela Davis, "often relied on indirection and irony to highlight the inhumanity of slave owners so that their targets were sure to misunderstand the intended meaning."[42] These slaves were Signifyin(g) on the trope of entertaining the master with slave revelry, at once under the disciplinary gaze of their owners and before the knowing eyes of their fellow slaves.

In "Walkin' Blues," Son House signifies on any number of tropes, including the hard-line notion of a split between performer and persona. Aesthetic analysis generally resists confounding performer and persona, especially when tempted to do so by that devious little first-person pronoun *I*. This is a particularly important concept when analyzing popular song, a primary trope of which is singing in the first person. The argument holds that an artist is creating voices and characters as much as she or he is creating fictionalized worlds, and that even if an artist claims to be portraying the self, there exists a fundamental divorce between creator and created. This is an important analytical principle that blues complicates and resists. As Gussow insists, "The black male blues singer, vocalizing the shared experience of his cohort, is the subject of his own song: his fears, his hopes, his sexual hungers and romantic losses, his financial setbacks, his aching body, the town he hungers to escape from, the town he dreams of fleeing to."[43] By attempting to give voice to the cohort, the blues *I* contributes to the performer's solicitation of identity, asking the community to recognize and accept expressions of shared experiences and feelings. McGinley's argument that "the *I* signifies multiply and simultaneously—and does not always refer back to the self, or to one's own identity position" elucidates the pronoun's subjective complexity. The precise referent of the blues *I* is never unambiguous, because the blues performer makes himself or herself the subject of song representationally rather than personally, performing insights and attitudes shared prominently throughout the multivalent blues community in the hope that audiences will recognize, support, and encourage the performer's right to do so. McGinley is certainly correct that "these performers were always greater than their autobiographical *I*," but the degree to which the performer is able to transcend the personal *I* relies on successful engagement with the audience.[44]

By signifying on the aesthetic notion that splits performer and persona, early blues sought to construct a broad, often indeterminate community through which the music could signify on the social dehumanization of the black body. Son House collapses the performer-persona distinction not in such a way that makes the song autobiographical, but rather in order to extend the emotive register of the song to the performer and the community that might accept his representation. He might have seemed to be participating in the familiar trope of popular music to sing about fictional or generic scenarios (familiar in his era through ragtime, "badman" songs, Tin Pan Alley, and other popular styles), but he signifies on that trope, covertly expressing feelings of pain, anxiety, fleeting joy, and hope. This method of concealing personal feelings of despair behind the trope of a performer/persona split is certainly not the only strategy blues artists used to covertly express themselves. Muddy Waters's "Hoochie Coochie Man," for example, is a song rife with sexual braggadocio. Waters's first-person persona insists that his birth was prefaced by a gypsy woman claiming that the child on the way is "gonna be a son of a gun" who will "make pretty womens jump and shout," before putting everybody on notice that "the whole world gonna know what he's all about"; finally, he announces his own presence and identity boldly:

> But you know I'm here
> Everybody knows I'm here
> I'm the Hoochie Coochie Man
> Everybody knows I'm here.

The identity crafted in Waters's song is unabashedly bold, forthright, and confident. This does not sound like the covert expression of a black man frightened of violent appraisal from white authorities.

The tone changes from House to Waters, but blues performative conditions remain consistent. Having begun his career as a Delta bluesman, it may seem like Waters is taking blues into new confident terrain with "Hoochie Coochie Man," recorded in 1952 when he was making a relatively good living recording at Chess Records in Chicago. But certainly "braggadocio blues" existed in the early years of Delta blues, and more importantly, Waters in "Hoochie Coochie Man" is Signifyin(g) just as much as Son House is in "Walkin' Blues." The difference is that under different social and economic conditions in 1950s Chicago, Waters conceals his complex personhood under the veil of confidence rather than dejectedness. The persona he projects is one of pride, power, and brashness, allowing him to conceal from a broad audience feelings of pain, bitterness, and anger that come with continued inequality, as well as the humor and joy bound up with both singing a sexually suggestive song and getting one over on the white society that does not decode his Signifyin(g). "Hoochie Coochie Man" thus replaces the dejected persona of "Walkin' Blues" with an arrogant braggart, but deploys the same Signifyin(g) technique to perform his complex humanity to the blues community. While performances of blues braggadocio may seem to present a fully realized person marked by self-confidence and aggression, these songs in fact only offer this as a guise to the white hegemony eager to believe the simplistic notion that the performer reveals black society's contentment with its conditions. The black human embodied in blues performances, however, is full of the sort of conflicted human complexity that early blues artists had little to no interest in demonstrating to white hegemonic society.

Blues is thus a humanist expression, one through which artists perform their humanity within a social sphere in the tentative hope that it will be recognized and ratified by response. The term *humanism* invites many condemnations of the history of uncritical, universalized humanism, but the model of humanism found in the blues is active, social, and agonistic in the manner proposed by Bonnie Honig. The very operation of blues as a pursuit of a socially defined humanity suggests that it treats the human not as a biological given but as a product of active discourse. Honig's notion of "agonistic humanism" accepts the limits of human subjectivity and universalism while recognizing nonetheless that the human engages in certain distinctive activities that can be productively theorized.[45] For Honig, foremost among those activities is the development of agonistic (rather than moralist or ethical) politics, but the aesthetic performance of self fits neatly into any list of distinct human activities. At bottom, although the human may not be wholly exceptional, universal, or unique, humans seem to be the only creatures that turn to art in an effort to engage with and work toward reconciling challenges of existence.

Of course, in order to develop social humanity, one must have access to a social sphere that is willing to offer engagement. Delta blues artists had no access to the political apparatus by which they were governed, and only limited access to any domain of the social sphere in which they lived. Honeyboy Edwards relates how a black man in the Delta could gain some limited social standing by proving reliable to whites: "Always, if the whites would ask me to do something, if I know it wasn't for long, I'd go out there and do it. I get into something they'll help me get out of it. You got to have somebody to speak for you at that time." But this ersatz benevolence had its limits: "Whites run it down there. . . . They treated us like we was property. Come all through slavery time and they still wanted us to be slaves."[46] Most often, the only social sphere reliably available to Delta blacks was a community of other Delta blacks. For blues artists, that community was made up of what Baraka and Salaam call *blues people:* southern blacks sharing in the community and ethos of blues.

Even with a supportive community, artists defying Jim Crow precepts in the Delta faced danger in what is best conceived of as a panopticon of white surveillance. But performers' success in coyly making references to sexual prowess, or fear of lynching, or political anger to a community of blues people who understand the innuendo suggests that the community recognizes the complex expression of the performer who is one of them, welcomed and supported by the social sphere. A major facilitator of this performative framework is the voice, another component of any Delta blues person's claim to humanity. The Signifyin(g) strategies of blues exist primarily in its manipulation of language, but beyond and before any language is the sound of the voice, a bodily expression of selfhood. Each person's voice arises uniquely from the particular material construction of their throat; in this, Adriana Cavarero argues, lies the resources for a philosophy of individual human uniqueness. Cavarero insists that the individual voice reveals "the uniqueness that makes of everyone a being that is different from all the others." The prelinguistic sound of the voice, which depends on the unique fleshy construction of throats, reveals the basic individuality that linguistic communities obscure. According to Cavarero, the voice contains "the simple vocal self-revelation of the existence, which ignores every semantic interference. The typical freedom with which human beings combine words is never a sufficient index of uniqueness of the one who speaks. The voice, however, is always different from all other voices, even if the words are the same, as often happens in the case of song."[47] This is also true when words are conventional or meant to misdirect, as is often true in blues.

Cavarero's ideas allow a closer examination of the vocal expression underlying the performance of blues. Like Cavarero's insistence that the history of philosophy has ignored vocality, evidence suggests that the disciplinary forces of Jim Crow did the same, ignoring the uniqueness of blues vocal expression. Son House and others could get away with defiant claims to personhood because they were not making their claims on the levels of logos and semantics, but of vocality and signification. The first sound from any singer is the voice; even if it is only a split second between the utterance of that sound, its shaping into word, and an interpretation of sound as language, logos and reception are nonetheless predicated on the sound of voice.

Vocality in the three-and-a-half-minute 1930 recording of Son House's "Walkin' Blues," for example, offers evidence of longing, weariness, bewilderment, and ultimately determination and wry humor. In the 1930 recording, in fact, all of these feelings are perhaps more perceptible than the semantic content of the lyrics, which unrefined recording equipment and House's wailing vocal style obscure. House's voice moans and warbles in a style recalling a field holler or arwhoolie, like the one Alan Lomax recorded on Parchman Farm by a man named Tangle Eye.[48] Tangle Eye's holler is almost pure vocality. Fittingly, Lomax describes the vocal performance in terms of instrumentation: "he sang in a high sweet voice that at times moaned like an oboe, then leapt into liquid yodeling cries with the fluidity of Sidney Bechet's clarinet." Lyrics can be distinguished in the recording of Tangle Eye, but this performer is keening more than singing. The song may very well have "told Tangle Eye's story," as Lomax claims, but the performance's most powerful expression is in the wailing of its singer. On a plane beyond the semantic content of lyrics, and beyond any Signifyin(g) suggested by lines like "Well it must have been the devil that fooled me here," lies fleshy vocality that is unique to Tangle Eye.[49] This is a work song performed on a prison farm, not a blues, but the connections between the wails of its vocalist and those of Son House should not be overlooked. The moans of the black worker crying out in pain and longing from the prison farm reverberate through the bluesman, Signifyin(g) on any notion of divorce between himself and his slave ancestors or his pained persona. Listening to sound, that is, unlocks the personal voice of a dehumanized black body performing his defiant humanity.

This humanity is not, however, a condition that can be demonstrably claimed by an epideictic performance for whoever may be listening. "Existence hangs on a push of the lungs," says Cavarero, "which is at the same time an invocation of the other. The voice is always *for* the ear, it is always relational" (emphasis in original).[50] The humanism of blues in fact exists only in a reciprocal matrix of exchange between performer, audience, and larger social context. At the same time that the performer is performing himself or herself, he or she is also performing the entire blues community. Despite the nearly omnipresent *I* as the subject of blues songs, the audience, according to Sherley A. Williams, "assumes 'we' even though the blues singer sings 'I.'"[51] The blues artist expresses pain, longing, and pleasure, speaking not only for himself or herself but for the broader community that shares and can identify with those feelings. Baraka says, "Blues was a music that arose from the needs of a group," and Lawson calls blues, succinctly, "the story of a people told from one person's point-of-view."[52] Audience recognition of the blues artist speaking for communal experiences thus becomes crucial to any felicitous performance of social humanity. Cavarero insists that what is at stake in her philosophy of vocal expression "is not a closed-circuit communication between one's own voice and one's own ears, but rather a communication of one's own uniqueness that is, at the same time, a relation with another unique existent. It takes at least a duet, a calling and a responding—or, better, a reciprocal intention to listen, one that is already active in the vocal emission, and that reveals and communicates everyone to the other."[53] Judith Butler agrees, suggesting that "our fundamental dependency on the other" reveals "the fact that we cannot exist without addressing the other and without being addressed by the other."[54] "To ask for recognition, or to offer it," argues Butler, "is precisely not to ask for recognition for what one already is. It is to solicit a becoming."[55] The other from whom blues performers solicit in the active, creative, and communal process of becoming is the audience. Innumerable people have played blues alone in a room, but such a performance does little to assert or instantiate social humanity. Blues demands an audience.

Reliance on audience shows up clearly throughout the performative history of blues tradition, as well as in the many call-and-response aspects of the music. A singer cries out, "hey hey!" the audience replies in unison, "hey, hey!" and everybody heads to sweet home Chicago. Of course, this technique is far from universal throughout or exclusive to blues songs, but it is a prominent example of the fundamentally antiphonal structure of blues, a trait that Baraka calls an "important aspect of African music found readily" in blues.[56] More significantly than other genres of music, blues operates on call-and-response, a reciprocal relationship between performer and audience. This is shown as true in call-and-response lyrics, in the implicit demand that a performer improvise within a song in the hopes of thrilling the particular audience of a particular show, but also within the most recognizable musical structures of blues. Regularly, traditionally structured twelve-bar blues songs follow a pattern whereby the singer's vocal performance over the first two bars of a musical line calls for an answer by an instrumental performance responding over the next two bars in licks that recall the singer's emotive expression. A singer will often even model audience response by responding to himself or herself: routinely the second line of blues lyrics repeats the first line, but with a change in emphasis or emotional register. When Son House sings, "I woke up this morning feelin' round for my shoes" for the second time, he changes "woke up" to "got up," adds a soulful "woo" to the middle line, and stretches the word "shoes" out over twice as many beats. Sherley Williams calls this repetition-with-a-difference "worrying the line," a technique that includes "changes in stress and pitch, the addition of exclamatory phrases, changes in word order, repetitions of phrases within the line itself, and the wordless blues cries which often punctuate the performance of the songs."[57] While worrying a line effectively adds emphasis and drama to the vocal performance, the technique also reveals antiphony lying at the core of blues structure, as a song progresses along a trajectory of repetition and response. Ideas are offered, modified upon reception, and further developed.

This antiphonal structure within the music replicates the antiphonal structure of the blues community, emerging in musical structures as well as performative dimensions. Blues' early years were fostered and supported not only by performers but also and perhaps more importantly by the communities that formed around those performers: like a preacher, a blues performer needs a congregation. Barry Lee Pearson calls early blues musicians "spokespersons for their community," but although musicians were certainly vocal and visible community members, this formulation is not quite precise enough, because the notion of spokesperson suggests a representative from within the community speaking to outsiders.[58] A better characterization of early blues musicians is as people striving for the position of griot. In certain West African traditions, the griot is a community elder and bard whose social function ranges from reporting news to mediating courtship rituals to recounting genealogies. Essential to the griot's performative work is uniting a culture; Thomas A. Hale says that a griot, "enables societies to cohere" and suggests that griots constitute "the social glue in society." Hale argues that by serving in part as keepers of folk tales and traditions, "griots provide deep insights into the values of a people and their social structure," but in order to do so in any meaningful way they need an audience to listen.[59] A griot, that is, must be recognized as such by the community. At least implicitly, a community needs to say, "Yes, we recognize your voice as a special link to our ancestors." The griot's call of identity requires a response.

The social position and performative role of the blues performer function similarly. West insists that most the basic task of a blues performer, who has "control over only voice and body," is to "sing in such a way that others want to sing with you," adding that this requires a kind of "Socratic courage beginning with tears."[60] The blues performer comes before a community and makes a claim. Through the musical language of signification and the presentation of unique vocality, the artist covertly says, "I am performing all the pain, suffering, fortitude, and humor constitutive of our humanity," and implies, "Please respond with your recognition" (compare the Responsorial Psalm of the Christian Mass, in which faith is performed in the antiphonal exchange between officiant and congregation; as Jon Michael Spencer, James Cone, Lawrence Levine, and others have shown, blues and the church are not quite the antinomies that cultural critics often make them out to be). As Comentale recognizes, blues denies any "traditional notions of identity or expressive consistency," offering instead "a much more flexible form of identity and exchange."[61] One cannot assert a consistent identity when one requires the engagement and ratification of a community; the flexibility that Comentale highlights underscores the antiphonal, improvisational process of blues identity formation. The performer calls with a provisional sense of human identity, but must negotiate that identity with the complex and varying responses of blues community members.

In short, the musician claims a tentative humanity in a performative call, but can only hope to receive the needed response from the community in order to ratify that humanity. "Hope wrestles with despair, but it doesn't generate optimism," claims West. "It just generates this energy to be courageous, to bear witness, to see what the end is going to be." A blues performer, whom West calls "a prisoner of hope," seeks sustainable social humanity when entering into the performative structure of blues, but is unable to be optimistic about an affirmative response.[62] Instead, the prisoner of hope must wait anxiously for ratification from the community and be prepared to improvise as needed based on community response. In order to signify effectively, one must have an audience who both understands the coded language and is willing to acknowledge that understanding. Performance functions within a social sphere, requiring the active participation of the people constituting that sphere, and so blues, constitutively performative, is at bottom communal.

Comentale helpfully demonstrates the stress blues places on community in his discussion of the "1969 television video of Son House performing 'Death Letter Blues'" at Carnegie Hall, graphically underscoring blues' demand for community by examining an exception. The author highlights the sheer physicality of the famous performance: "His weathered hand beats against the steel, over and over again. . . . The movement spreads to his entire body, which heaves and jerks in forceful counterpoint, until his face finally crumples in pain—eyes closed, teeth clenched—as if wincing against the very sound of his song." This performance came long after House's developmental blues years, when revivalists rediscovered his music and delivered him to a national audience. According to Comentale's insightful analysis, however, "Son House's return seems less like a personal triumph than a brutal reenactment, a whitewashed conjure act of the racial violence the singer had long since left behind."[63] This performance likely provided House with the largest audience of his career, but the pain Comentale recognizes results from the singer calling out his trauma to a Carnegie Hall audience who, familiar with blues as music but not as a social expression of selfhood, is unprepared to respond with recognition and identification. In this case, any hope House may have had of receiving a ratifying response to his performed humanity was dashed by the absence of a blues community.

In keeping with a seemingly paradoxical aspect of blues, House might have assuaged his frustration by joking about it. Indeed, the communal support blues performers often seek is in reference to suffering, but much of blues' performative humanism nonetheless traffics in humor and playfulness. Too often blues is conceptualized as a music of depression and woe, a notion overlooking the ludic qualities underwriting the music. Pearson argues that "blues artists are witness to a world that embraces hard times and good times, and as masters of transformation they can find humor in the least likely places," and Salaam insists that one of the most salient characteristics of blues people is that "we laugh loud and heartily when every rational expectation suggests we should be crying in despair."[64] Langston Hughes puts it most directly: "Sad as Blues may be, there's almost always something humorous about them—even if it's a kind of humor that laughs to keep from crying."[65] Ellison argues a direct tie between the ludic aspect of blues and black oppression: "The blues speak to us simultaneously of the tragic and the comic aspects of the human condition and they express a profound sense of life shared by many Negro Americans precisely because their lives have combined these modes. This has been the heritage of a people who for hundreds of years could not celebrate birth or dignify death and whose need to live despite the dehumanizing pressures of slavery developed an endless capacity for laughing at their painful experiences."[66] This concept underscores the necessity of blues performers bringing vibrant joy to their communities, and suggests that doing so is a key condition upon which the ratification of the performer's social humanity depends. Honig insists that agonistic humanism draws "not only nor even primarily on mortality and suffering, but also on natality and pleasure, power (not just powerlessness), desire (not just principle), and *thumos* (not just *penthos*)" and that conceptualizing humanity in this manner allows for "a pleasure-based counter to grief attuned to the limitations of solidarity forged in sorrow." Much sorrow runs throughout the blues community, but a community sustained by such notions limits its viability and its potential to offer support and reprieve. Honig points to the often overlooked fifth stasimon in *Antigone* when the Chorus, just as the play's tensions grow to their most intense, offers an invitation to all the players "to go to the feast of Dionysus and forget, in dance" as a primordial moment of the humanist pursuit of pleasure over and against suffering.[67] Sophocles's Chorus, in that moment, suggests that everybody go laugh to keep from crying.

The humanism of blues thus traffics very directly in notions of pleasure and joy. Yet, as with all components of the agonistic humanist model, the joy delivered by a performer is provisional, dependent on the response of the community and the performer's improvisational engagement with that response (and the community's response to the improvisation, and so on antiphonally throughout the blues matrix). Stephen K. White's concept of weak ontology helpfully elucidates the humanist operation of the blues community. White argues that weak ontology prioritizes the understanding of self and other but deemphasizes absoluteness of conviction. Instead of a stalwart devotee to ontological certainty, one committed to a continuous project of self-understanding is best modeled as "a traveller who has a rough sense of the direction in which she must head but is also crucially dependent on the insights of those she meets along the way for clues as to her ultimate destination."[68] Neither the blues performer nor the members of the blues community are at all certain of their ultimate destination, how to get there, or even that the voyage is worth the trouble. And so they need each other. The performer requires the audience to respond to his or her call claiming a humanity founded in vocal uniqueness expressing basic human fears and joys, and the members of the blues community require the centralizing force of the performer in order to provide a beacon of their own humanity.

Toward a Blues Aesthetic

If it is true as Cavarero claims that "the voice is the way in which the exquisitely human uniqueness emits its essence," then the specific blues voice began as the way for blues people to emit and articulate their essence.[69] This chapter opened by initiating a search for a blues aesthetic, a framework in which to conceptualize the nature and dynamics of blues music that might help clarify how August Wilson was guided by the same blues ethos. Certainly there are any number of exceptions that do not fit so snugly into this framework, but a handful of key elements that contribute to what Wilson found in blues have emerged.

The first important condition of blues is that it is performative, an essential and easily overlooked characteristic of much popular music. Like drama, blues is only fully realized in performance with an audience. This condition is thus deeply implicated in the second constituent condition of blues, which is that it is community based. Performance and community are so important to blues because, much more so than other forms of music, it is antiphonal to its core. From musical structures, to lyrics, to performance traditions and beyond, blues relies on a performative call in search of a community response. Blues is also ludic, an underremarked quality of a genre that is too often characterized as depressed or maudlin despite profound senses of play and joy. This has as much to do with the covert Signifyin(g) of lyrics—getting one over on society at large—as it does with the music's danceable rhythms, ribald humor, and life-affirming sense of exuberance. Countless lyrics about pain, loss, and anger notwithstanding, as Richard Wright insists, "the most astonishing aspect of the blues is that, though replete with a sense of defeat and down-heartedness, they are not intrinsically pessimistic; their burden of woe and melancholy is dialectically redeemed through sheer force of sensuality, into an almost exultant affirmation of life, of love, of sex, of movement, of hope. No matter how repressive was the American environment, the negro never lost faith in or doubted his deeply endemic capacity to live."[70] Born in a time of near-totalizing terror and fear, blues bears the marks of an aesthetic release that laughs to keep from crying, in Hughes's terms. Recognizing blues humor ought not diminish attention to the horrific conditions of its early years, but it should provide a clearer understanding of the art's social function.

Finally, then, blues turns out to be at once socially responsive and deeply humanizing. Paul Garon says that "we see in [blues] one of the few modern American poetic voices through which humanity has fiercely fought for, and managed to regain, a semblance of its true dignity."[71] As Garon recognizes, blues' concern with the various trials and triumphs of black American life contributes to a broad social project of developing individual and community identity. Its originary performers turned to the music and to the community in order to articulate not only their feelings about the social conditions under which they lived but also to seek out a social recognition of their dignified humanity. Jim Crow was an apparatus of dehumanization, and so in order to respond in any meaningful way, those being oppressed needed to assert humanity. Blues was not the only method of doing so deployed by blacks under Jim Crow—for many the church provided a humanizing society and lynching plays served a similar function—but those who turned to blues and the blues community found there a structure supportive of social humanity. Blues is certainly not a guarantee of social recognition, and even less so a form of agitprop social activism, but it is deeply and foundationally concerned with the humanity of blues people.

As the next two chapters demonstrate, these qualities pervade Wilson's work because he was deeply committed to a blues ethos as both a man and an artist. In the social and aesthetic conditions of blues, Wilson found the necessary tools for both examining and productively contributing to the black American experience. His treatment of that experience is neither mollifying nor fatalistic, but rather clear-eyed, empathetic, and hopeful; as Shannon argues, "a powerful blues dynamic" in the playwright's work "sets an appropriate tone of despair while also affording Wilson's characters buoyancy as they try against devastating odds."[72] Such buoyancy comes from a blues sense of shared suffering and shared strength in the community. Wilson's characters regularly struggle, but his dramaturgy suggests that characters from across the *Cycle* are in that struggle together, and that fostering community is a path forward toward clear, sustainable black identity. This distinctively blues ethos permeates the work of Wilson, bluesman to the core.

2
"I Am the Blues"
August Wilson as Bluesman

BLUES HAS LONG BEEN part of the discussion of August Wilson's work. Having his first popular success with *Ma Rainey's Black Bottom,* a play about a blues band, and constantly professing profound indebtedness to blues, Wilson positioned himself throughout his career as immersed in blues aesthetics. But he was no musician—"I don't play an instrument. I don't know any musical terms. And I don't know anything about music," he confessed—nor was he involved in music production.[1] As a result, critics regularly characterize Wilson as a dramatist influenced by blues music rather than as a bluesman. Harry J. Elam, for example, argues, "The blues for Wilson continue to offer a methodology for negotiating the difficult spaces of African American existence and achieving African American survival"; Jay Plum says that for Wilson "the blues are a supportive force that allows listeners to transcend their hardships"; Sandra G. Shannon insists that the playwright's process is "aided by the melancholy strains of blues lyrics, a poet's sensitivity, and extraordinary intuition"; "Indeed, the womb from which Wilson's plays were born was [the historical] Ma Rainey," suggests Randy Gener; and Paul Carter Harrison writes that "Wilson's memory has fashioned a vernacular voice that resonates, with archetypal sonority, the rhythms of West African 'talking drums' and the riffs of Delta blues guitars."[2] Each of these critics make compelling arguments that treat blues as a musical repository from which Wilson drew influence, and the playwright as an artist working in one medium (drama) who is heavily influenced by another (music).[3]

Recognizing blues as an ethos that finds purchase in a variety of aesthetic modes, however, allows for productive recognition of Wilson as a bluesman who produced direct blues expression. Certainly music has been the predominant expression of this ethos: amid uncertainty and oppression in the early years of blues, Delta musicians called out claims to their complex social identities, hoping to receive from the social sphere a collaborative response that ratified identity through recognition and support. Those artists begat musical followers and continue to inspire musicians throughout the world. But "lest we be terribly mistaken," cautions Kalamu ya Salaam, "we must understand two factors: (1) not all african americans are blues people, and (2) the blues aesthetic is an ethos of blues people that manifests itself in everything done, not just in the music."[4] As Salaam insists, blues is more expansive than a musical genre. At its core is the conviction that aesthetic expression of particular challenges and values shared by and performed before a community can facilitate the development of selfhood. Bessie Smith mobilized this ethos in music, but so too did Wilson in his drama. The work of Bessie Smith is a particular expression of blues through music rather than blues a priori, as Wilson's work is blues drama. Both of these artists and others in a variety of media invoke an ethos that transcends and precedes its particular expression in any given art. At bottom, blues is an aesthetic philosophy provoking and underwriting responses to challenging social environments in a wide range of artistic modes, including Wilson's drama.

In one regard, calling Wilson a bluesman might seem a simple claim: he constantly claimed influence from blues, blues themes pervade his work, and blues music appears frequently in his plays. Yet, if blues aesthetics is the particular expression of a larger ethos, then essential to the task of theorizing Wilson's work as blues drama is recognizing evidence of a blues ethos guiding the playwright. Wilson looked out over a twentieth century full of oppressive dehumanization and poorly defined identity for himself and his community of black Americans, and he turned to art as a response. This is the impulse of a bluesman. Like all blues artists, however, a sustainable identity for Wilson as bluesman must come through antiphonal performance of self in the uncertain hope of receiving ratification from his audience. The *American Century Cycle* contributes to this performance, but throughout his career the playwright made a call of identity more directly in interviews that he treated as opportunities for performative self-crafting. While it might seem that his responses to questions offer only information and context about his life and work, they in fact show Wilson actively constructing a self that is guided by the blues principle of social identity crafting. Both the content of his narratives and the particular stories he chooses to highlight show an artist who considers the community an essential contributor to the self, and who attempts to use his public forum as a venue for identity formulation. This active, sustained performance extends to Wilson's dramaturgy, an aesthetic expression of the blues ethos that guides his engagement with society.

Still, using the interviews as a rubric for understanding the *Cycle* plays would be tenuous. Evidence of Wilson responding to the world in a certain way during interviews does not necessarily suggest that such a response emerges in his work. Two other non-*Cycle* works strengthen this link: his polemic speech, "The Ground on Which I Stand," and his dramatic memoir, the monologue play *How I Learned What I Learned*. The former has been variously derided, praised, and dissected since its 1996 delivery, and the latter has received almost no critical treatment to this point. Neither has been examined as evidence of its author's dramaturgy, leaving a critical lacuna that this chapter seeks to address. The interviews show a man shaping his life through the lens of blues experience; "The Ground on Which I Stand" shows that man demanding American theater rise to the challenge of supporting blues expression; and *How I Learned What I Learned* demonstrates how this playwright executes those demands himself. This constellation of extra-*Cycle* work shows that the ten *Cycle* plays arise from the blues ethos of an artist who approached drama as an aesthetic contribution to a sociocultural search for identity. Rather than simply taking the playwright on his word that blues is a primary influence, this chapter endeavors to uncover and reveal a complex portrait of August Wilson as bluesman.

Wilson's Signifyin(g) Interviews

In his frequent interviews, Wilson signifies on the trope of offering passive responses to journalists' questions in such a way that allows him to use the venue for active performances of himself as bluesman. Those who take Wilson's interview responses as glosses to understanding his plays are duped.

Far more important than what he says is the manner in which he reads his biography as a blues odyssey, calling out as a bluesman in hopes of a ratifying response from his audience. Wilson characterizes his own black experience within a blues framework: out of pain and recognition of injustice, he created art as a means of response, expression, and self-actualization. Thus, when he says that his first hearing of blues music made him think "this spoke to something in myself. It said, this is yours," he is suggesting that the voice of blues attitudes resonates with his life experience.[5] He is characterizing himself as what Salaam dubs a blues person, who "manifest[s] a blues sensibility, a post-reconstruction expression of peoplehood culturally codified into an aesthetic."[6] It would be a fallacy to claim that one who thinks like a blues musician is by necessity a blues person, but in his interviews Wilson goes further, performing a blues sensibility in his methods of active engagement with society.

Wilson's many interviews and public appearances returned frequently to similar topics and stories, with clear patterns emerging through which he demonstrated a blues mentality underwriting his engagement with the world. One topic that Wilson never seems to have brought up on his own is his white father; still, his treatment of this topic shows a commitment to identity crafting that is active and social rather than passively received. The fact of his white father suggests to some that as a maturing young man, Wilson had the opportunity to identify with either his maternal or paternal heritage (or some combination thereof) and chose to embrace his blackness rather than his whiteness. Pointing out that an adult Wilson "neither looks nor sounds typically black," Henry Louis Gates, for example, suggests that Wilson was "black first and foremost by self-identification."[7] Bill Moyers raises the issue in precisely these terms to Wilson in a 1988 interview: "You had a white father. And yet you chose the black route, the black culture, the black way. Could you not just as easily have chosen the patriarchal way?"[8] Moyers, Gates, and others suggest that the combination of Wilson's white parentage and light complexion afforded him the potential to identify as white.

Moyers's question, like Gate's charge, is built on the presumption of free self-fashioning, the notion that how social beings identify is dictated by the free choice to say, "This is who I am. Treat me as such." Wilson responds to Moyers by rejecting this premise: "Well, no, because the cultural environment of my life was black. . . . The cultural environment of my life, the forces that have shaped me, the nurturing, the learning, have all been black ideas about the world that I learned from my mother."⁹ In another interview, Wilson rejects any notion of predetermined identity. "You're from an interracial background, aren't you?" asks Dennis Watlington, garnering the curt response "my father was white, if that's what you mean."¹⁰ Interviewers regularly note Wilson's reticence to explore the issue: "His eyes say: Next question, please," notes Dinah Livingston after relaying a similarly curt response to a question on the topic.¹¹ When speaking about the issue during his Town Hall debate with Robert Brustein, Wilson again seems annoyed and eager to move past the subject: "obviously, if you look at me, obviously the slavemaster visited the slave quarters, OK, so it's very obvious. [. . .] My father was German. Uh. Yeah, what about it? I don't know. I don't know what else you—The cultural environment of my life is black."¹² Whenever the issue of his mixed-race heritage came up, Wilson consistently cited his cultural environment as more constitutive of identity than biology.

The potential of Wilson's racial ambiguity and his treatment of the issue in interviews reveal the important blues condition of socially defined selfhood underwriting his notion of identity. Race for Wilson and for the blues ethos turns out to be performative in much the same way that Judith Butler theorizes gender. Insisting that "gender proves to be performative—that is, constituting the identity it is purported to be," Butler defines the concept of gender as "the repeated stylization of the body, a set of repeated acts within a highly rigid regulatory frame that congeal over time to produce the appearance of substance, of a natural sort of being."¹³ For Butler, while sex might be biological, gender is determined by engagement with the social sphere; for Wilson, while his genealogy might be biological, his race is determined almost entirely by engagement first with the domestic sphere and then with the social sphere. Society treated him as black, his cultural environment was black, he adopted black mores, and he considered himself fundamentally black as a result. His constant annoyance at the question suggests on the one hand that Wilson considered his performance at some point concluded, that he felt his performance of identity had been ratified by the community and he had no interest in continuing down that particular path of inquiry. But in another important aspect, his aggravation suggests an annoyed awareness of his persistent need to perform black selfhood. This makes his social performance of his identity a constant and dynamic performative project, one that demands active attention.

Wilson's refrain-like response to the question of his racial background— that he is black because the cultural environment of his life was black—

therefore argues for identity as fundamentally social, crafted in interaction between the self and the community. He supports this by highlighting stories where his understanding of self developed antiphonally with the community as the most formative experiences for his racial identity. He reports being the only black student at Central Catholic High School, for example, where he received daily notes on his desk telling him, "Go home, nigger"; he says that the principal often had to escort him through a schoolyard full of white students eager to fight him.[14] He regularly tells other stories of attending the black church in his neighborhood, being refused a bag for his purchases at Woolworths, and joining a community of black artists. By telling these stories, he seeks to make clear that well before he wrote a word about the black American experience for the theater, the regulatory forces of his social sphere were treating him as a black American with all the attendant bigotry by whites and support by blacks. Thus any notion of choice—as posited by Moyers, Gates, and others—is overridden by the power of social experience. As Shannon recognizes, "Due to childhood circumstances in his native Pittsburgh . . . Wilson had no choice but to fashion his identity from the culture surrounding him and to define his manhood dictated by his fate."[15] Wilson repeatedly clarifies that he participated in the social performance of his blackness and ultimately embodied that blackness within a social sphere that allowed little room for anything other than the dichotomy of white and black. He shows that from an early age, he saw identity as defined in dialogue between self and society, recognizing himself as an active social being.

The Hill District may have offered Wilson no other racial identity than blackness, but he makes sure repeatedly in interviews to tell childhood stories highlighting how he learned about and participated in the dialectical identity crafting that shaped him as a black man. He insists, for instance, that his mother, Daisy, modeled for him how to negotiate productively the interaction between self and other. He does this through frequent recounting of the story about his mother winning a washing machine from a radio contest. When the station discovered their winner to be black, they denied her the promised new washing machine, offering a voucher for a used one instead. Wilson's mother refused: "She told them exactly what they could do with their certificate, and she didn't want no used washing machine because she was due a brand-new washing machine like they said on the radio."[16] Wilson here reports recognizing an example of identity crafting at a formative age. In the dialogue between Daisy and society, the radio station claimed Wilson's mother to be of lesser value than a white person. She could have chosen to accept the certificate for a used machine, acquiescing to the social statement, but she refused to ratify any notion of her lack of value, preserving dignity and selfhood. Wilson's frequent retelling of this episode from his youth reveals that this moment of instruction in responding to white identity denial was influential for his future social self-crafting. He sees his most significant black role model actively responding to bigotry in a way that says more about her sense of selfhood than it does about her desire for increased comfort. His deep admiration for his mother and frequent retelling of this story suggest that for Wilson, social blackness is tied up in the constant struggle, not necessarily to get by or to get one over on oppressors, but rather to establish and support a clear social identity.

By telling another favorite story about the ending of his formal education, Wilson shows that as a young man he incorporated lessons like this from his mother into his own interactions with regulatory social forces. He says that for a high school research paper assignment he wrote a twenty-page, thoroughly researched essay on Napoleon: "I was real proud of it," he asserts.[17] Wilson says that the paper's quality made his teacher suspect that Wilson had not written it himself and he found himself accused of cheating: "He had written A plus on it or an E, and he said, 'I'm going to give you one of these two grades,'" depending, it seems, on whether or not Wilson could prove that he wrote the paper himself. Wilson says he refused to play along: "I had my bibliography and my footnotes, and I felt that's all the explanation I should give." Wilson says that his refusal "to prove to him that I'd written the paper, other than to say that I had written it" prompted the teacher to fail the essay, whereupon Wilson says he "tore the paper up and threw it in the wastebasket and walked out of the school."[18] He suggests that he would not accept this slight to his dignity, and instead left school and never returned.

By frequently telling this story, Wilson crafts his younger self as somebody at once deploying the influence of his mother and finding his own voice in the process of social identity crafting. In both cases, the act (accepting the used machine, offering a defense against cheating) would justify the racist premise, and neither Daisy nor August had any intent of doing such a thing. Wilson treats his younger self as a nascent playwright developing a notion of social identity, suggesting that this experience provided early recognition of the role played by self and society in crafting identity. He could have passively allowed his white teacher to brand him as untrustworthy, but his refusal to participate in the unjust situation was an active response to the social attempt at creating his identity for him. In telling his story of leaving school, Wilson crafts his younger self as recognizing that he does not need the white establishment to sanction his intelligence in order for him to operate as an intelligent individual.

Importantly, however, he does not simply storm out of school and never seek education again. To have done so would have been to acquiesce to the white establishment by acknowledging that the white-controlled schools provided the only means of intellectual development. Instead, Wilson reports taking himself to the public library, where he continued his education through black literature (Shannon suggests that at least initially his library trips forestalled "deciding how and when to inform his mother of his decision" to leave school).[19] "I discovered the Negro section of the library," he says. "I read *Invisible Man,* Langston Hughes, and all the thirty or forty books in the section, including the sociology. I remember reading a book that talked about the 'Negro's power of hard work' and how much that phrase affected me. [. . .] Looking back, I see that I had never seen those words together: 'Negro power.'"[20] By telling the story of turning away from white teachers in favor of black literature, Wilson shows himself redefining the dialogue of his social becoming. He shows that rather than engaging with the white hegemony that sought to define him downward, he began a conversation with a community invested in his confidence and success. As his awareness of being awed by any notion of black power reveals, the conversation with the black community was very different from the conversation with the white community, having a profound effect on the young Wilson: the call he made to a different social sphere was returned through the literature with support and encouragement. For an adult Wilson speaking to an interviewer, the juxtaposition between his experiences with his white teacher and his reading of black authors suggests that as he reflects on his own development, he recognizes the dialogic dimension of identity.

And yet the sparsity of the public library's black literature selection underscores the limited options available to a young Wilson for engagement with writers. A collection of thirty to forty books, spread among literature and sociology, does not make for an extensive catalog of black experiences. Wilson reports finding such a catalog in blues. He offers evidence of his blues ethos most clearly in his reflections on the sense of identity ingrained in blues. In what might be the playwright's most frequently told childhood story, he relates discovering blues music through a chance encounter with a Bessie Smith song called "Nobody in Town Can Bake a Sweet Jelly Roll Like Mine": "I recall I listened to the record twenty-two straight times. Just over and over. I had never heard anything like it," he says. He admits being "stunned by its beauty," but says that his time spent with Smith's record elicited more than aesthetic appreciation: "There was an immediate emotional response. It was someone speaking directly to me. I felt this was mine, this was something I could connect with that I instantly emotionally understood, and that all the rest of the music I was listening to did not concern me, was not a part of me. But this spoke to something in myself. It said, this is yours."[21] In this and similarly phrased responses, Wilson crafts his younger self as in formative dialogue with blues on the level of identity, claiming that his selfhood developed through consistent engagement with a blues ethos. From his white teacher to the black authors to Bessie Smith, Wilson suggests that he moved through a spectrum of interlocutors with whom he found increasingly specific identification. His characterization of himself listening to Smith shows the song speaking to Wilson as a black man approaching society through a blues ethos. Between the lines of Smith's performance, Wilson heard a blues response to the world, and in recounting his profound connection to the song, he attempts to mark himself out as a member of the community of blues people with Smith and others. "With my discovery of Bessie Smith and the blues," he says, "I had been given a world that contained my image, a world at once rich and varied, marked and marking, brutal and beautiful, and at crucial odds with the larger world that contained it and preyed and pressed it from every conceivable angle."[22] He says that blues affected his worldview, but by making such a claim he performs a blues mentality and espouses a blues ethos.

He seeks to develop this identity further by insisting that engrossing himself in the blues musical tradition profoundly affected his view of black America. He says that blues showed him "that there was a nobility to the lives of blacks in America which I didn't always see. At the time I was living in a rooming house in Pittsburgh. After I discovered the blues, I began to look at the people in the house a little differently than I had before. I began to see a value in their lives that I simply hadn't seen before. I discovered a beauty and a nobility in their struggle to survive."[23] He thus constructs a performative scenario in which blues makes a call for recognition of identity and humanity, and upon hearing that call he offers a ratifying response not only to blues performers but also to the black people in his immediate social sphere. Others might have claimed a deep connection to the novels and poetry at the library, but for Wilson, "Blues is the best literature we have" because "the blues and music have always been at the forefront in the development of character and consciousness of black America," or more simply, "culture is in the music."[24] Most importantly for Wilson, the period during which he became immersed in blues was the time "I began to discover myself as a black man in relation to the world."[25] Consistently in interviews, Wilson shows himself finding in blues the key to his own identity as a person and later as an artist.

Part of this process is participating in the performative framework of blues with a view to engendering similar participation from his own audience, which Wilson attempts to do by demonstrating that his aesthetic ethos aligns with that of blues. He says that "the blues are important primarily because they contain the cultural responses of blacks in America to the situation that they find themselves in. Contained in the blues is a philosophical system at work."[26] He treats the blues tradition not as a static repository of time-stamped ideas, but as full of active cultural responses constantly relaying and advancing the dynamically performative black response to evolving, frequently oppressive social spheres. In Wilson's view, the goal of blues is locating humanity within that cultural response. He argues, "The music provides you an emotional reference for the information, and it is sanctioned by the community in the sense that if someone sings the song, other people sing the song. They keep it alive because they sanction the information that it contains."[27] In these responses to interviewers' questions, Wilson recognizes blues performers' appeal for a social humanity and responds with a ratification that contributes to the humanization of blues performers, himself, and other members of his social sphere. Moreover, he models his aesthetic philosophy for blues art: in his response to blues musicians, he makes a call to his audience to recognize the quest for social humanity motivating his own work. At bottom, then, the body of interviews and other self-reflexive work are a broad performance by Wilson in which he seeks at once to self-craft his identity as guided by a blues ethos, engage with the tradition of blues art, and call to his audience in search of a ratifying response for his identity as bluesman.

Standing on the Ground of Social Theater

This complex performance of self continues in "The Ground on Which I Stand," a speech through which Wilson makes more explicit claims about his blues community, his identity as person and artist, and his concept of the importance of theater to the blues aesthetic community. In the speech, delivered as the keynote address of the Theatre Communications Group's eleventh biennial conference in 1996, he articulates his understanding of the black American experience in its social and artistic dimensions. Standing before an audience of his peers, Wilson presents himself as an artist deeply concerned with the state of his community, making a call through his speech in search of a response ratifying him as a spokesman and agent of change for that community. Although the response was far from univocal—the speech garnered comparable amounts of praise and condemnation—most important in understanding Wilson's blues identity is recognizing that his expectations for theater are to perform, examine, and foster active social humanity.[28]

"The Ground on Which I Stand" shows Wilson's belief that black theater is an active process of communal identity formulation. In the speech, he defines himself as "a race man," which he says means "simply that I believe race matters. That is the largest, most identifiable, and most important part of our personality. It is the largest category of identification because it is the one that most influences your perception of yourself, and it is the one to which others in the world of men most respond."[29] In the American social landscape, however, he sees the responses to race as problematically unequal, suggesting that blacks and whites "stare at each other across a divide of economics and privilege that has become an encumbrance on black Americans' ability to prosper and on the collective will and spirit of our national purpose" (16–17). He suggests that this sense of social inequality extends through privilege, economics, and theater.

The foundation of this rift as Wilson sees it is white society's systematic denial of black humanity, and he identifies his own socio-aesthetic mission as working to rebut such an outlook. He says that the ground on which he stands is in part "the ground of the affirmation of the value of one's being, an affirmation of his worth in the face of the society's urgent and sometimes profound denial" (11). For Wilson, theater, with "its daring and its sometimes lacerating, and often healing, truths" provides an invaluable mechanism for responding to such dehumanization through an active performance of self (10). "Theatre can do that," he insists. "It can disseminate ideas, it can educate even the miseducated, because it is art—and all art reaches across that divide that makes order out of chaos and embraces the truth that overwhelms with its presence and that connects man to something larger than himself and his imagination" (45). At bottom, he identifies theater as a vehicle that can precipitate the journey he sees black America making "from the hull of a ship to self-determining, self-respecting people" (38).

Yet, the foundation of Wilson's speech is a concern that the state of American theater mirrors the racial disenfranchisement of society, and his anger over this condition reveals a fundamental belief in theater as blues expression. He is mad not simply because black theater artists have too few places to work, but because this lack denies the black community a necessary venue for social becoming. Treating American blackness as a distinct culture with a specific history that demands artistic examination, he reveals his belief that theater is a vehicle for self-actualization. He worries that the lack of funding for black theater denies black America an opportunity for the formation of identity. Objecting to theater-funding models he decries as racist and calling color-blind casting "an aberrant idea that has never had any validity other than as a tool of the Cultural Imperialist who views their American Culture, rooted in the icons of European Culture, as beyond reproach in its perfection," he insists, "We do not need colorblind casting; we need theaters. We need theatres to develop our playwrights" (29, 33). His thesis is that theaters will develop the talent of black artists who will be able to work toward establishing the distinctive identity of black Americans, whereas color-blind casting of white plays denies the opportunity for call-and-response identity crafting to the black community.[30] He wants his audience to recognize black humanity neither as some inferior rendition of white humanity nor as assimilated into white culture and cut off from the history of black experience, but as fully actualized within itself.

Wilson insists that such a recognition of black identity hinges on the lineage of black Americans from slaves: "The term black or African-American not only denotes race, it denotes condition, and carries with it the vestige of slavery and the social segregation and abuse of opportunity so vivid in our memory" (16). He seeks to demonstrate the crucial distinctiveness of black art, showing that black theater has its own important tradition stretching back to the performances of African slaves: "I stand myself and my art squarely on the self-defining ground of the slave quarters, and find the ground to be hallowed and made fertile by the blood and bones of the men and women who can be described as warriors on the cultural battlefield that affirmed their self-worth" (20). His sense of the most valuable black art being in dialogue with slave culture underwrites his notion that distinctively black theaters are essential because they are best equipped to foster that dialogue.

Although critics like Robert Brustein and Henry Louis Gates derided Wilson for what they read as an argument for stark separation of theater based on race, the speech calls instead for theaters dedicated to actively fostering and engendering black culture. The sticking point for Brustein, Gates, and others is Wilson's insistence that black drama should happen in black theaters supported by black artists, and that black actors should not play roles written for whites. The unifying term that Brustein and Gates use to characterize this position is *separatism*, a notion that they both relate to separate-but-equal segregation. This objection is not without merit—certainly Wilson is calling for a separate and equal space—but its premise is the very assumption that Wilson endeavors to expose and deconstruct: a presumption of white universality. When the issue was raised in response to the speech, he pointed out that "universality, of course, is conferred on white artists automatically, and never, never is it suggested that white playwrights like David Mamet or Terrence McNally are limiting themselves to whiteness, and that they are being confined in their art by pursuing white themes," and that nobody ever said to Chekhov, "you are limiting yourself to Russian. You should write about the more universal."[31] In this way, Wilson argued that seemingly all nonblack playwrights have the freedom of cultural specificity without being branded separatists. Elam correctly insists that Wilson's claims offer "a prescription for decentering American normative whiteness and reflect a politics of difference that offers not separatism, but a recognition of diversity"; May Joseph calls this diversity "African American cultural sovereignty."[32] As Elam recognizes, Wilson makes a classic poststructuralist move: he demonstrates that the presumed universal is in fact a social and political construction, and then shows that those same social and political forces disempower the marginalized segment not included in the universal. "Wilson's black particularism," says Elam, adopting Harold Cruse's term in rebuttal to the notion of separatism, "asserts black self-determination against the hegemony of the white-controlled culture industry."[33]

The space between the playwright and his critics highlights the ethos underwriting Wilson's dramaturgy. He is neither calling for segregated theater nor suggesting that only black theaters can produce black plays; he seeks support for theaters dedicated to the exploration of black history and culture so that black Americans might be better able to develop sustainable identity. This notion of thorough imbrication between performance and identity is why he is so upset with the concept of colorblind casting. He insists that "to mount an all-black production of a *Death of a Salesman* or any other play conceived for white actors as an investigation of the human condition through the specifics of white culture is to deny us our own humanity, our own history, and the need to make our own investigations from the cultural ground on which we stand as black Americans. It is an assault on our presence, and our difficult but honorable history in America" (*Ground*, 30–31). Wilson would not likely deny the universality of themes like aging, regret, father-son strife, and compassionless capitalism that structure Miller's play, but he would probably be quick to point out that very few black men in the middle of the century had the job of a traveling salesman with a car and a house in Brooklyn—those are components of what he dubs white culture. Willy Loman's black counterpart is a garbage man living in a working-class neighborhood, and for Wilson that characterization is a more honest and fruitful exploration of the black experience. Pronounced economic and social privilege underlies such pillars of American drama as *Long Day's Journey into Night* or *Cat on a Hot Tin Roof* that would for Wilson ring false for the contemporaneous black community, regardless of how universal their transcendent themes remain. Black Americans have a very different history than the Lomans, Tyrones, or Pollitts, and so to filter black life through white characters' experiences is to presume falsely that their experience is common. Stephen McKinley Henderson says, "August Wilson wrote ten plays about what black characters in other plays do when they go home," and in this sense, Wilson's speech calls for a space where black theater artists can examine their culture's distinct homes.[34]

"The Ground on Which I Stand" thus argues that theater has a duty to perform honest humanity, and that part of theater's task is assembling a social community for the examination of and engagement with a notion of self. The speech reveals that Wilson brings a blues sensibility to bear on his expectations of theater. His sharp focus on humanity and social identity in a speech about theater given to a conference of theater professionals makes explicit his conviction that drama and performance are media of identity examination and crafting. He calls for funded black theaters because he considers the process of existential humanization crucial for his culture and because he believes the theater is a space where that important cultural work can happen. He calls blues "a flag bearer of self-definition" for black Americans, and he treats theater the same way.[35] He treats art as a tool of identity crafting in a way that has been expressed for generations in blues, and suggests that theater works toward that same goal. For Wilson, theater is blues expression.

Wilson as Blues Practitioner

Although the *Cycle* plays work within this blues framework, a clearer picture of Wilson as bluesman turning to theater for communal identity crafting arises from his dramatic memoir, the monologue play *How I Learned What I Learned*, written in collaboration with Todd Kreidler and originally performed by the playwright in 2003. By foregrounding Wilson's investment in the identity-crafting potential of theatrical performance, *How I Learned* shows Wilson actively participating in theater as a place of performative becoming within an antiphonal community. "I was, and remain, fascinated by the idea of an audience as a community of people who gather willingly to bear witness," said Wilson, emphasizing his investment in theater as a space of productive community.[36] *How I Learned* shows the playwright attempting to harness this space of active witnessing for his own social becoming and illuminates the performative strategy of characters throughout the *Cycle*. Elam argues that in the play Wilson "situates himself as a character within his African American cycle," suggesting that Wilson treats himself and his life's journey not unlike that of Troy Maxson, Wining Boy, or any of his many other characters.[37] While this is certainly true in terms of the play's narrative exploration of Wilson's struggles with racism, romance, history, and the search for his song, a slightly different way of thinking about Wilson's performativity in *How I Learned* may be more productive. Rather than placing himself within the *Cycle*, he demonstrates how the *Cycle* characters are always already part of the American social sphere with which *How I Learned* engages, eroding barriers between those characters' fiction and his reality, and making his dramatic persona a catalyst for the antiphony between stage and social sphere. Mary L. Bogumil suggests that the play can be read either as a bildungsroman or, perhaps more fruitfully, "as a *künstlerroman,* a growth of a character as an artist," which would show how "Wilson through this fictional reenactment actively engaged the audience to participate in and accept this instability of self as an operative trope of identity."[38] As Bogumil recognizes, *How I Learned*'s primary investment is the performative process of identity crafting catalyzed by Wilson's narrative of self. Accordingly, the play functions as a conduit between Wilson's dramaturgy and the dramatic work of his *Cycle* plays. It is a stylistic outlier that casts the social operation of the *American Century Cycle* into sharp focus.

In the monologue, Wilson tells the story of his physical and psychological emergence from his mother's house in Pittsburgh, chronicling the lessons he considers most important to his formative years. The notion of "how" in the play's title becomes more precisely "from whom" as the body of the play moves primarily through Wilson's interpersonal experiences, chronicling many of the important people that gave shape and direction to a young artist. Notably absent are artistic influences like Amiri Baraka, Romare Bearden, and Lloyd Richards, and in their places are Wilson's mother, ex-girlfriends, former bosses at menial jobs, and the junkies, fledgling artists, and wise elders of Pittsburgh's Hill District; Kreidler says that part of Wilson's desire in writing the play was "to show, as he did in the majority of his plays, that the Hill District community was the 'best offstage character.'"[39] This is not the story of a successful playwright navigating the world of theater, but rather of a young poet, struggling to reconcile his profound senses of dignity and purpose with the challenges of being black and poor in twentieth-century America. Very little of what he says about his life in the play focuses on himself alone; rather, all the stories are about his experiences with other people. It is clear that, for Wilson, the operation of learning about one's self and animating those lessons in a productive process of becoming relies on an antiphonal relationship with others in the community. That these experiences became a monologue play makes it equally clear that he considered the process of ratifying this becoming dependent upon sharing the experience performatively with an audience. *How I Learned* is thus prototypical of the blues dramaturgy underwriting the *American Century Cycle*.[40]

Personal stories and Wilson's reflections on the journey of his early life dominate the play, but first Wilson reflects on his ancestry by pinpointing the beginning of his personal history as the moment the first African slaves arrived on American soil in 1619: "My ancestors have been in America since the early seventeenth century." By opening in this fashion, Wilson makes clear his connection to the history of Africans in America, but he also identifies historical roots as the foundation of his social existence. As blues artists evoke all the tradition's voices with each performance, Wilson makes explicit that black American history is constitutive of his social self. After linking his history to the arrival of American slaves, Wilson immediately proceeds to a bit of humor: "And for the first two hundred and forty-four years we never had a problem finding a job."[41] From the very beginning of *How I Learned*, therefore, Wilson demonstrates two fundamental blues characteristics: cultivation of a dialogue with one's ancestors and biting blues humor. Yet, as Ralph Ellison influentially argues, wry blues humor does not assuage suffering but precipitates personal progress through direct engagement with suffering: "The Blues is an impulse to keep the painful details and episodes of a brutal experience alive in one's aching consciousness, to finger its jagged grain, and to transcend it, not by consolation of philosophy, but by squeezing from it a near-tragic, near-comic lyricism."[42] Wilson opens his monologue by fingering the jagged grain of slavery with a joke and then moving on in the next line to engage suffering directly: "But since 1863 it's been hell." At once obliquely and directly, Wilson points to the slave trade and its legacy as the foundation of black American suffering, refusing to espouse any romantic notion of emancipation and equality. "It's been hell," he continues, "because the ideas and attitudes that America had toward slaves followed them out of slavery and became entrenched in the nation's psyche. Ideas that said that Blacks were sub-human, and that they were lacking in moral personality, that they were unbaptizeable, that they were lazy, shiftless, watermelon-eating, chicken-stealing, oversexed, loud, menacing appendages to the polite, civilized society that the Europeans had wrestled from, what the Honorable Elijah Muhammad called 'the wilderness of North America.' This is, after the polite, civilized Europeans had killed all the Indians" (7). With this analysis of black America's social history, Wilson argues that his performance of self is in dialogue with a genealogy of suffering. Between the lines of the play's opening moments, Wilson therefore introduces himself as one immersed in a blues ethos who is turning to the theater in order to express and perform his social self before a community. From the outset of *How I Learned*, Wilson aligns his aesthetic mission with early blues artists.

At the play's opening, Wilson establishes the conditions to which he is responding, and he moves on from there to narrate a number of specific events in his life: moving out of his mother's house, quitting several jobs in the face of racist affronts to his dignity, dating and losing various women, and spending time with a number of influential friends. Some of these friends he finds among "a group of poets and painters at the Hill Arts Society" (13). This is an artist collective that Wilson also references in interviews: the community among which he wrote poetry and developed as an artist and person. But in *How I Learned* there is no mention of poetry readings or peer-review workshops or the like; there are instead stories about life lessons he gleaned from time spent with men like Chawley Williams, who taught him to value silence, and Cy Morocco, an illiterate musician manqué who showed Wilson the value of dedicating himself to his craft of writing.

Ultimately, Wilson characterizes his engagement with the Hill Arts Society as engendering his development as a dignified person with self and social awareness. He calls the men of the society "people who became my life-long friends and, ultimately, sanctioned my life and provided it with its meaning" (13). He had spent his young life having the voice of his selfhood rejected and derided by any number of different social forces, but through antiphonal social engagement with the men of the Hill Arts Society, a young Wilson learns about himself and his place in the world. In relating that story in *How I Learned,* Wilson the performer is claiming before the theatrical community an investment in the active and perpetual process of social becoming through antiphonal exchange. When telling this and other stories, the narrator of *How I Learned* is performing the self, implicitly claiming, "This is who I am, and this is how I became so." The connection between this implicit claim and the play's opening section recalling slavery's legacy underscores the long tradition of black dehumanization in America, suggesting that a particularly powerful way of rebutting such dehumanization is to perform the self for an audience.

This is a blues impulse and a blues performative structure: in response to dehumanizing oppression, the artist makes a performative claim of selfhood before a social community in the uncertain hope of receiving a ratifying response of humanization in return. Late in the play, Wilson tells a story of receiving advice from a community elder: "'I've been watching you for about six or seven years now,'" says the man, "'See, and you going through life carrying a ten-gallon bucket. And if you go through life carrying a ten-gallon bucket, you always going to be disappointed. Cause it ain't never going to be filled. [. . .] Get you a little cup and carry that through life. And that way somebody put a little bit in it and then you have something." Wilson reports dutifully replying "Yes, sir" to his elder, but then says to *How I Learned*'s audience: "I do want you to know that since then I have been working on it and I have got it cut down to about a gallon bucket. But, I do want you to know this also. That it ain't never going to get down to that little cup. See, and it ain't never going to get down to that little cup because I deserve more" (43). Wilson is not asking simply to be seen and acknowledged, but to be recognized as a valuable person, and ratified by the community as such. Delta blues artists went before their audiences repeatedly and powerfully in order to make an assertive call that would elicit a vigorous response of ratification. Wilson here suggests that his project is similar: as he does for black Americans in the *Cycle,* he calls for a recognition of substance that goes beyond simple acknowledgment with the confidence that such recognition is deserved. *How I Learned What I Learned* turns out to be a blues play: the narrator is not singing or playing harmonica, but he is entering into the mode of blues performance. In response to social oppression and the search for identity, the artist makes a performative claim of selfhood before a community in the uncertain hope of receiving a ratifying response of social humanization in return. Wilson's regular reference to the notion of community sanction reveals his investment in social engagement and collaboration in the creation of the subject. As a window into Wilson's blues dramaturgy, *How I Learned* reveals that, for this playwright, theater is a social art, and a vehicle to perform the task of catalyzing social becoming.

His choice to write a play for a self-crafting memoir is of a piece with his dramaturgical and social investment in theater. Repeatedly in interviews, Wilson confessed an interest in moving toward fiction after the completion of the *Cycle,* but his choice of theater for his memoir suggests that he considers it the most efficacious venue for identity crafting. When speaking about poems and stories he had written, he says, "I never sought sanction outside the sanction I would place on my own work. I never sent my poems or my stories off to be published. For me, it was the sheer joy of writing them"; elsewhere he says that "if there is such a thing as public art and private art, then poems are private."[43] This indicates that the primary difference between drama and other genres of writing for Wilson is the search for sanction from audiences, the community of theater artists, and society at large. Wilson's predominate form of writing therefore actively sought sanction in a way that would ratify his work as a writer and his identity as a black American. *How I Learned* and the conditions of its creation therefore reveal most clearly what it is Wilson wants out of theater. For this playwright, theater is a social art through which one is able to perform the self in search of sanction from the community. Ultimately, *How I Learned*'s window into Wilson's dramaturgy reveals that he looked to theater as a vehicle to catalyze the process of social becoming. The monologue sought to do this for himself, but the *Cycle* plays seek to do so for the much broader social self of black Americans.

Existential Bluesman

Wilson reads the social history of blues' originary production as a means of performative self-crafting: "I saw the blues as a cultural response of a nonliterate people whose history and culture were rooted in the oral tradition. The response was to a world that was not of their making, in which the idea of themselves as a people of imminent worth that belied their recent history was continually assaulted."[44] Placing blues squarely in the lineage of ex-slaves and their descendants, Wilson recognizes not a specific musical sound but a cultural response, a means of social self-expression, and a method of social becoming.

It is unsurprising therefore that like Cornel West, Wilson, who was in no way a musician, had no reservations claiming, "I was, after all, a bluesman." "Never mind I couldn't play a guitar or carry a tune in a bucket," he admits, "I was cut out of the same cloth and I was on the same field of manners and endeavor—to articulate the cultural response of black Americans to the world in which they found themselves."[45] Wilson saw his plays as written in the same manner as songs performed by Son House or Bessie Smith, and he understood his aesthetic project as seeking the same goal of black cultural response. An insightful analyst of his work, the playwright's comments underscore the most important elements of his dramaturgy. He never says exactly how blues functions as "the wellspring" of his art in his plays; perhaps the most specific he ever gets is to claim "the music is made up of black life, and the plays are likewise made out of the same thing the blues are made out of. So they are blues. I am the blues."[46] While certainly the musical numbers and musician characters are clear reference points, blues is embedded deeply in the plays' ethos and dramaturgy. Blues sensibilities define his understanding of and approach to the world, and blues aesthetics guides his expression.

To be sure, Wilson was deeply concerned with the beleaguered state of black identity in America. He insisted that "the battle since the first African set foot on the continent of North America has been a battle for the affirmation of the value and worth of one's being in the face of this society that says you're worthless."[47] Consistently referring to himself as a black nationalist committed to the precepts of self-respect, self-determination, and self-defense, Wilson deployed art in an attempt to address all three of these notions. In order to do so, he traveled the road marked out by generations of bluesmen before him, calling blues "life-affirming music that guides you throughout life."[48] Wilson's project is not to write plays in dialogue with blues music; it is to create blues expressions of self and cultural identity. As the next chapter will demonstrate, the *American Century Cycle* turns out to be a complex blues opus, thoroughly invested in the social project of black American humanization.

3

August Wilson's Blues

TWO OF AUGUST WILSON'S most mystical scenes invoke the Middle Passage. In one, a vision of black bones people walking out of the sea onto American soil floors Herald Loomis. In the other, Citizen Barlow sails from Pittsburgh on a tiny paper ship made from Aunt Ester's slave Bill of Sale to the City of Bones, a settlement under the Atlantic Ocean populated by the souls of dead Africans who were tossed off slave ships before making landfall in America. Both Loomis and Citizen are in existential quandaries, unsure of who they are or where they fit into a world that seems to them harsh and inhospitable. In response, a playwright invested in helping his characters progress along journeys of self-discovery and self-invention decides to send these two on mystical voyages that unite them with a community of ancestors. These visions prove crucial vehicles for allowing both characters to find their voices and to understand better how they might find space for themselves within a crowded, dynamic social sphere.

The most obvious spaces to explore the operation of blues in Wilson's plays are the recording studio of *Ma Rainey's Black Bottom* or the backyard of *Seven Guitars*. Ma Rainey might be the *American Century Cycle*'s resident blues sage—saying famously that the blues are "life's way of talking. You don't sing to feel better, you sing because that's a way of understanding life," and that "the blues help you get out of bed in the morning. You get up knowing you ain't alone"—and Floyd Barton the flawed Wilsonian bluesman par excellence.[1] Critics like Sandra G. Shannon, Harry J. Elam, and Steven C. Tracy have proved that following the trail of Wilson's blues influence directly to his most vivid representations of blues music is an enlightening approach to specific plays.[2] But an approach to Wilson's blues dramaturgy broader than the scope of where blues music enters his plays shows how the visions of Loomis and Citizen are deeply ingrained with Wilson's blues thinking, and are in fact more prototypical of his blues dramaturgy than even the musical interludes scattered throughout the *Cycle*. Loomis and Citizen are in search of identity, and as the previous two chapters demonstrate, this urge and its performance lie at the core of blues sensibilities.

In this way, the *American Century Cycle* invites more holistic thinking about how a blues ethos animates Wilson's work. "The blues is more than a pastime for Wilson's characters," recognizes Shannon. "It is their universal means of communicating on the one hand and a means of healing emotional wounds on the other."[3] "The blues in the *American Century Cycle* is the existential metaphor for identity and freedom," argues Riley Keene Temple in a similar vein, calling blues "the song the Wilson men and women must find to know who they are."[4] Even stronger than metaphor, blues performativity proves the only path to existential fulfillment for Wilson's characters, a fundamental force that transcends music and its performance. The playwright treats blues less as a musical preference than as a guiding philosophy, undergirding his expectations of theater. As a result, approaching the entire *Cycle* through the lens of blues opens productive new insights into the plays and their social commentary. Blues, that is, proves to be the key to unlock the social performativity of Wilson's plays. Turning to history as a means of examining, commenting on, and affecting the performative present, Wilson enters into a similar aesthetic sphere as that of blues musicians: using art to express himself to a community in the uncertain hope of ratifying his social humanity. Simultaneously, he shepherds his characters into that aesthetic sphere, allowing them to make similar claims to their communities. Characters from Levee through Harmond Wilks are deeply invested in projects of communal identity crafting, even if they are not quite as aware of that fact as are Toledo, Elder Joseph Barlow, and others. And yet these characters are not simply making claims of social humanity within their own fictive world. Instead, the collection of characters that make up Wilson's *Cycle* stand in for Wilson's vision of the black American community, the experiences of which he hoped would be recognized, accepted, ratified, and embraced by his audience.

Wilson marks out his world in terms of a blues ethos: blues is the organizing metaphysics of the *American Century Cycle*. For his characters, this means that relative success or failure in their pursuits depends on how well they align themselves with the conditions of that ethos. To varying degrees, Citizen and Loomis willingly—if fearfully—participate in the performative events that advance their journeys toward social becoming, and in each case the character makes important advancements along that journey by play's end. Characters like Levee or King Hedley II actively resist participating in a blues-inflected social sphere and suffer as a consequence. At bottom, Wilson's aesthetic project shares blues music's originary concern with the attempt to claim a social humanity among a community of blues people, and as such the *American Century Cycle* operates in a clear mode of blues expression. The previous chapter sought to define Wilson as bluesman; the current chapter sets out to examine the implications of his art operating under a blues metaphysics within a community of blues people.

This argument departs from existing discussions of Wilson's blues influence that focus on the specificity of blues music inflecting his plays rather than a blues ethos writ large. Aside from the number of critics who focus their discussions of Wilson's blues on an examination of specific plays—such as Shannon's influential claim that *Ma Rainey's Black Bottom* "can be viewed as a dramatic rendition of a blues song" or Tracy's argument that "*Seven Guitars* exemplifies Wilson's comments about the importance of blues to his work"—the two most extensive examinations of the subject come from a seminal 1993 essay by Jay Plum and a chapter in Elam's 2006 important book on Wilson.[5] Both critics consider Wilson's blues influence as reflective of his treatment of history. Focusing on Wilson's insight into the Eurocentricity of hegemonic American history, and insisting that Wilson "views the blues as an empowering text that records African American experience," Plum argues that blues music offers the playwright an alternative medium through which he might examine the black experience in America: "the blues provide a mediational site where the contradictions between the lived and recorded experiences of African Americans might be resolved."[6] Because he considers Wilson's work as concerned primarily with offering a rendition of black history counter to the one in white-dominated textbooks, and because he recognizes the centrality of blues to Wilson's dramaturgy, Plum finds the project of establishing a subject position out of oppression to be at the heart of Wilson's investment in blues.

Elam's analysis places a similar emphasis on Wilson's process of rethinking black American history. He argues that "Wilson (w)rights history through performative rites that pull the action out of time or even ritualize time in order to change the power and potentialities of the now. This process of (w)righting history necessarily critiques how history is constituted and what history means."[7] Like Plum, Elam sees blues music as pivotal to Wilson's reinvestigation of black history with a view to resisting its hegemonic marginalization. "Throughout the work of August Wilson," he argues, "music, most particularly the blues, functions as both metaphor and metonym, as vehicles for cultural transmission and re-membrance."[8] For Elam, blues music and its essential characteristics of improvisation and cultural engagement provide Wilson with tools to rewrite black American history, aligning it more accurately with its own modes of cultural transmission: instead of reading history books, Wilson's characters sing songs and tell stories.

Both critics offer important insights into the presence of blues music in Wilson's plays and the influence of a blues ethos on his dramaturgy, both treating blues almost exclusively as music. Plum's essay is concerned primarily with the places in Wilson's earliest four plays where music proves prominent. And while Elam's chapter offers enlightening discussions of plays without musical interludes, it does so through musical metaphors: "If *Jitney* is a jazz jam session, then *King Hedley II* embodies the feeling of a jazz opera in which the characters' arias reveal their loves and losses."[9] For both critics, as for many others, blues is primarily music, and its influence on other art forms like poetry, drama, or painting is found in the musicality of that art.

Following Kalamu ya Salaam's caution that "the mere thought that the blues is mainly music is a grossly euro-centric misconception" and treating blues music as only a particular (if certainly the most pronounced) aesthetic manifestation of a broader ethos allows recognition of how that ethos permeates every aspect of the *Cycle*.[10] Elam supports his thesis that "Wilson's history cycle reveals an African American continuum that is always in process, stretching back into Africa and reaching into the future" by arguing that blues musicality provides a conduit and a vehicle for this continuum: blues both stretches into the distant past and "is amplified in the performative now."[11] This important insight becomes more valuable by acknowledging that blues animates this process at every turn. Certainly the men singing about Parchman Farm in *The Piano Lesson* amplify their historical continuum in the performative now, but so too do Loomis and Citizen in their visions, and so does Harmond Wilks by marching out to join the community protest, and Rose Maxson in her rejection of Troy. Throughout the *Cycle,* characters seek identity and freedom by making performative claims of selfhood in contexts that are separate from musicality but nonetheless saturated by blues. More universally than through music, Wilson defines his *Cycle* within a metaphysics of blues, examining how black American life looks when operating through this distinctively black American ethos.

Blues Foundations in *Joe Turner's Come and Gone*

In creating a blues world in the *Cycle* plays, Wilson constructed chains of repetition and revision of characters and the situations in which they find themselves. Among the most distinctive characteristics of blues aesthetics, repetition with a difference stresses important aspects of a blues composition within an antiphonal structure; the first utterance makes a call, and the repetition responds by repeating the call with an added emphasis. Anybody who sees or reads any given three or four plays from the *American Century Cycle* in a short time frame would likely recognize prominent themes, plot points, tensions, and characterizations that Wilson weaves throughout his plays. These patterns demand recognition of the most pronounced repetitions while attending to the nuances of differences within them. *Joe Turner's Come and Gone,* for instance, invites an investigation into the importance of a character like Herald Loomis, so bound and determined to prove his individuality and self-sufficiency, appearing on the heels of similar characters like Troy Maxson and Levee. Repetitions like these reveal precisely how and to what ends Wilson deploys a blues aesthetic in his plays, and so attention to their specifics will unpack the *Cycle*'s blues performativity.

Rather than moving through the *American Century Cycle* in any exhaustive or methodical way—either by date of composition or by setting—this chapter begins with a close examination of *Joe Turner's Come and Gone,* the play Wilson considered his signature, treating it as a thematic foundation from which to explore outward, tracing the nature and import of the *Cycle*'s blues methodology.[12] *Joe Turner,* that is, shows how Wilson explores the complex and troubled desire to forge community among an amalgam of disparate characters, who share little more than the quality of being black in America. Recognizing that *Joe Turner* builds around "collaborative confrontations," Soyica Diggs Colbert's assertion that "the play features conflicts whose resolutions require uneasy alliances" captures the tense and anxiety-ridden process of social becoming, for the individual selves as well as for the blues community.[13] Seth Holly's boardinghouse proves to be a stage for many different performances of self—Temple calls the play "a tableau of human longing"—each of which engages uneasily but necessarily with the broader community of the play.[14] In these performances, Wilson's call of blues performativity begins to emerge. He will offer a number of responses to that call in other plays, but ultimately he seeks from the theatrical audience and from society at large a response ratifying the social humanity of his characters, of the communities they hope to represent, and of himself.

Joe Turner develops out of a tension between intimacy and opacity. The audience meets eleven different characters in the boardinghouse—a space defined in part by ephemerality—but never comes to know any of them in great depth. The one possible exception is Rutherford Selig, the sole white character, who narrates much of his family history; that the white character has the most legible backstory reflects Wilson's concern for black Americans' divorce from their history. Wilson suggests in the play's opening stage direction that its black characters are of a piece with participants in the Great Migration: "From the deep and the near South the sons and daughters of newly freed African slaves wander into this city. Isolated, cut off from memory, having forgotten the names of the gods and only guessing at their faces, they arrive dazed and stunned, their hearts kicking in their chest with a song worth singing."[15] Most distinctive about these people is not where they have been or where they are going, but their state of mind: "Foreigners in a strange land, they carry as part and parcel of their baggage a long line of separation and dispersement which informs their sensibilities and marks their conduct as they search for ways to reconnect, to reassemble, to give clear and luminous meaning to the song which is both a wail and a whelp of joy" (6). He does not identify any of the play's characters by name in this opening note, and he will ultimately reveal very little about their backstories—Seth was born in the North, and Loomis was a Southern sharecropper, but even those details are vague. The uncertainty surrounding the characters keeps audiences always at arm's distance, never able to know these characters and their experiences fully.

And yet this pronounced opacity is porous enough to allow for a certain degree of intimacy with the current plight of each character. "August's characters are defined by speech," points out Phylicia Rashad, a definition that characters seek through performance.[16] Through language, Seth reveals his struggles to define himself as what he considers a respectable northerner in contrast to the new wave of southern blacks whom he derides. Mattie Campbell shows herself terribly heartbroken after being abandoned by her man. Bynum offers himself as at peace with his spiritual sense of purpose. Similar details emerge from the rest of the characters as well: Wilson shares just enough details to allow for an understanding of the characters' desires, struggles, and drives, but not enough to understand these characters as fully developed people. Access to that understanding lies beyond details of characters' lives; it requires audiences' good-faith participation in characters' blues performance. This is an important blues technique: the audience is never granted enough information to understand the blues artist fully, but is invited to learn more by engaging with subtext and performativity, in the uncertain hope of developing empathy for the artist's struggles and sharing the artist's joys.

This technique allows Wilson to stress his characters' performative essence, the characteristics that contribute most directly to what Bynum calls their song. Bynum's concept of one's song refers to the sense of self among each character, and characters' ability to perform their respective songs speaks to their abilities to embody their selves within a social sphere that embraces them. Kim Pereira suggests of these characters that "Wilson investigates their poignant yearnings for meaningful relationships and their struggle to sing the song of their true identity," arguing that all the play's characters exist along a "path to self-discovery."[17] But Wilson's blues dramaturgy presupposes and prioritizes a self that is social, defined in concert between the self and others, rather than a metaphysical notion of a "true identity." Any self-discovery in Wilson must be a process of social becoming, engendered in the performative process of dialogue with the social sphere. Colbert is more precise: "Bynum describes Loomis' loss of identity as his inability to 'sing' his song. Although metaphorical, the imagery emphasizes the importance of embodied practice; it is not just that Loomis has forgotten his purpose, but that he has lost the ability to materialize it through action."[18] The most important interfaces between these characters and their various audiences are their social performances.

In *Joe Turner* as throughout the *Cycle*, Wilson's blues communities expect and foster antiphonal performance that seeks out and plays back to a response. Knowing one's song is not enough without performance. Bynum, for example, sings a song of binding: "I chose that song because that's what I seen most when I was traveling . . . people walking away and leaving one another. So I takes the power of my song and binds them together" (16). Bynum does not discover binding as his true identity; rather, he becomes a binder because he responds to a condition he recognizes in the social world. He comes to perform this community function only after traveling on a spiritual journey with a mysterious stranger he met along the road who told him "to come and go along the road a little ways with him [. . .] he was gonna show me the Secret of Life." After leading Bynum into a strange meadow, the man takes on the characteristic that comes to define him in Bynum's memory: "I turned around to look at this fellow and he had this light coming out of him. I had to cover up my eyes to keep from being blinded. He shining like new money with that light." From his father Bynum learns that this shiny man was "the One Who Goes Before and Shows the Way." His father reveals that there are "lots of shiny men and if I ever saw one again before I died then I would know that my song had been accepted and worked its full power in the world and I could lay down and die a happy man. A man who done left his mark on life" (14–15). In the final lines of the play, Bynum finds that he can in fact lay down and die happy: "Herald Loomis, you shining!" he says. "You shining like new money!" (86). Loomis's new glow comes only after his guidance at various points throughout the play by Bynum, combined with his own determination to understand his place in the world more fully. Bynum, that is, leaves his mark on life by engendering Loomis's shine.

A detail that the play does not make explicit is the fact that throughout the entire play Bynum is shining like new money. The shiny man that Bynum meets along the road leaves his mark on life by imparting his shine on Bynum, and Bynum continues the tradition by leading Loomis into shininess; Sinikka Grant helpfully relates the condition of shininess to "some kind of 'enlightenment,' a self-recognition or self-knowledge."[19] The play's final lines carry with them a tone of awed surprise from Bynum, as if he expected to be able to help Loomis find peace but never thought that such a project would allow Loomis to shine. This is because Bynum does not entirely understand the condition and function of shininess himself. He hires Selig "the People Finder" to locate for him the shiny man he met along the road, but grows frustrated by Selig's inability to track him down: "You around here finding everybody how come you ain't found my shiny man?" (13). Bynum presumes that in order to see another shiny man, he must track down a man that is already shining. But the play suggests instead that the mysterious shiny man imparted on Bynum a distinct shine, and in order for him to see another shiny man before he dies he too must reveal his shine to another on whom he will impart shininess.

Wilson's blues dramaturgy helps to explain this unusual dynamic. Willfully stretching the bounds of realism—Mary Bogumil calls the play "a world where the natural and supernatural coexist and impinge upon one another"—Wilson mystifies his bluesman into a transcendent shiny man and places the demand on him to perform his song to the community in order that the community might recognize and ratify him as a shiny man and that he might pass along this performative potential to others.[20] When Bynum follows his shiny man he both constitutes and participates in the blues community, providing this man with an audience to participate in his performance of self. Bynum's resultant finding of his own song both ratifies the social existence of his shiny man and sets Bynum himself on a performative project. "Shiny man" becomes in this context synonymous with "bluesman," one who has a song of the self to perform for the community with the goal of benefiting both the performer and the audience in an antiphonal process of giving, receiving, and giving back.

Having found the bluesman and entered into his performative space, Bynum is more advanced along his blues journey toward selfhood than are the other inhabitants of Seth's boardinghouse, but he is nonetheless actively engaged in the process of performing his song and searching out ratification from the community. The others do not readily recognize his shine; he must work to reveal it to them. This dynamic appears most directly in his scenes of council. He seems to understand that Jeremy's calling is to play music for the community, for example, and he urges him to go play at a club downtown, despite Jeremy's fear of being arrested: "That's where the music at," Bynum tells the young guitarist. "That's where the people at. The people down there making music and enjoying themselves. Some things is worth taking the chance going to jail about." Bynum is working here on binding Jeremy to his song, that of the blues musician engaging with community, but Jeremy is trapped in the space of his hormonal self-interest: "They got some women down there, Mr. Bynum?" (23). Later, when Jeremy's fixation on sexualizing women continues, Bynum tries to steer the young man toward a productive understanding of a relationship:

> Jeremy: She a fine woman too. Got them long legs. Knows how to treat a fellow too. Treat you like you wanna be treated.
>
> Bynum: You just can't look at it like that. You got to look at the whole thing. Now, you take a fellow go out there, grab hold to a woman and think he got something cause she sweet and soft to the touch. Alright. Touching's part of life. [. . .] I ain't just talking about in the way of jumping off into bed together and rolling around with each other. Anybody can do that. When you grab hold to that woman and look at the whole thing and see what you got . . . why, she can take and make something out of you. [. . .] That's a foolish thing to ignore a woman like that.
>
> Jeremy: Oh, I ain't ignoring her, Mr. Bynum. It's hard to ignore a woman got legs like she got. (45)

Bynum here is continuing to perform his song, but in his failure to get through to Jeremy he is not succeeding in establishing a productive engagement with community.

He fares a bit better with Mattie Campbell, who asks him to fix it so that Jack Carper, the man who abandoned her, returns. Mattie is uninterested in how Bynum might return Jack or in any great reasons for the binding; she just wants her man back: "Make him come back to me. Make his feet say my name on the road. I don't care what happens. Make him come back." Bynum refuses the binding job on the terms Mattie begs, offering her a consoling wisdom instead: "Jack Carper gone off to where he belong. There's somebody searching for your doorstep right now. Ain't no need you fretting over Jack Carper" (26–27). Mattie listens, and takes the charm Bynum gives her to help her forget, but when Mattie and Jeremy end up in a brief relationship that ends with Jeremy abandoning her for the more vivacious Molly Cunningham, the play reveals that neither Mattie nor Jeremy has come to a clear understanding of self.

Bynum's success is Loomis who, through his engagement with the blues community of the boardinghouse guided by Bynum, comes to a more complete understanding of self. When Loomis interrupts the Juba ritual in a rage, he offers a bit of insight into his constant vexation: "You all don't know nothing about me. You don't know what I done seen. Herald Loomis done seen some things he ain't got words to tell you." Loomis is defined by a vision of the world he cannot articulate, but when he is in this moment struck down by the reappearance of that vision, it is Bynum who crawls to join him on the floor and coax Loomis toward speaking out the vision: "What you done seen, Herald Loomis? [. . .] Tell me about them bones, Herald Loomis. Tell me what you seen. [. . .] What happened, Herald Loomis? What happened to the bones? [. . .] You just laying there. What you waiting on, Herald Loomis?" While Seth offers Loomis only hasty judgment— "Nigger, you crazy! [. . .] You done plumb lost your mind!"—Bynum provides him an audience, a community representative who will engage with his performance of self (50–52).

Through his engagement with the play's other characters, and particularly with Loomis, Bynum reveals himself to be primarily in service of others. He is an elder and a sage whose own journey is defined by its contribution to enabling the journeys of others through their own self-discovery and social performance. Certainly Bynum is still engrossed in the project of discovering and performing his own self, but his particular song shapes the social self in reference to its function of guiding others as he was guided by the One Who Goes Before and Shows the Way. This essential characteristic makes Bynum a Wilsonian blues griot, a character that appears throughout the *American Century Cycle*. From Toledo through Elder Joseph Barlow, Wilson repeatedly invokes the blues griot as a means of examining the various twisted paths his characters travel (or fail to travel) toward a sense of self-understanding.

The griot is a West African figure with a long history whose chief social function is offering wisdom and guidance to the community primarily through passing along stories and songs that keep oral traditions alive; a griot "enables societies to cohere" through performance, serving as "social glue."[21] Robert Palmer suggests that griots "belong to a particular social caste" made up of singers and musicians who perform a number of social functions, one of which is to "memorize long epic genealogies that constitute a kind of oral history of their people."[22] Thomas A. Hale argues that "the griot as historian emerges as a 'time-binder,' a person who links past to present and serves as a witness to events in the present, which he or she may convey to persons living in the future."[23] The griot is a receptacle of social and aesthetic history who passes along that history through performance as a way of galvanizing a society. As Hale argues, the performance of the griot should affect its audience: "The individual who hears his or her genealogy recounted at a ceremony or in an epic is transformed from a member of the audience to the living product of those who went before."[24] Described elsewhere as a figure that "combines the functions of living history book and newspaper with vocal and instrumental virtuosity," and a master of "extemporizing of current events and chance incidents with 'devastating' and 'formidable' local knowledge," the griot critiques the present by existing as a living conduit to the past, providing a vehicle through which the community may consult and engage with the experiences of its ancestors.[25] These are functions crucial to Wilson's aesthetic project, which seeks to revitalize how black Americans think about their lives by inviting them to reassess their dialogue with history. According to Hale, the griot is "the human link between past and present," but rather than simply recounting history, the griot offers "a reading of the past for audiences in the present, an interpretation that reflects a complex blend of both past and present values."[26] Wilson objected to the white supremacist narrative of American history books and looked to oral and aesthetic traditions for the most thorough account of black American history. Such a journey into uncharted territory of history demands a confident and nimble guide, and so Wilson provides griots, characters whose chief function is to guide and support others finding and singing their songs.

Crucially, however, Wilson does not import this figure wholesale from Africa. In the work of Wilson, even a powerful figure like the griot bears scars of the Middle Passage and the early American black experience. Wilson's griots must be "blues griots" because, like their playwright, their history begins when the first African slaves reached American soil, which means that it is a history in dialogue with enslavement, brutality, forced disjuncture, oppression, and hard-fought joy. Colbert argues that "the Middle Passage in Baraka's and Wilson's theater resists the belated dichotomy of oppression and resistance," suggesting that "a philosophy of history emerges in relation to political configurations situated outside the oppression/resistance dichotomy."[27] Wilson's blues griot embodies the awareness of and resistance to the reductive simplicity of this dichotomy. The blues griot dwells in the political and social complexity of the black community experience, guiding others down their own paths through that complexity. The griot's job is to provide a conduit to the past, but for Wilson's American blues griot that past is just as murky and winding as it is for everybody else in the community. This figure is thus a blues griot because it shares with all other characters an investment in the process of social becoming, wrestling with uncertainty and fear through the performance of self before a community. Wilson's blues griots have no answers, but they have the wherewithal to guide others as they forge ahead into uncertainty. The blues griot proves to be an essential component of Wilson's blues dramaturgy, as the playwright repeats and revises the figure throughout the *Cycle*.

In *Joe Turner*, Bynum's most direct investment is in the mysterious figure of Herald Loomis, a character who arrives at Seth's boardinghouse on a journey in search of his wife. Yet, as is clear by the play's conclusion, this journey is much more about Loomis exploring himself after finding that his "vision of the world and of himself is at odds with reality," as Bogumil aptly puts it.[28] Unlike his blues griot counterpart, Loomis takes an active, forceful approach to his search for selfhood. In the character's introductory stage direction, Wilson writes, "He is at times possessed. A man driven not by the hellhounds that seemingly bay at his heels, but by his search for a world that speaks to something about himself." Loomis is marked as an outsider from the community in any number of ways, from his dark attire, to his gruff demeanor, to his refusal to take any solace or joy from community rituals like mealtime or the Juba. Wilson's stage direction suggests that the reason for this self-exclusion is that Loomis is on a single-minded search for the self, one that refuses any encounters he might consider distractions. Wilson says that Loomis, instead of working within the social framework of the boardinghouse, "is unable to harmonize the forces that swirl around him, and seeks to recreate the world into one that contains his image." Loomis has little idea of who he is or how he fits into the world around him, but for much of the play he seems quite certain that any answers to that dilemma lie elsewhere: "Whichever way the road take us, that's the way we go" (18–20).

The road has brought Loomis to the boardinghouse, but he has difficulty fitting in with this community. That becomes most vivid as the final moments of *Joe Turner* grow tense and potentially violent when Loomis comes to believe that Bynum has bound him to the road these past few years, and Martha tries in vain to sooth him by spouting theological platitudes. In this moment, Loomis's only urge is to reject confinement by others and their institutions: "Everywhere I go people wanna bind me up," he protests. "Joe Turner wanna bind me up! Reverend Tolliver wanna bind me up. You wanna bind me up." The *you* here is Bynum, so this listing of Joe Turner, Reverend Tolliver, and Bynum suggests white society, the Christian church, and Africanized spirituality as forces which Loomis sees competing to be the controlling interest in restricting his ability to create his self. Still, the play ends on a high note for Loomis: He tells Martha that he plans to make his own world, and he slashes his chest claiming, "I don't need nobody to bleed for me! I can bleed for myself" (83–85). Loomis leaves the boarding-house in triumph, ready to take an active, agential role in creating the world around him and his own place within in.

Still, the prevailing dramaturgy of the play and the *Cycle* makes clear not only that Loomis will need to exist among an active community in the future but also that he has been able to arrive at this moment of awakening only through his extended engagement with the community of the boarding-house. Wilson writes in the stage direction that Loomis finds his song to be the "the song of self-sufficiency," and Loomis seems to believe that his blood has cleansed him of the influence of the social forces seeking to restrict him. Certainly he has shaken off a number of the foreign influences competing for the right to control him, and he has arrived at a place of confidence in his self, but "self-sufficiency" is misleading. To be self-sufficient suggests that one requires only the self for happiness, productivity, and existence; in this case it suggests that Loomis is ready to make his way in the world relying only on himself. But in Wilson's world governed by a blues metaphysics, such a strategy would lead to disaster. Despite Wilson's exultant stage directions that usher Loomis offstage—"fully resurrected, cleaned and given breath, free from any encumbrance other than the workings of his own heart and the bonds of his flesh, having accepted the responsibility for his own presence in the world, he is free to soar above the environs that weighed and pushed his spirit into terrifying contractions" (40)—the character's self-actualization finds root in his commitment to the blues community.

That commitment comes through engagement with the blues griot. Loomis arrives deeply affected by a double trauma: one is his terrifying vision of the bones people walking on the water, and the second is the rupture to his life caused by his capture and imprisonment by Joe Turner. He reveals both as he tells his story to Bynum and others in the room. The blues griot at once elicits a performance of self and engenders an audience to receive and respond to this performance. In the processes of these performances, Loomis gradually becomes more of a social human. Days after the call-and-response revelation of his vision to Bynum, Mattie addresses him not as a mysterious stranger but as a person with a story to tell: "Did you really see them things like you said? Them people come up out the ocean?" As they speak in brief, halted sentences, each becomes more intrigued by the other before Loomis gives voice to the implicit sexual tension: "Come here and let me touch you. I been watching you. You a full woman. A man needs a full woman. Come on and be with me." Mattie's response is telling: "I ain't got enough for you. You'd use me up too fast." Having watched Loomis reveal his vision and continue to engage with the boardinghouse community in the subsequent days, Mattie judges him not as a mysterious and inaccessible other but as an all-too-human man whose life force she cannot equal. The scene concludes with Loomis trying and failing to touch Mattie before lamenting, "I done forgot how to touch" (72–73). Loomis has not yet reached a level of full social humanism that will allow him intimacy, but this scene with Mattie is an important moment on his way toward the play's climax, one that reveals how he is gradually becoming more of a social human through his participation in the social sphere.

Loomis thus needs the social sphere, but he is almost entirely unaware of this fact. His resistance to the notion of being bound up signals the urge for individualism and self-sufficiency that drives him. He does not want to understand the world or find a place in it; he wants to craft a world of his own: "I been wandering a long time in somebody else's world. When I find my wife that be the making of my own" (69). This desire marks Loomis with a spirit of resistance, a character that Wilson dubbed a warrior. Like Levee and Troy Maxson before him, and characters like Boy Willie, Sterling Johnson, Floyd Barton, and King Hedley II after him, Loomis desires above all to act on the world rather than to be acted upon. He sees the power of the white hegemony keeping blacks placated by oppressing them into predefined spaces, and he refuses to take on a role drafted for him. Wilson's warriors stand out from their communities because that is precisely what they intend to do. They see others living a life that they have little interest in sharing, so they seek to define one for themselves.

Although their playwright has great respect for these characters, few of them fare well in their journeys. This is because they mostly refuse engagement with their social sphere, and Wilson's blues dramaturgy is built on the social dynamics of the blues community. Loomis ends his play on a high note, shining like new money, but in order to engender that shine in another, allowing him to lay down and die a happy man, he will have to engage with a community, showing the way for others to gain their shine. This prototypical Wilsonian warrior ends his play in a liminal space between warrior and blues griot: he shines because his social humanity has been ratified by his community, but he now faces the call to greater social service for the blues community. Thus, *Joe Turner* concludes in terms far more open-ended than climactic. A bluesman like Loomis never stops needing the community for engagement.

Wilson's last stage direction before blackout reinforces the play's open-endedness: "Loomis turns and exits, the knife still in his hands. Mattie looks about the room and rushes out after him" (86). The implication seems to be that after Loomis finds his song, Mattie suspects strongly that it is harmonious with her needs and desires, and hurries out so as not to lose her chance at finding her song through Loomis. Earlier, Bynum tells Mattie that "Jack Carper gone off to where he belong. There's somebody searching for your doorstep right now" (27). The conclusion of the play suggests that Mattie judges Loomis to be that somebody and is overcome with the desire to requite his search. But it is only a moment or two later that the lights go down, revealing nothing about how or even if a relationship between Mattie and Loomis develops. The play shows that Loomis finds his song, but does not indicate if Mattie has found hers, or if Loomis will be another ill-fated romantic venture for her. In either case, it seems clear that Mattie feels that her song must be a duet with a man. Her partner will be neither Jack Carper nor Jeremy, and it may or may not be Loomis, but her voyage through life to discover her place in the world is shaped by the search for a man to be her companion. Her female counterparts in the play are in similar positions, defined primarily by their relative position to men in their lives. Bertha's happiness with "love in one hand and laughter in the other" (79) has its source in her partnership with Seth, and Molly Cunningham may not arrive at the boardinghouse in search of a man, but she is immediately sexualized and engages with the play's community almost entirely in terms of sexuality.

Critics often accuse Wilson of misogyny and occasionally of the lesser charge of underdeveloping women. Neither critique is misplaced. Wilson's work is primarily interested in the experience of blacks in America, but in ways similar to the myopic masculinity with which bell hooks charges the civil rights movement, Wilson's focus on race tracks specifically to black masculinity.[29] The *Cycle* plays revolve around the tension between the blues griot and the warrior—both usually men, with one notable exception, discussed below—with a view to how the warrior's angst and anger will come to influence the struggles of the play's social sphere. Women become much more of a plot element than a play's focus, providing an aspect of romantic or domestic tension to the plot. As Shannon argues, African American men "are the thinkers, the doers, the dreamers" in Wilson's "theatrical universe," and "revolving around them in seemingly expendable supporting roles are wives, mistresses, sisters, children and other relatives."[30] "Simply put," recognizes Elam, "women are not the focus of Wilson's project."[31] This is evident enough in *Joe Turner:* Mattie, Molly, Bertha, and even Zonia and Martha are compelling characters, but their primary function seems to be to provide context for an understanding of the play's men (even Bertha's name, appearing after Seth's in the dramatis personae, carries the moniker "his wife").

Despite the secondary position of women in Wilson's work, the *Cycle*'s blues dramaturgy allows productive theorization of their characterization in the plays. Mattie, for example, comes to the Seth's boardinghouse looking for a clearer fulfillment of a selfhood that she defines in terms of an interpersonal relationship: "All my life I been looking for somebody to stop and stay with me," she tells Bynum while appealing for him to make Jack Carper return to her. It does not take long for Jeremy to make romantic advances on the attractive single woman who has just arrived: "A woman like you need a man. Maybe you let me be your man." But Mattie resists initially, presuming (rightly, as it turns out) that Jeremy wants only a fling. Mattie has entered into the boardinghouse community not in search of romance or sex, but rather for a man with whom she can identify herself: "I just can't go through life piecing myself out to different mens," she says. "I need a man who wants to stay with me." But once Jeremy's charm combines with the revelation that he is a musician, Mattie becomes more receptive:

> Mattie: I got me a room up on Bedford. Me and Jack had a room together.
> Jeremy: What's the address? I'll come by and get you tonight and we can go down to Seefus. I'm going down there and play my guitar.
> Mattie: You play guitar?
> Jeremy: I play guitar like I'm born to it.
> Mattie: I live at 1727 Bedford Avenue. I'm gonna find out if you can play guitar like you say.

Given the new information that Jeremy plays guitar, Mattie begins to think he might be a suitable (or at least exciting) man to whom she could bind herself for social identification. She might become "Jeremy's woman," as Bertha is "Seth's wife." Immediately she begins to speak of herself in obsequious terms regarding Jeremy: "I got to get home and straighten up for you. [. . .] I got to get home and fix up for you" (27, 29).

In this moment, Mattie's call for the recovery of her man is returned by the community in a way that she did not anticipate but that nonetheless allows her to continue her journey of self-crafting and self-discovery as best as she understands it. After Jeremy abandons her to run off with Molly, Mattie begins to reassess herself in dialogue with Loomis: "I ain't never found no place for me to fit. Seem like all I do is start over" (72). In the space of the play, Mattie's antiphonal development engages primarily Bynum, Jeremy, Bertha, and Loomis, each of whom contributes to her evolving sense of self. By the play's conclusion, her social identity—either in relationship to a man or on her own—has not been ratified by the community and so it remains uncertain and opaque. She runs after Loomis hoping that more engagement with him will better shape her conception of self.

Mattie Campbell, like many of Wilson's women, is confused and wandering along her journey of selfhood, which she seems to understand best as defined in reference to a man. Bertha and Seth Holly seem to have a strong marriage, but this is more of an exception than a pattern for romantic relationships throughout the *Cycle*. Wilson's men are regularly unfaithful, and his women are most often defined by how they manage their own selfhood in relationship to the men they do not trust. These blueswomen are in the double bind of existing in a world that all but demands a woman enter into a relationship with a man while only providing them with untrustworthy men. This plight defines the position of female characters in the *Cycle*'s blues community. The warrior seeks to define himself outside community bounds, but women often seem all too aware that they must seek identity within the limiting strictures of romance. How they negotiate this bind reveals much about conditions giving shape to their plays' social spheres.

Developing his style through short pre-*Cycle* plays (including an early version of *Jitney*), and then in the full-scale development of *Ma Rainey* and *Fences*, Wilson arrived in *Joe Turner* in new and distinctively Wilsonian territory; he was insightful in dubbing it his signature play. With its large ensemble cast, meandering plot line, mysticism, and musicality of dialogue, the play contains all of the most distinctive elements of Wilson's blues dramaturgy and proves a useful touchstone for the genealogies running throughout the *American Century Cycle*. The play is a boisterous interlocutor with all the *Cycle* plays that precede and follow it, affecting an understanding of *Ma Rainey* as much as of *Radio Golf*. It is in *Joe Turner* that Wilson comes most fully into his own style, and so it is in this play that solid groundwork exists for the complexities of his blues dramaturgy.

Because Wilson was so invested in exploring what he called the four-hundred-year-old autobiography of black people in America, his dramaturgy necessarily focuses on people and their interpersonal experiences. In developing that dramaturgy, the playwright constructs a number of genealogical strands throughout his plays, strands that are not necessarily biological (although those do exist) but rather cultural. Boy Willie, for example, is a warrior descendant of Loomis, Troy, and Levee; Holloway is a blues griot with heritage from Doaker, Bynum, Bono, and Toledo; Vera's blueswoman struggle is in dialogue with Risa, Berniece, Mattie, and Rose. The term *character type* seems relevant here, but it is not quite precise enough to capture Wilson's strategy. For Wilson's characters are defined not by their relationship to some metaphysical type but rather by their thorough imbrication with each other, showing what Wittgenstein would call "family resemblances."[32] As a blues musician repeats and revises lyrics and musical constructions within songs and throughout his oeuvre, so too does Wilson repeat and revise certain prominent formulations throughout his blues *Cycle*. Close attention to these formulations will reveal how a blues aesthetic allows Wilson to explore twentieth-century struggles to identify and perform black American selfhood, as well as the call Wilson's plays make to audiences in their performative present seeking out a lasting sense of social humanity for their characters and the playwright.

Cultivating Community and Offering Guidance: The Blues Griot

Bynum is more or less at peace because he is in sync with the harmonies of his social sphere; his introductory stage direction says that "he gives the impression of always being in control of everything. Nothing ever bothers him. He seems to be lost in a world of his own making and to swallow any adversity or interference with his grand design" (10). But Bynum's world is not of his own making: the social sphere of *Joe Turner* bears the influence of any number of external and contextual factors. Bynum may *give the impression* of always being in control of everything, but that illusion comes from his comfort at navigating the twists and turns that his social sphere presents him.

Throughout the *American Century Cycle,* Wilson recasts his blues griot character with varying levels of this sort of comfort, often dependent upon varying levels of respect received from other members of the blues community. *Ma Rainey*'s Toledo, for instance, never achieves the levels of peace and influence that Bynum does. This is in part because of the attitudes of the other members of his community—as Shannon points out, his bandmates take his "uninvited" lessons on various topics "as an insult"—but more so because Toledo is never able to harmonize himself effectively with the forces of his social sphere.[33] Whereas Bynum gives off the appearance of peace and control, Wilson says that Toledo "is self-taught but misunderstands and misapplies his knowledge."[34] The only literate member of Ma's band, Toledo has a nearly constant drive to share knowledge with his community, seemingly in hopes of awakening their awareness of the world. But his ineffectiveness in this endeavor becomes clear from his first substantive dialogue with a bandmate, when he tries to wax philosophical to Levee about the nature of change. The exchange begins as Levee arrives and comments that the band room has been rearranged: "Damn! They done changed things around. Don't never leave well enough alone." Toledo seizes on an opening to impart some knowledge: "Everything changing all the time. Even the air you breathing change. You got, monoxide, hydrogen . . . changing all the time. Skin changing . . . different molecules and everything." Levee has no sense of Toledo's point or purpose: "Nigger, what is you talking about? I'm talking about the room. I ain't talking about no skin and air." Toledo recognizes that he and Levee are on entirely different wavelengths, but he does not attempt to bridge the gap: "Hell, I know what you talking about. I just said everything changing. I know what you talking about, but you don't know what I'm talking about." As Toledo gets more abstract, Levee gets more concrete: "That door! Nigger, you see that door? That's what I'm talking about. That door wasn't there before." Toledo tries again to make his point with a different example, but receives the same vociferous resistance from Levee, causing the elder musician to end the conversation: "I'm gonna ignore you cause you ignorant" (15–16).

This exchange sounds in many ways similar to the discussion between Bynum and Jeremy about women, with a similar failure of communication between the two men. In both cases the elder blues griot attempts to elucidate some of life's complexities to the impetuous youngster who sees only what is before his eyes. More telling than the similarities, however, are the elements of the scenes that make them a distinct expression of a recognizable form; to repeat with a difference is to put added stress on that difference. The comparison is especially helpful in elucidating Toledo's struggles for a fully realized identity. Bynum ultimately does not get through to Jeremy, but he continues to try making his point with a variety of metaphors hoping to meet Jeremy on similar conceptual ground. Their conversation ends not by Bynum resolving to ignore Jeremy but by the interruption of Molly's arrival, a complication that only thwarts Bynum's purposes further. The scene's final line, when Jeremy has finished ogling Molly and tells Bynum, "I think I know what you was talking about now," is full of comic irony because Bynum has tried his best, only to be misunderstood (48). In this light, Toledo's resolution to ignore Levee at the end of their exchange reveals in this griot a lesser degree of patience, and a greater resistance to engaging with his community. The actor playing Toledo might turn his back on his bandmates as he delivers the line pronouncing Levee's ignorance; his silence for a full page of the script might even suggest sulking.

While all the *Cycle*'s journeys toward self-realization and social humanization are complicated and perilous, Toledo's is especially so. It ends in his destruction rather than his gaining the ability to perform his song of selfhood within the blues community, in part because he never manages to engage fully with the community on its own terms. Rather, he attempts to impose his learning and knowledge on those around him, at times seeming aloof in his intelligence, and at others seeming frustrated that the community does not respect what he has to offer. When he bets that Levee does not know how to spell *music,* for example, and Levee retorts, "I can spell it, nigger! M-U-S-I-K. There!" Toledo is triumphant for only a moment before he realizes that neither Cutler nor Slow Drag is able to confirm Levee's mistake. "Here go your dollar back, Levee," he says. "I done won it, you understand. I done won the dollar. But if don't nobody know but me, how am I gonna prove it to you?" (18–19). Toledo enters into this bet in order to prove Levee's ignorance and his own intellectual superiority, but the episode leaves him frustrated that the community provides him no recourse to prove that superiority. Reactions to his later insistence that "that's the trouble with colored folks . . . always wanna have a good time. [. . .] There's more to life than having a good time" show all three bandmates dismissive of the would-be blues griot. Slow Drag tells him that "just cause you like to read them books and study and whatnot . . . that's your good time. People got other things they likes to do to have a good time," and Cutler dismisses the notion of reforming the urge for good times: "Niggers been having a good time before you was born, and they gonna keep having a good time after you gone." When Toledo points out that the problem with this is that while folks are having good times, "Ain't nobody talking about making the lot of the colored man better for him here in America," Levee retorts snidely, "Now you gonna be Booker T. Washington." Despite Toledo's continued urging for his bandmates to recognize what he sees as the problems with an obsession with good times, Slow Drag ultimately encapsulates the community's conviction by saying, "Well, the colored man's gonna be alright" with or without Toledo's knowledge (30).

Rather than being accepted into the community as an asset for education and guidance, Toledo gets dubbed a "cracker-talking nigger" and summarily dismissed by his associates (22). He becomes a blues griot manqué, a character whose social humanity the community never fully ratifies and who, as a result, never effectively engages with his community. He does not recognize their social humanity because they refuse to ratify his, and the blues community of *Ma Rainey* remains disjointed. Without an effective blues griot as a grounding influence, the band never gels, no room is made for Levee the warrior, and the play ends in a tragedy punctuated by Cutler underscoring the inability of this particular blues community to function independently of white society: "Slow Drag, get Mr. Irvin down here" (92).

Toledo's desire accents his ineffectiveness as a blues griot: he clearly wants the others to act in accordance with a respect for what he has to say. Their resistance prevents him from coming to a full sense of himself because his call of identity is as an influential counselor. Conditions are different with several of his descendants in the Wilson griot genealogy. Bono, Doaker, and Holloway all are blues griots, and none are particularly influential. Bono warns Troy several times about the perils of getting involved with Alberta, but despite Troy's lip service—"Yeah, I hear what you saying, Bono"—his message never gets through.[35] Similarly, Doaker is a fount of sound advice and guidance for his niece and nephew about how to deal with the family piano, and he is the resource Wilson uses to deliver *The Piano Lesson*'s exposition about the instrument's torrid history, but ultimately Doaker's presence has little influence on the drama's outcome. Berniece, Boy Willie, and Sutter's ghost need to work out their conflicts between the three of them, and they have little time for the blues griot.[36]

Unlike Toledo, however, Bono, Doaker, and Holloway are accepted and respected by their communities. Effectiveness turns out to be not an adequate rubric for assessing Wilson's blues griots.[37] Evidence that their calls of identity are received and returned with ratification exists in the willingness of their communities to listen to and engage with what these men have to say. Holloway, for example, holds court in a corner booth of Memphis's restaurant, where the regulars are willing to listen to and consider his advice and guidance. He retells folk stories and contextualizes the community's struggles, and in general gives dimension to the community dynamic. He may not be overly influential to the play's plot, but he nonetheless proves influential to the thinking of the fellow members of his blues community.

This sort of influence defines Wilson's blues griot par excellence: Aunt Ester. The physical embodiment of black people's long history on American soil, Aunt Ester is the ultimate repository for wisdom and guidance of ancestors; Shannon calls her "Wilson's living metaphor of black experience and the model for present and future black cultural identity."[38] Much of what defines Holloway as a griot is his following of Aunt Ester, and the same is true in slightly different terms for the Elder Joseph Barlow. When she shows up on stage in *Gem of the Ocean*, the *Cycle*'s penultimate play, Aunt Ester bears not only the ancestral wisdom of generations of black Americans but also the influence of all Wilson's blues griots preceding her. Her dramatic lineage, that is, comes down through the genealogy of Toledo, Bono, Bynum, and all the rest.

Wilson refers to Aunt Ester as the mother of all the *Cycle*'s characters, and Shannon calls her "the supreme matriarch, Earth Mother, and healer," all of which underscores her identity as the *Cycle*'s most powerful blues griot.[39] As the resonance of *ancestor* in her name suggests, her social function is like that of a conduit between the past and the present of her social sphere. As Shannon recognizes, "Aunt Ester personifies African American historical reality that is—in the interest of sheer survival—spoken into being and kept alive in the testimonies from within the community."[40] Shannon underscores an important two-part process of the blues griot's work: preserve the past through performance, and engender its survival by provoking responses to that performance. Aunt Ester embodies the blues griot as powerfully in *Two Trains Running*, when she never appears on stage, as in *Gem of the Ocean*, which focuses in large part on her presence. Both Memphis and Sterling go to consult her in *Two Trains*, and both gain a greater sense of selfhood. "I talked to her a long while. Told her my whole life story," says Sterling.[41] He reports that Ester speaks to him in aphorisms—"I cannot swim does not walk by the lakeside. [. . .] Make better what you have and you have best"— and tells him that he's "got good understanding."[42] After this encounter, new confidence replaces Sterling's brashness. He is finally able to woo Risa because he speaks to her directly, explaining his life experiences rather than simply trying to impress her with bravado. More importantly, rather than treating the rally honoring Malcolm X as the most important expression of social unity, he makes the much more concrete gesture of stealing a ham to place in Hambone's casket. This latter action reveals in Sterling a new dedication to his immediate social sphere that replaces the abstract sloganism he had avouched hitherto. His meeting with the blues griot, that is, awakens him to how duty and connectedness to his community can assuage his feelings of nonbelonging, and he immediately begins to perform that connection. Upon returning from Lutz's store bloodied from his theft of a ham, Sterling Johnson begins to shine like new money.

As *Gem* reveals, Ester's griot methods involve awakening her audiences' sense of ancestry in order to contextualize their present troubles within a lineage of noble struggle. Sterling tells her his life story, and she helps him recognize how he fits into his blues community; the task of performing that community awareness rests with him. The awareness of community works as a balm to sooth and a jolt to energize. Citizen Barlow's visit with Aunt Ester in *Gem of the Ocean* is more extended than Sterling's, but he too comes to a sense of peace from learning of his interconnectedness with an ancestral community. In fact, after Ester eases Citizen's guilt for killing a man by telling him how judgment lies with God, Citizen dozes into a peaceful sleep, soothed by the voice of the blues griot. "You on an adventure, Mr. Citizen," Aunt Ester tells her sleeping visitor. "I bet you didn't know that. It's all adventure."[43] Temple argues insightfully that Aunt Ester's house "is a sanctuary—not a shelter. A shelter is a place of protection from the elements—from the storms. A sanctuary, however, is where you go for sustenance—for strength."[44] Citizen can sleep peacefully, as Sterling can carry himself with more confidence, because Aunt Ester offers them the sustenance of empathetic engagement with their performances of selves, and in the sanctuary overseen by their blues griot, Sterling and Citizen gain strength.

Citizen's adventure, like that of his ancestors and fellow blues people, is a tumultuous journey into selfhood, one that must traverse the terrain of the social sphere. Ester has Black Mary make up the guest room for Citizen because his particular journey will require gaining an awareness of his membership in and duty to a community. Aunt Ester will guide him along that journey in a pilgrimage to the City of Bones, but Black Mary assures Citizen,

"You got to help yourself. Aunt Ester can help you if you willing to help yourself. She ain't got no magic power." "I got me. That's all there is," says Citizen before traveling to the City of Bones and learning about his ancestral community; "That ain't never gonna be enough," Black Mary assures him.[45] It is only well after Citizen makes his pilgrimage that he begins to recognize his investment in shared community struggles, telling Solly that he will accompany him on his getaway flight from Caesar. "You're on the battlefield now," Solly tells him, ratifying his social humanity as an important member of this community.[46]

Both Sterling and Citizen are turned onto new senses of purpose in their lives after meeting with Aunt Ester, revealing much about Ester as blues griot. Griots that precede her in the *Cycle* attempt to service their communities as she does by contextualizing struggles within the fabric of history and society. Any success, like Bynum's, is limited, and occasionally failure like Toledo's is catastrophic. Endowing Ester with the genealogical markers of all her predecessors by the time she makes it to the stage in *Gem*, Wilson crafts a blues griot that can be successful primarily because she has both the awareness of her circumstances and the respect of her community. Not even Bynum has either to such extent.

Aunt Ester's success as blues griot results from her ability to perform the role so effectively that she gains widespread ratification within the broad community, from 1839 Wylie Avenue, throughout the Hill District, and down through the generations. The Ester Tyler of *Gem* will soon die, but Black Mary will succeed her as Aunt Ester, and the name and community performance will carry with it the social humanism accrued over generations. As Black Mary points out, Aunt Ester does not have magical powers and does not claim to. Her importance comes from an unmitigated willingness to engage with both her present community and its long ancestral lineage, consistently performing ancestral links for her social sphere.

Through the figure of the blues griot, then, Wilson signals much about the condition of particular plays' social spheres. It is telling that his blues griots are most effective in the earliest decades of the *Cycle* when his characters are more in touch with their ancestral roots and the memory of slavery is more vivid. Toledo faces a deck stacked with the urge for modernization, and both Doaker and Bono offer guidance to characters who are burning to show their individuality from any sense of community, past or present. By the time the *Cycle* reaches the 1980s, Wilson offers his bleakest portrait of black American life by killing Aunt Ester with no Black Mary to step into the role and thereby creating what Bogumil aptly calls "a spiritual lacuna within the community."[47] The social sphere of *King Hedley II* has grown so fractured that it rejects the call of its griot, refusing to ratify her social humanity or to pay much attention at all to a possible alternative in Stool Pigeon.[48] Like Toledo who is destroyed in part out of rebellion against his griot guidance, Aunt Ester can no longer exist without a community to guide. As the *Cycle* reaches the 1990s in *Radio Golf,* Wilson's Pittsburgh is without a blues griot, the Hill District is declared blighted, and Aunt Ester's house is on the verge of destruction.

But when Elder Joseph Barlow, the son of *Gem*'s Black Mary and Citizen Barlow, enters Harmond Wilks's office, he begins to perform the blues griot song sung by his mother, grandmother, and the generations of Aunt Esters that preceded them. Elder Joseph had always been accepted and welcomed by his social sphere—he says people would always give him money because "[t]hey don't want to see me want for nothing"—but his engagement with Harmond Wilks is where he begins truly to affect the community.[49] On behalf of himself, his daughter, and the house's history—which is to say, on behalf of his present and future stretching back through generations of his ancestors—he makes a call to Harmond to recognize his voice as a social human with a right to his ancestral line. It takes most of the play, but ultimately Harmond returns that call and heads out to join the chorus seeking broader recognition for the humanity of the people of the Hill District. "Harmond Wilks is standing! Harmond Wilks is shining!" observes Temple, recognizing the successful work of Elder Joseph as blues griot.[50] The responsibility to support another's journey into the enlightenment of shininess now becomes Harmond's, and the productive development of Wilson's blues people can carry on through the work of the griot. *Radio Golf* and the *Cycle* both end with a sense of hope that even without its griot par excellence, the blues community might still be able to find and heed the guidance of the griot's legacy.

"I'm Gonna Do the Right Thing for Me": The Warrior's Threat to Blues Community

Bynum is at peace with the world, but Loomis is racked by angst and confusion. Bono is satisfied as one who gives advice in the genuine hope that it will be accepted, but Troy demands to be heard and respected. Toledo wants his community to be in touch with their ancestry, while Levee wants nothing more than to forge a new path for himself. Doaker is dedicated to living through family history; Boy Willie wants to appropriate and reshape that history. Levee, Troy, Loomis, and Boy Willie presage characters like Floyd, Sterling, Booster, and King Hedley II who feel the powerful urge to change their place in the world for the better. They have little interest in understanding their own plights or those of their communities, and less patience for a gradual shift in social dynamics. Instead, they are focused on their own troubles and their plans to assuage those troubles. Fundamentally solipsistic, the Wilsonian warrior believes that he deserves better out of life and seeks to improve his social existence, often aggressively.

The Wilsonian warrior therefore troubles the blues metaphysics of the *Cycle,* providing the greatest source of tension for Wilson's dramaturgy. The blues community that is defined in large part by a commitment to shared struggle finds itself disrupted when forced to compensate for an aggressive presence determined to reshape social power dynamics. Eileen Crawford describes this tension as "a special emphasis on the boy/men who are misdirected, misunderstood and misbegotten by the society in which they hope to thrive and prosper but yet are incapable of being directed and guided by that black community. They are the asocial nonconformists who the community, in all its dignity and seriousness, has yet to figure out, especially how to challenge their destructive energies."[51] As Crawford recognizes, the warrior exists in discord with the community, and the tension surrounding him arises from uncertainty about whether or not warrior and community can find harmony. Indeed, not only has the community yet to figure out the warrior, but the warrior is at a similar loss in understanding the community. In *Ma Rainey's Black Bottom, Seven Guitars,* and *King Hedley II* this tension ends in tragedy; in *Gem of the Ocean* tragedy leads to rebirth (Stool Pigeon insists that this is also true in *King Hedley II*); in *Fences* and *The Piano Lesson* the warrior spirit must make way for the cohesion of the family. In each of these cases and others, tension and resolution depend on the degree to which the blues community and the warrior can find harmony. The warrior's call is one of individuality, self-sufficiency, and powerful agency, but his great weakness is failing to realize that this call requires a ratifying response from the blues community. Whereas the blues griot seeks to harmonize with the rhythms of the social sphere, the warrior tries to overpower and dictate those rhythms. That desire leads without exception to trouble, but the condition that Wilson's *Cycle* finds so fascinating is how the blues community responds to that trouble either by supporting the warrior along his journey or by rejecting his call and assuaging the trouble by refusing him admission into the functional blues community.

The central conflict in each of the *Cycle*'s first three plays is greatly influenced by how well the warrior character engages with the wisdom and guidance of the griot. Loomis is able to stand up and bleed for himself because he listens and responds to Bynum. The same can certainly not be said about the relationships between Levee and Toledo or Troy and Bono.[52] Levee has no interest in anything Toledo has to say because, as he professes, "Levee got to be Levee," and that means that he dictates his own course of action.[53] Levee fails to realize that any success or glory he may gain must come through the community vehicle of the band. As Cutler makes clear, "this ain't none of them hot bands. This is an accompaniment band."[54] "Refusing to recognize the limits of his own talent or the social limits imposed on him," recognizes John Timpane, "[Levee] is trying to construct a romance of a meritocracy in which he will be surely rewarded."[55] Levee's drive that Timpane underscores is prototypical of the warrior: he believes himself to be better than the people and conditions surrounding him, and strives to transcend that community. Levee's refusal to accept his reliance on the blues community is so great that he strikes out violently against the community rather than embrace his need for his bandmates. His murder of Toledo is a desperate exclamation that he needs neither the community nor Toledo's ancestral wisdom in order to define his own existence. Wilson said he admired Levee's warrior spirit, but he still does nothing as a playwright (other than perhaps concluding the play) to assuage the damage Levee has done to the community and himself. Wilson's blues dramaturgy will brook no rejection of the blues community, and Levee must suffer the consequences.

Much of the prevailing scholarship on Wilson's warrior characters suggests that their anger and angst are rooted in a struggle to embody their socially imposed ideals of manhood. Keith Clark, for instance, argues that Wilson's plays interrogate "a culture consistently devoted to denying black men the emotional space to express and experience hurt." Clark insists that "in America's deformed and deforming perspective, black men are denied an interiority, an emotional and psychic complexity that undermines their presumed bestiality" and that the *American Century Cycle* in part "chronicles the catastrophic consequences of black men's obliviousness to their psychic malaise as well as the curative responses some men fashion to resist it."[56]

In a similar vein, Elam, pointing out that "for black men, the emblematic status as 'all that is dangerous' too often becomes internalized," argues that "Wilson's representation of black men addresses their historical stigmatization within American society as well as their internalized oppression."[57] For Clark, Elam, and others, the warrior spirit in these characters is a symptom of internalized social expectations for black manhood before it becomes the cause of strife within the plays' communities.

In a distinct but similarly popular strain of argument, critics often theorize Wilson's warriors as in dialogue with the Eshu/Legba/Signifying Monkey tradition of African and African American folkloric tricksters. According to Paul Carter Harrison, this figure "mediates the obstacles that threaten survival and harmony with wit, cunning, guile, and a godly sense of self-empowerment which accord him extravagant transgressions. Alogical and nontraditional—at least more adept at improvisation—he is unimpressed with social constraints established for mortals of average size." Harrison insists that Levee, Troy, and Loomis "each owe their pedigree to the trickster."[58] In accepting this argument, Pereira argues that a lineage connecting warriors to the trickster "focuses attention on the cosmological dimension of Wilson's plays as it intersects with the mundane struggles of his characters."[59] This concept underscores how deeply Wilson's warriors feel a separation from their social spheres, which they consider mundane encumbrances on personal quests of higher order. By situating this character in a lineage with Eshu, whom Pereira characterizes as "the trickster deity who rails against the status quo and the rigidity of rule and order, preferring the freedom of individual will," critics contextualize warriors' struggles as resulting from a refusal to define their life journeys within the confines of a rigid social sphere.[60] The warrior as trickster is a character who seeks above all to get one over on the society that would seek to define him downward.

According to the Clark/Elam approach to the Wilsonian warrior, Levee lashes out because Sturdyvant's refusal to allow him to record his songs forces the young musician to run up against the limit of his masculine self-crafting, a limit out of sync with the expectations he had formulated in accordance with society's fabricated and imposed standards. According to the Harrison/Pereira alternative, Sturdyvant's refusal forces Levee to recognize that he has been the object of a trick rather than its agent. In both cases, Sturdyvant's refusal reveals to Levee a reality out of sync with his own self-imposed expectations for his relationship to the social sphere.

While both of these approaches offer insightful treatments of Wilson's warrior, both run into problems when considering the warrior as a character in dialogue with a community. In general, analyses through the lens of masculinity or the trickster treat the warrior in isolation from his immediate community. As a result, they encounter the same problem that plagues the warrior himself: overlooking how deeply the other people in his immediate social sphere affect him. When Loomis arrives at Seth's boardinghouse, he does so out of the necessity of needing a place to rest himself and his daughter; he is not in search of a community. Still, any ground gained in his project of understanding his place in the world, and any hope of continuing to do so, come in dialogue with a blues griot and the community. Loomis's warrior plight thus ends well, whereas Levee's does not, precisely because Loomis learns to engage with and accept the influence of his community. Within Wilson's blues dramaturgy, few realizations are more valuable. Men like Levee, Troy, Floyd, and King Hedley II never come to this realization, and the blues community is unable to support their journeys.

Wilson's warriors struggle because their instincts for individuality place them at odds with a social system that is irreducibly antiphonal and community based. This formulation is perhaps most clear at the beginning of *Joe Turner* and the conclusion of *Ma Rainey*. Loomis is an outsider vexed in large part because he carries himself as one who is not part of any community. When he returns to the boardinghouse to find the rest of the characters sharing the communal elation of the Juba, his alienation becomes vivid; his anger is a symptom of his stark inability to understand or participate in community. It is only once Bynum helps Loomis enter into a dialogue with his ancestral community that he is able to open a dialogue with his contemporaneous blues community. His extended struggles are grounded in his debilitating self-definition as a loner. The same is true of Levee who, at the conclusion of his play, refuses to amend his self-definition as an individual who does not rely on his community. Backed into a corner with his ideals crumbling, he can either turn to the blues community for an antiphonal reevaluation of his identity or fight for his self-contained individuality. His warrior spirit leads him to the latter.

Thus, although Wilson confesses to admire the warrior spirit, its presence in the *Cycle*'s blues communities is most often destructive. Floyd's only desire from the opening of *Seven Guitars* is to get out of his Pittsburgh community and into what he considers a more fruitful community in Chicago. Like Levee before him, Floyd believes that he can lead himself and others to success if only his community would follow and support him. Unlike Levee, when Floyd's plans flounder, he continues to take active steps toward achieving his goals. Rather than turning to the blues community for support, however, Floyd's robbery of the loan office of Metro Finance and his violent covetousness of his loot show a sharp increase in his urge for individuality on his journey toward self-identification. "I'm going to Chicago," he pronounces defiantly. "If I have to buy me a graveyard and kill everybody I see. I am going to Chicago. I don't want to live my life without. Everybody I know live without. I don't want to do that. I want to live with. I don't know what you all think of yourself but I think I'm supposed to have."[61] An individualistic warrior spirit drives Floyd, but for much of the play he operates under the guise of community leader, a performance that seems to fool even himself. Calling Floyd a "blues hero," David L. G. Arnold underscores the tension within the community and outside it that defines the guitarist: "As a member of his community, he raises a unifying, glorious voice, but as an individual beset by ambition, an artist whose art is tainted inasmuch as it is bent to slake the commercial thirsts of the white producers, he loses sight of what Wilson sets up as better priorities." "Floyd could be a vital part of his community," adds Arnold. "He sets up a call and gets a response (his record's popularity), but his inability to follow through and make his final comment, to fill out the call and response paradigm of the blues, renders his efforts ultimately tragic."[62] As Arnold and others recognize, the conflict between Floyd as musician and Floyd as person makes for dangerous tension.

Floyd's community position is problematic in ways similar to Troy's: his community looks to him as leader, a role he accepts while nonetheless embodying the drives of individualistic warrior. In a striking reversal of *Ma Rainey*'s conclusion, Floyd is killed by Hedley, the blues griot enraged at having been ignored for so long—"Having been made to wait too long, John the Baptist kills his Christ," says Tony Kushner of this moment[63]—but as the play's brief prologue and epilogue show, Floyd's absence works to engender a stronger sense of community among his social sphere. "In being so eager to get to Chicago and leave his community behind," argues Brenda Murphy, recognizing that what she calls "the tragedy of *Seven Guitars*" finds its roots in Floyd's schism from his community, "Floyd was in a sense cutting himself off from the people and floating off into the sky, as the image of the funeral angels suggests. Hedley's deed simply gave concrete existence to the action."[64] Without the destructive presence of the individualistic warrior, the blues community can function more harmoniously.

In comparison, Troy's death has an ambivalent effect on the community of his family. On the one hand, Cory and Raynell share a touching moment of family bonding, fused by the spirit of a blues song that Troy had learned from his father and sung to his children. On the other hand, as Wilson himself points out, "At the end of *Fences* every person, with the exception of Raynell, is institutionalized. Rose is in a church. Lyons is in a penitentiary. Gabriel's in a mental hospital and Cory's in the marines."[65] The play's conclusion suggests that the loss of Troy was for the Maxson family a loss of its organizing center, and that in the wake of such a loss they turned toward other institutions for guidance and structure. This conclusion reflects tellingly on Troy as a warrior throughout the play. For Troy conceptualizes himself not necessarily as part of or separate from the community, but as a pure giver who supports his social sphere fully. "Woman," he tells Rose, "I do the best I can do. I come in here every Friday. I carry a sack of potatoes and a bucket of lard. You all line up at the door with your hands out. I give you the lint from my pockets. I give you my sweat and my blood. I ain't got no tears. I done spent them. [. . .] That's all I got, Rose. That's all I got to give. I can't give nothing else."[66] At various points in the play, other characters confess to thinking of Troy in much the same manner that he thinks of himself, as a leader and guide. Bono tells him that early in their relationship he thought, "My man Troy knows what he's doing . . . I'm gonna follow this nigger . . . he might take me somewhere. I been following you too. I done learned a whole heap of things about life watching you" (60). Cory tells his mother on the morning of Troy's funeral, "The whole time I was growing up . . . living in this house . . . Papa was like a shadow that followed you everywhere. It weighed on you and sunk into your flesh. It could wrap around you and lay there until you couldn't tell which one was you anymore. That shadow digging in your flesh. Trying to crawl in. Trying to live through you. Everywhere I looked, Troy Maxson was staring back at me" (87). And when Rose is infuriated by Troy's selfish appeals for understanding upon his confession of adultery, she tells him, "I held on to you, Troy. I took all my feelings, my wants and needs, my dreams . . . and I buried them inside you" (67). Troy defines his existence by the self-crafted narrative of a benevolent field guide through life for his social sphere, and at least for a time his closest relations buy into this narrative and follow their guide.

The problem is that Troy styles himself as a blues griot when in fact he is a warrior, and his family makes the strategic error of following the warrior down a dangerous path designed for individuality, not communal strength. His claim to give Rose and the family all he has to give is simply not true; the play's opening scene makes clear that at least some amount of his energy has been going toward courting Alberta. The unfinished fence around his family's yard stands as a vivid indicator of Troy's incomplete commitment to Rose, Cory, and the social sphere that forms around his back porch to include Bono and Lyons. "In the final analysis," says Pereira, "we cannot judge him on a socially realistic level without considering also the mythological perspectives of his actions. In his magnificent struggle to nurture his family, he represents the purest strain of the survival instinct in the African-American race."[67] This sounds very much like what Troy himself might say in defense of his warrior self-interest. While there may be in Troy a struggle to nurture his family, the force that makes that struggle magnificent is the force pulling him toward self-interest.

Any nurturing that comes from Troy in fact comes contra his overwhelming drive for personal advancement. When he attempts to explain his adultery to Rose, his language reveals how thoroughly self-centered are his pursuits; he confesses that his interest in Alberta has little to do with her, but rather with how their relationship gives him "a different understanding about myself. I can step out of this house and get away from the pressures and problems . . . be a different man." His baseball metaphor similarly centers on himself and his social coup in establishing a secure life against oppressive odds: "I fooled them, Rose. I bunted. When I found you and Cory and a halfway decent job . . . I was safe." But of course the warrior spirit is not satisfied standing safely on first base: "Then when I saw that gal . . . she firmed up my backbone. And I got to thinking that if I tried . . . I just might be able to steal second. Do you understand after eighteen years I wanted to steal second?" (65–66). Even while living the domestic life and providing for a family, Troy is simply a dormant warrior.[68]

Wilson's warriors thus exist at odds with the blues metaphysics governing his plays. His dramaturgy expects that characters beset by a shared struggle turn to the unifying forces of the social sphere in order to engage in a communal act of responding through social identity crafting. The warrior intends to do no such thing. He seeks instead to impose his self-crafted identity on those around him, and to carry himself through life in the manner he deems most fitting to his goals. Levee's community never accepts him; Troy's enables him to the detriment of all; and Loomis's manages in the end to get through to him, helping him become a more fully realized social human. Throughout the *Cycle,* Wilson's warriors thus experience a wide variety of degrees of success. Somebody like King Hedley II, a character who finds his lineage not necessarily from his namesake in *Seven Guitars* but rather from warriors like Levee, Troy, Loomis, and his biological father Floyd, has absolutely no interest in listening to his community's response to his identity crafting, and he dies having failed to impose himself in any way. He says that "the next motherfucker that fucks with me it's gonna be World War III," but he does not make a profound impact on his society.[69]

Significantly, he makes no distinction of who that motherfucker might be: his aggression is ready to act out on anybody, be they family, friend, foe, or oppressor. "I ain't sorry for nothing I done," he says defiantly. "And ain't gonna be sorry. I'm gonna see to that. 'Cause I'm gonna do the right thing. Always. It ain't in me to do nothing else. We might disagree about what that is. But I know what is right for me. As long as I draw a breath in my body I'm gonna do the right thing for me."[70] This sounds like the Wilsonian warrior's creed. Troy tells Bono something similar about his infidelity to Rose: "I ain't ducking the responsibility of it. As long as it sets right in my heart . . . then I'm okay. Cause that's all I listen to. It'll tell me right from wrong every time" (61). Boy Willie similarly claims to find moral grounding within himself: "I don't go by what the law say. The law's liable to say anything. I go by if it's right or not. It don't matter to me what the law say. I take and look at it for myself."[71] Wilson's dramaturgy demands that characters participate in the antiphonal social operation of their plays, but the warrior defines his call-and-response as at all times self-reflexive.

And yet, this presumed self-reflexivity is debunked by the near constant vexation of Wilson's warriors. Troy's life falls to shambles once he tries to reconcile his urge for individuality with his ill-formed commitment to his family. Early in the play, his quarrels with Rose and Cory find their roots in Troy's perception of a discord between the identity he crafts for himself and the manner in which his family relates to him, which he considers disrespectful to his self-styled identity. He gets so angry when Cory tries to walk past him without excusing himself because Troy deems himself as deserving such courtesy. But his call for respect is not returned with a ratifying response, and the dissonance of his song vexes Troy. This same sort of dissonance fuels *Jitney*'s central agon, as Booster tries to explain to his father that the murderous actions he took to craft his identity were done with a view to preserving the family name, but Becker staunchly refuses to accept such a claim:

> Booster: I thought you would understand. I thought you would be proud of me.
> Becker: Proud of you for killing somebody!
> Booster: No, Pop. For being a warrior. For dealing with the world in ways that you didn't or couldn't or wouldn't.

As he says, the warrior spirit ushered Booster to prison, but he has spent his twenty years reflecting and realizes now that his murder was an individualist act: "I did it for myself. But it didn't add up the way I thought it would. I was wrong. I can see that now."[72] Even though Booster arrives at his father's jitney station far more at peace with himself than many other Wilsonian warriors, the play's father-son tension is a symptom of the most common problem troubling warriors: Booster attempted to impose his identity on the community rather than engaging in the communal act of self-crafting.

From their position of discord, however, Wilson's warriors underscore the pervasiveness of the blues ethos running throughout the *American Century Cycle*. The antiphonal and communal rhythms of this ethos give constantly evolving shape to the *Cycle*'s social sphere, one that always adapts as blues people engage performatively with the sphere's matrix. The warriors' vexation signals the ultimate refusal of the plays' social spheres to engage the individualistic call of the warrior spirit. In *Radio Golf*, the final vision of Harmond exiting his office to join the community's fight to save Aunt Ester's house shows that the blues social sphere is infinitely accommodating to new voices that share in its communal struggle. But the warrior's fundamental blindness is the extent to which those around him share his struggle. He sees himself on a solo journey, beset by troubles that nobody else understands. Characters like Loomis and Boy Willie travel through their troubled journeys and discover that they are not alone; Levee, Troy, and Floyd never learn the necessity that Wilson's dramaturgy places on community. Paradoxically, the warrior's constant frustration with his community's not accepting his self-crafted identity betrays an awareness that an identity requires social ratification, but rarely does he recognize these conditions. Instead, Wilson's warriors constantly test the limits of the blues social sphere's willingness to accept what is imposed on it by force. The regular failure or forced reevaluation of this quest demonstrates how fundamental a blues ethos is to the social operation of Wilson's *Cycle*.

Searching for Identity within a Conservative Romantic Imperative: The Blueswoman

The tenor of Floyd's wooing of Vera in the long second scene of *Seven Guitars* is that in order for him to succeed in life the way he desires, he needs the love and support of Vera: "A man that believe in himself still need a woman that believe in him. You can't make life happen without a woman."[73] Vera has heard this tune before, and she is skeptical that his ways have suddenly changed to such a degree that he will not run off with another woman this time like he did previously. Unlike *Joe Turner*'s Mattie Campbell, whose only desire is to define herself in terms of a man, Vera initially resists the idea of a woman needing a man. She tells Floyd that she has longed for him, but she is by no means eager to have him back. After resisting for much of the play, however, Vera eventually agrees to join Floyd in Chicago with one proviso: "I went down to the Greyhound Bus Station too. Here. See that? What that say? It say 'One way . . . Chicago to Pittsburgh.' It's good for one year from the date of purchase. I'm gonna put that in my shoe. When we get to Chicago I'm gonna walk around on it. I hope I never have to use it."[74] The nuance of difference between Mattie and Vera thus lies not in whether they desire a relationship with a man, but rather in the relative position of power they maintain within that relationship. Vera maintains for herself a level of agency: she gives in to Floyd's advances, but she preserves in her shoe for a year the power to extricate herself.

As many critics have recognized, there exists little space for feminine agency in Wilson's plays: his women are defined almost entirely by their relationship to men. Arguing that "Wilson has created an array of powerful African American women," Shannon nonetheless locates that power most directly in his women's capacity to nurture others.[75] Certainly there is little room within the *Cycle* for a woman to express a warrior spirit. Ma Rainey may seem like a warrior because she is so assertive, but that is because the play so frequently shows her asserting herself within a white space. When she is alone with Cutler and when she alludes to her ability to abandon Chicago in favor of her southern fans' support, Ma reveals that she is deeply invested in the black blues community. And certainly the *Cycle* is far more focused on the struggles of men than it is on the constant plight of women who are affected by men's actions. As Berniece makes clear, rarely do Wilson's men consider the degree to which their actions cause turmoil for the women around them.

Although the blues community is supportive of the project to develop female social humanity, it nonetheless restricts the forms that that humanity might take. As is particularly evident with characters like Berniece, Risa, and Vera, who can resist the advances of men only temporarily, the *Cycle* views women in the particular role of a man's lover. As *Joe Turner*'s dramatis personae dubs Bertha "[Seth's] wife," so too could nearly all the *Cycle*'s women be dubbed "His wife/love interest." As Elam points out, however, "the question is how and to what degree they are able to achieve self-definition given their relationship to the men in their lives."[76] The *Cycle*'s social sphere limits women's options while still expecting that they will participate in the communal performance of identity, humanization, and shared suffering. The task of combating identity effacement is thus far more complicated for Wilson's women than it is for his men.

Berniece, for example, begins her play feeling betrayed by love. Having lost her husband to a botched robbery, Berniece is in no mood to rush back into a romance. When Avery raises the issue of marriage to her, as it seems he has done before, she tells him directly, "I ain't ready to get married now. [. . .] I got enough on my hands with Maretha. I got enough people to love and take care of." In this moment, Berniece vocalizes a call of identity to the social sphere—one she has apparently made repeatedly in the past—but she is denied a ratifying response. "Who you got to love you?" responds Avery accusingly. "Can't nobody get close enough to you."[77] Earlier, Doaker also refuses to ratify her identity as a woman without a man, telling Wining Boy that Berniece "still got Crawley on her mind. He been dead three years but she still holding on to him. She need to go out here and let one of these fellows grab a whole handful of whatever she got. She act like it got precious."[78] For Doaker, Avery, and the broader community they represent, the only social humanity available to Berniece is conservative femininity defined by the relationship to a man. "You trying to tell me a woman can't be nothing without a man?" objects Berniece to Avery. "But you alright, huh? You can just walk out of here without me—without a woman—and still be a man."[79] Berniece is correct that in Wilson's world Avery lacking a woman does not carry the same social stigma as Berniece's status as a single woman, but Avery also distinguishes himself from Berniece by actively seeking rather than shunning romance.

Throughout the *Cycle*, there exists an implicit expectation that most characters actively participate in the social practice of seeking a romantic or sexual partner. Boy Willie and Lymon are both single, for example, but both have scenes of courtship. Wilson seems to expect that his younger characters fulfill a duty of seeking out some semblance of love, romance, or sex. Cory has no clear romantic investment throughout *Fences,* but the play does suggest that his teenage hormones are active: "I'm talking to Jesse. [*Into phone.*] When she say that? [*Pause.*] Aw, you lying, man. I'm gonna tell her you said that" (41). And evidence of his commitment to the romantic imperative comes when he returns from the Marines on the day of his father's funeral:

> Lyons: I hear you thinking about getting married.
> Cory: Yea, I done found the right one, Lyons. It's about time. (85)

Seven-year-old Raynell seems excused from the expectation for romance that Wilson places on his characters, but *Joe Turner*'s Zonia and Reuben are about the same age, and their roles are defined in part by a progression into the social ritual of romance.

Berniece's refusal of Avery's advances might seem to make her a female warrior. Her social sphere offers her one path toward realized humanity, and she staunchly resists. She resists, that is, until Lymon tries a different tactic of courtship. The late-play scene between Lymon and Berniece that concludes with a kiss shows Berniece, having been denied ratification for full social humanity as a single woman, beginning to acquiesce to antiphonal feedback from her community. By participating in the courtship with Lymon, Berniece changes course on her journey toward selfhood and begins to harmonize with her blues community. When she plays the piano and calls to her ancestors, she makes a similar change, no longer rejecting the piano and its history by refusing to play it, and by doing so she helps secure the safety of her brother and their blues social sphere. Kissing Lymon is far less dramatic, but it similarly shows Berniece participating in rather than denying rituals of her social sphere.

This is a troubling method for Berniece to have to follow in order to begin to achieve social humanity. She appears to have little interest in Avery, but his implication that a woman needs a man (an implication made also by Jeremy, Sterling, Floyd, and Citizen to the respective targets of their romantic advancements) turns out to be more true of *Cycle* society than one might hope. The only two female characters in the *Cycle* that are neither currently involved in some sort of romance nor have been in their past are the children Raynell and Maretha. The only other woman who has no romantic activity during her play is *Seven Guitars'* Louise (that is, if her opening the play with a sexually suggestive ballad is not romantic activity), but Wilson makes clear that she has fulfilled her romantic responsibility in the past with Henry, the man who walked out on her. Not even advanced age excuses women from the demand for romance: the elder Ruby in *King Hedley II* plans to marry Elmore, and at 285 years old, Aunt Ester flirts with Solly in *Gem:* "Come on and let's get married. You always talking about getting married. I done had four husbands I might as well have five."[80] With few exceptions, Wilson's women exist under the expectation of participating in romance, and their potential for social humanity seems contingent upon such participation.

Put differently, Wilson's women are defined by the potential of their genitalia, a concept that the playwright uses when introducing Risa in the scene directions of *Two Trains Running:* "Risa is a young woman who, in an attempt to define herself in terms other than her genitalia, has scarred her legs with a razor."[81] Risa shares Berniece's disdain for romance, but hers is both more extreme and longer standing. According to Holloway, Risa is "one of them gals that matured quick. And every man that seen her since she was twelve years old think she ought to go lay up with them somewhere," and Wolf says that she has not been involved with a man "in six years that I know of." Risa's refusal of normative romantic relationships is so aberrant in her community that after she cut her legs, "They had her down there at Western Psych" attempting to ascertain why she would go to such extremes to avoid something that seems to her society so natural. "Something ain't right with a woman don't want no man," says Memphis, voicing the opinion of the community. "That ain't natural. If she say she like women that be another thing. It ain't natural, but that be something else. But somebody that's all confused about herself and don't want nobody . . . I can't figure out where to put her."[82] Even in his perspective limited by heteronormativity and homophobia, Memphis can grasp the concept of a homosexual relationship because at least it is a romantic partnership; he simply cannot wrap his head around the notion of sexual individuality. The sense of compassion Risa feels for Hambone is telling: she is the only character that can empathize with his plight because she is a social outsider like him. "Most people don't understand Hambone," she says. "That's 'cause they don't take the time. Most people think he can't understand nothing. But he understand everything what's going on around him. Most of the time he understand better than they do."[83] Risa could very well be talking about herself here. Nobody understands her because nobody takes the time to think outside the confines of normative relationships and desires for women.

The collection of people who fail to stretch their thinking about interpersonal relationships in regards to Risa must therefore include Wilson. When Risa's individuality falters in favor of a romance with Sterling, she, like Berniece before her, enters into the normative social practice of romance that defines the existence of Wilson's women. Risa's expression of desire for Sterling contributes to closure in *Two Trains Running*: the blues community is finally able to accept Risa as socially human, ratifying her identity as a functioning member of the social sphere.

If to this point the blues social sphere of Wilson's *Cycle* has seemed like some egalitarian space, then the condition of women should reveal the fallacy in that notion. There turns out to be little room for female individuality in the *Cycle*. Elam points out that the most distinguishing characteristic of Wilson's women is "their relationship to and even need for a man. It is a paradox that Wilson seems to recognize, and yet does not step outside of, in his depiction of women."[84] Elam finds evidence nonetheless of "the ways these women express agency within the limitations of male dominance."[85] Doris Davis goes further, arguing that Wilson's "female characters function, in fact, as integral counterparts of the blues and African folklore motifs that envelop his male protagonists. Moreover, while they do not hold center stage, at their strongest, they represent the center of wisdom. They know their songs intuitively, for the 'ground on which they stand,' to paraphrase Wilson's famous speech, is that of self-knowledge."[86] But Wilson's blues dramaturgy has little interest in self-knowledge without the performance of self, and self-knowledge rarely breeds agency in any of Wilson's women. They may have wisdom—Berniece and Aunt Ester certainly do—but a causal relationship between wisdom and a productive performance of self within the *Cycle*'s blues social sphere is untenable. The obvious women who express female agency in the *Cycle* are Ma Rainey and Rose Maxson; the former dominates her recording session, and the latter asserts her individuality by pronouncing Troy "a womanless man" in response to his admission of infidelity.[87] But both gain access to agency only after participating in the social practice of a romantic relationship. The blues community of *Fences* had long since ratified the identity of Rose as a family matriarch, and so there is no need to amend that beyond the household, where she had gained a certain amount of power at the cost of Troy ceding his. Ma flaunts her sexuality at all times, both through bawdy, suggestive lyrics and by insisting on the attendance of her female sexual interest, Dussie Mae. Ma may not be participating in heteronormative, procreative romance, but she does embrace her identity as a sexualized woman. As Rose and Ma make clear, any journey for agency and identity for Wilson's women comes through their active participation in romance.

The journey of women toward identity thus reveals much about the expectations and limitations of the *Cycle*'s social sphere. Most of the *Cycle*'s women find their identities in the relationship with men, whether that be in marriage, like Bertha, Tonya, or Mame, or not, like Mattie, Vera, Ruby, Black Mary, and others. But in their journey from resistance to acquiescence, Berniece and Risa reveal how limited the paths open to women are and how essential it is for women to follow one of those paths. Ultimately, Wilson's blueswomen expose a paradoxical conservatism running through the *Cycle*. Certainly the blues impulses of Wilson's characters work counter to hegemonic white society, and certainly the concepts and attitudes that are most influential in the *Cycle*'s society are far different from those of the dominant culture, but Wilson's counterculture world is shot through with conservative notions of gender roles.[88] "When you have the males, you have to have the females," says Wilson, revealing the limited scope of his thinking about gender. "What happens is the male goes off to the battle, if you will, and when he comes home, the woman nurses his wounds, binds him up and sends him back off into the battle. That's the role defined by this relationship that has enabled us to survive."[89] This conservatism is consistent with the blues musical tradition, which contains thousands of songs by blueswomen dominated by subjects of lost love or romance. As Angela Davis and Hazel Carby have shown, however, recasting love and sex through a defiantly feminist lens was a means for early blueswomen to seize agency otherwise denied them. When jilted by love, for example, the persona of blueswomen's songs rarely becomes some sort of weak damsel, and Ma Rainey and others would often assert their independence from men by singing about homosexuality. But even this strategy does not free them from a primarily sexualized identity. Elam calls this condition in Wilson's plays "the dialectic of feminist assertion and traditional conformity," which is a tension running all but universally through blues art's expression of femininity.[90] Whether they are sexually assertive or heartbroken and in search of a new love—positions that correspond precisely to Wilson's Ma Rainey and Mattie Campbell—blueswomen exist along a spectrum defined by that relative position to sex and romantic partnership.

Characterizing women reductively, the *Cycle* nonetheless frequently shows women keenly aware that their personhood is in reference to men.

Mattie is a paradigm of somebody who recognizes and does all she can to satisfy this restraint, revealing the attendant psychological turmoil in the process. Rose also reveals that she has lived her life to the moment of Troy's admission of infidelity completely in terms of her marital relationship: "I held on to you, Troy. I took all my feelings, my wants and needs, my dreams . . . and I buried them inside you. I planted a seed and watched and prayed over it. I planted myself inside you and waited to bloom. And it didn't take me no eighteen years to find out the soil was hard and rocky and it wasn't never gonna bloom. But I held on to you, Troy. I held you tighter. You was my husband. I owed you everything I had. Every part of me I could find to give you" (67). For eighteen years, Rose's call to her community was for the precise identity she is granted in the dramatis personae of *Fences*—"Troy's wife" (4)—and that identity has been successfully ratified because, as she points out, she has defined herself entirely in reference to her husband. She may very well have the authority to dub Troy a "womanless man" at the end of this scene, but such agency has only come through a long dedication to Wilson's romantic imperative. Mattie is on a desperate search for a husband to whom she might dedicate herself like Rose did, because she recognizes that her social personhood is contingent upon just such a relationship.

As he moves through the *Cycle*, Wilson experiments with women less committed to romantic partnership, but he continually instantiates this demand. Berniece and Risa follow directly on the heels of Rose and Mattie; the *Cycle* moves from those fully committed to the female demand of romantic partnership to those most adamantly opposed. But the romantic independence of Berniece and Risa ultimately loses out, and both end their plays on a path toward participation in a structured system of romance. With romantic independence seemingly futile, the *Cycle* moves to Vera, Ruby, Rena, the elder Ruby, and Tonya, all of whom are defined almost entirely by their relative positions to a romantic relationship. When the *Cycle* arrives at *Gem of the Ocean* Aunt Ester emerges as much more of a spiritual maternal figure than a sexualized woman, but even this blues griot recalls that she has had passed lovers, has born children, and in her flirtations with Solly that the sexualized aspects of her identity have not waned fully with age.

Two of Wilson's final women, Black Mary and Mame Wilks, find room for some agency but nonetheless maneuver within romantic demands. "You got a woman in your hands. Now what?" Black Mary says to a stunned Citizen as she places her head on his chest. "What you got? What you gonna do? Time ain't long, Mr. Citizen. A woman ain't but so many times filled up. What you gonna do? What you gonna fill me up with?" Overpowering Citizen's lame courtship, Black Mary shows the potential for women's power within the limited space of their identity formation. If she is to become the next Aunt Ester, Black Mary must learn assertiveness and self-confidence. She shows the beginning of these characteristics here (and when she talks back to her mentor). Still, the hapless Citizen encapsulates the ultimate futility of Black Mary's grab for agency: "I'm a man. I can't change that. You a woman. A man's gonna have his way with a woman."[91] By the time the *Cycle* reaches what Wilson characterizes as the soullessly capitalistic 1990s, Mame believes that her own identity as a successful woman will come via her husband, and she aggressively attempts to secure that success through his political capital. Nonetheless, when she feels betrayed by his change of political course, she might psychologically break from Harmond in order to look elsewhere for her own identity crafting—"I can't live my life for you"—but she cannot bring herself to abandon him: "I'm still standing here, Harmond. I still love you."[92] Even though she is determined to shape her own professional future, the imperative of romance that Wilson places on his women limits Mame's options for independence.

Throughout the *Cycle*, then, Wilson's blueswomen remain mostly confined within the conservative social structure that expects them to commit to and define themselves by a romantic relationship. Still, the characters are marked by a bluesy repetition with revision. According to Kushner, "If August Wilson, as he exists in his plays, can be called a patriarchal conservative, he isn't a dogmatist or an ideologue. He is, he was, a dramatist, which is to say a dialectician."[93] As Kushner highlights, Wilson, although working within confined structures, created women on dialectical journeys of becoming. Every female character would desire to be as powerful as Ma, but the *Cycle* offers instead a collection of wives like Bertha, searchers like Mattie, and man-grabbers like Molly. In this repetition with revision, Wilson shows his limited female characters constantly testing new avenues for agency, making newly shaped calls to the social sphere in the uncertain hope of a ratifying response. Like their warrior counterparts, the rebellious calls of Berniece and Risa are denied, but by the time the *Cycle* reaches Black Mary and Mame, women have begun to find some limited means of asserting agency; the *Cycle*'s women characters find various ways of responding to and maneuvering around those limitations. Still, the shared struggle of Wilson's women turns out to stem from the lack of independence available to them.

Wilson's Theater as Blues Dialogue

Wilson's *Cycle* consistently explores many familiar characters and tensions as it meanders across the twentieth-century landscape. In doing so, Wilson is not constructing some historical survey of how black American life evolved from decade to decade, but rather offering a complex portrait of the many components of black American life in the performative present. Taken holistically, the *Cycle* does not offer Toledo, Bono, Bynum, and others as several different versions of a blues griot, but rather as a multidimensional, complex image of this social figure that resists conscription. The same is true of his warriors, women, and other characters: the concept of a four-hundred-year-old autobiography of blacks in America requires constant repetition and revision in light of antiphonal feedback from the blues community. It is not a history written and codified in a textbook, but one that exists only through embodiment in the performative present. To perform Wilson's plays at any point is to continue the ongoing investigation of black Americans in light of their long history of struggle stretching back ultimately to the blood memory of Africa.

The repetition and revision running throughout the *Cycle*, that is, constitute a continual process of Wilson looking to the blues community of his audience for ratification of his version of American blues people, with all their splendor, faults, challenges, and triumphs. The versions of blues people offered by Muddy Waters or Langston Hughes or Zora Neal Hurston, for example, are all quite distinct from each other and from Wilson's. As the previous chapter demonstrates, Wilson viewed theatrical performance as a means of communal identity crafting: his plays give a stage to his version of blues people in order to perform themselves, hoping that a community of shared suffering and strength will recognize its characteristics, respond to its call, and ratify its social humanity. C. Patrick Tyndall's argument that "Wilson's black art functions as a healing tool and guide for the African American community" is certainly an accurate description of the work's aspirations, but in order for Wilson's plays to work as such a tool and guide, their voice requires acceptance and ratification from the community.[94] Mark

William Rocha has likened this theatrical technique of Wilson's to the Signifyin(g) performance of "loud-talking." According to Gates, "One successfully loud-talks by speaking to a second person remarks in fact directed to a third person, at a level just audible to the third person. A sign of the success of this practice is an indignant 'What?' from the third person, to which the speaker replies, 'I wasn't talking to you.' Of course, the speaker was, yet simultaneously was not."[95] Rocha proposes "loud-talking as the paradigmatic metaphor for the African American theater in general and for August Wilson's history plays in particular," and argues that during Wilson's plays the characters, the performers playing them, and Wilson are all "consciously loud-talking on the audience."[96] Rocha insists that Wilson's intent is "to bring an indictment against the theatrical audience with the expectation that public exposure to the third party of the characters onstage will force the audience to accept rather than dismiss the charges" and to compel the mostly white audience to "tacitly admit its failure of social responsibility."[97]

This model extends to the process through which Wilson loud-talks on whites while also covertly performing black humanity to his black audiences. Like trickster bluesmen and blueswomen from the Mississippi Delta, that is, Wilson offers in his art several planes of expression for several different audiences. Addressing his white audiences in ways that Rocha decodes, Wilson also deploys the methods of blues to speak to his blues community. Certainly, as Rocha insists, "Wilson's signifyin(g) in effect breaks the fourth wall of the proscenium stage," but in doing so, the plays signify on a variety of social tropes, including the continually evolving conception of social humanity for black Americans.[98] Wilson does not posit a simple answer or stable model for that humanity, offering instead his plays and the *Cycle* as continual participants in the performative, antiphonal process of shaping and ratifying that humanity in response to ever-evolving social forces.

Ultimately, then, the blues metaphysics giving shape to Wilson's dramaturgy reveals the social project deeply invested in his plays. Throughout the *Cycle* there exists a performative expression of self that requires both the covertness afforded by art and the community garnered by performance. To recognize Wilson's plays as blues expressiveness thus reveals how important it is that they call to their audience in an appeal for response. These are not plays that hope simply that their audiences remember their characters and ponder their themes at home after showtime; they are performances hoping to arouse response and continued dialogue. That seems a peculiar notion for a collection of plays that traffic so overtly in the realist, traditional methods of Western theater, but these methods are again expressions of Wilson's Signifyin(g). He tropes the trope of Western theater by using its form to engender a lasting call-and-response between a theatrical audience and the continued performance of the plays throughout the *Cycle*.

PART II
Performance, Identity, and Reimagining American Drama

4

"God A'mighty, I Be Lonesomer'n Ever!"

Eugene O'Neill's Aesthetic of Whiteness

AUGUST WILSON HAS NOT in any material way affected Eugene O'Neill, a playwright who lived and worked nearly half a century before Wilson's career. But the critical lens of Wilson's work casts an illuminating backward light on the force of individualistic whiteness running throughout O'Neill's plays. Both playwrights' characters struggle with the construction of sustainable identity vis-à-vis the collective social other, a master theme of American drama. Wilsonian warriors like Troy Maxson and Levee frequently fail to impose their constructed senses of self upon their communities, while characters who succeed in progressing toward clearer identity, like Sterling Johnson and Booster, do so by eventually beginning to listen to and engage with antiphonal forces. But characters in O'Neill like Brutus Jones, Lavinia Mannon, and Larry Slade struggle in their attempts to control and sustain their identities in unique ways that Wilson's lens reveals to grow out of an aesthetic of whiteness at work in O'Neill's plays. The operation of race in O'Neill—of whiteness as an ethnicity undergirded by structures of power and privilege—becomes far more evident once considered in light of the distinctive approach deployed by Wilson's black characters to negotiating the dynamic between self and community. In Wilson, community strength and support are paramount: those who eventually commit to community's necessity like Citizen Barlow and Harmond Wilks fare far better than those like Floyd Barton and King Hedley II who resist it. Wilson's lens helps show that any dedication to sociality in O'Neill is fleeting, and usually disingenuous.

The importance of black community in Wilson's work, that is, throws into relief the regular disregard shown for social engagement in O'Neill's plays, and highlights how the presumption of individualism finds root in the racial identity of O'Neill and his characters. Thinking backward through Wilson therefore helps unpack O'Neill by showing that the earlier playwright's characters are not simply Americans struggling with challenges of money and desire and family and so on, but that they are affected distinctively by the force of whiteness guiding their attitudes and decisions. Well known is the playwright's interest in the downtrodden and disrespected—immigrants, laborers, prostitutes, drunks—but approaching O'Neill via Wilson allows a consideration of the overlooked factor of whiteness at work in O'Neill.

The centrality of this component in O'Neill's work finds root in a life steeped in the privileges of whiteness, beginning with a riotous youth. As a young man he was tossed out of Princeton University, drowned himself in dive bars, proved prodigal with his father's wealth, and once fled the country to escape the responsibility of an unplanned pregnancy. He was even rebellious when he turned his attention most directly to theater, working with the Provincetown Players, an aesthetically experimental and politically radical group of New York bohemians who defined themselves in antagonist opposition to the commercial theater. Still, in 1920, not yet thirty-two years old, O'Neill won the Pulitzer Prize for *Beyond the Horizon,* and he would go on to become the most celebrated dramatist of his age (three more Pulitzers and a Nobel were to come). Drunken, abusive radical though he frequently was, O'Neill did not jeopardize a comfortable future in American society. He was, after all, a heterosexual white man in a society that cherished little more than people like him.

The freedom O'Neill enjoyed in the early twentieth century to explore himself through exploit, philosophy, radicalism, and art without imminent danger of violent repercussions is a privilege afforded by, perhaps first among others, his whiteness: he could wander into a reprobate lifestyle with confidence that the American social order would welcome him back. By contrast, in the same epoch, a black artist like Muddy Waters found himself on a constant quest for the protections of social legitimization, a struggle from which whiteness for the most part excused O'Neill. Other markers of privilege—maleness, cis-gendered heterosexuality, wealth, able-bodiedness, et cetera—are similarly important in securing O'Neill's social position, but whiteness underpins them all; it is even powerful enough to overcome his family's Irish-Catholic immigrant experience, which O'Neill bore like a proud scar. He may have seen himself as a cultural, political, and philosophical outsider, but his race would always preserve for him access to the privileged, empowered majority. The privilege that attends upon white existence is not news, but recognizing how operative whiteness was for O'Neill's success broadens and productively complicates an understanding of O'Neill's life.

The distinctively African American dramaturgy of Wilson helps reveal how the power of that whiteness is similarly operative throughout O'Neill's work. Wilson's imperative of black community helps show by contrast that at the core of O'Neill's aesthetic of whiteness is an ethos of self-sustaining individualism, the hallmark of twentieth-century American white masculinity. Ironically, even though O'Neill rejected most mainstream American cultural investments, his rebellion led him to only a different brand of individualism. He shunned expectations of education, domesticity, and professionalization in favor of riots and the sea, and from the outset of his career he shared with his Provincetown colleagues an attitude that Brenda Murphy dubs "intense iconoclasm and individualism" learned largely from Nietzsche.[1] John Patrick Diggins argues that "Nietzsche made O'Neill aware of the distinction between freedom and democracy, between the potential strength of the self and the actual weakness of the people," and suggests that "the former Catholic O'Neill took to Nietzsche, the dragon slayer of doctrines who wandered in a world without any truth to live by or a God to live for."[2] In Nietzsche, O'Neill and his closest intellectual collaborators found an individualist imperative insisting that projects of self-actualization turn inward. Whiteness sustained the privilege that allowed O'Neill to dwell in this world of radical politics and subversive philosophy. Contemporaneous black blues people like Muddy Waters did not have the luxury of expensive educations and time to ponder the mysteries of philosophy subsidized by wealthy families. Eminently vulnerable and in crises of self-definition, blues people turned to the shared strength of each other in ways that would have a lasting impact on August Wilson.

The individualist drive in O'Neill's work therefore signals the powerful influence of whiteness that runs counter to Wilson's blues ethos. As previous chapters demonstrate, Wilson took from blues the imperative of community. He understood blues as a distinctively black, communal mode of response to the African American experience, with all its struggle, rewards, failures, and endurance. In Wilson's work, as in the blues tradition, individuals address the larger community in the search for empathy, shared strength, and most of all the formulation and ratification of identity. Thus the blues metaphysics of Wilson's *Cycle* insists that a good-faith engagement with other people is constitutive of productive identity crafting. The only path to a clear and sustainable sense of self in Wilson is to solicit identity through call-and-response with the social sphere.

Conversely, the clearest mark of whiteness pervading O'Neill's oeuvre is his characters' consistent shunning of other people's influence on the self. As this chapter demonstrates with a discussion of Brutus Jones, because O'Neill saturates his plays with the experience of whiteness, the condition underwrites many of the playwright's black characters as much as their white counterparts. His characters regularly reject the call to community, attempting to handle crises on their own terms. This frequent presumption of self-sustainment—the ability to exist largely independently of the social sphere—rejects the collaborative force of community with a hubris born of the white American experience. This attitude shows up in Wilson when black characters like Roosevelt Hicks or Caesar Wilks give themselves over to assimilation with white culture, a move that their playwright treats as disastrous to black identity and menacing to black community. There, the ethos of whiteness has encroached on the black community in ways that help reveal the more pervasive force of whiteness in O'Neill. Whereas characters in Wilson like Boy Willie, Harmond Wilks, and Sterling Johnson are tempted by individualism before reaffirming a commitment to black community, O'Neill's work cultivates an aesthetic of whiteness that inspires his characters to face crises of identity largely on their own terms.

That drive leads often to tragedy in O'Neill, a mode that Wilson regularly intimates without fully embracing. Tragic events certainly happen in Wilson's *Cycle*—Levee's murder of Cutler, Hedley's of Floyd, for instance—but for the most part the playwright concerns himself with the long arc of African American history and community. Since his plays are always in dialogue with each other, loathsome tragic events are not catastrophic, because the community that constitutes the *American Century Cycle* can grow from them and progress. O'Neill's plays, like his characters, look almost entirely inward, and so his sense of tragedy carries a greater force of doom. The persistence of tragedy throughout O'Neill's work in fact demonstrates that whiteness in his plays has deleterious effects on those who cannot overcome its drive for individualism. Whiteness tells these characters that they need not rely on the community for productive humanity—often that other people are a threat to one's sovereignty—and this commitment to individualism leads consistently to tragic gloom. Whiteness proves corrosive: it tells these characters that independence and individualism are admirable, operative, and tenable, but breaks that promise by leading them consistently to social and existential disaster. Although characters seem convinced of their ability to exist on their own terms, they cannot shake the need for sociality. Early in the development of modern American drama, this trend shows the premium the form puts on a functioning dialectic between self and community.

The corrosive effects of whiteness on sustainable social identity run throughout O'Neill's work, growing more pronounced during his career as characters' presumptions of individualism become more pervasive. This trend is clearest in a series of O'Neill's most desperately individualistic characters: Yank from *The Hairy Ape,* Brutus Jones, Lavinia Mannon, Ephraim Cabot, Larry Slade, and Mary Tyrone. In unique ways, each is deeply committed to a self-crafted notion of identity that crumbles when challenged. Their failure to manage the dialectic between the self and other people is emblematic of the O'Neillian tragedy of individualism.

The structural tension pitting privileged presumptions of individualism against social demands for engagement with other people emerges first in early plays such as *The Emperor Jones* and *The Hairy Ape*. Both plays center on a boisterous and physically imposing man, characters who dominate their plays as they seem to have done to other people throughout their lives. Yank is the biggest and loudest member of the stokehole crew, while Jones has manipulated himself into power he retains with lies and violence. But O'Neill introduces both at moments of crises, times when their seemingly irrefutable dominance meets a challenge. These challenges come as the reach of each man's social sphere expands, weakening not only his authority but also his conceptions of self. O'Neill's aesthetic of whiteness shows itself in these characters' aggressive fights to reassert their weakening identities. Rather than engage other people in dialogue, they persist in efforts to overpower their adversaries, aloofly presuming no need for dialogue to reclaim identities to which they believe themselves entitled. This may seem like the strategy of Wilson's warriors, but Floyd, Boy Willie, and the rest are in fact desirous of community, even if their strategies for cultivating it are flawed. Yank and Jones seek to subdue community. Whiteness even underwrites the actions of the African American Jones, who eschews the sort of communal engagement evident in many of Wilson's black characters and opts instead for the particular white individualist strategy of early O'Neill.

In the middle of O'Neill's career, this trend evolves as the playwright turns his attention from the domineering character who spends his play on a desperate quest for social ratification to self-indulgent characters who attempt to excise the need for sociality. On the surface, Ephraim Cabot is not much different from Jones or Yank: he is overbearing toward others in his social sphere and entirely confident in his position of dominance. But whereas his two predecessors spend their plays on the defensive, Cabot spends the majority of *Desire Under the Elms* convinced that he controls his farm and family, a hubris that only increases when he finds out Abby is pregnant and wrongly presumes himself the father. Cabot spends the entire play certain of who he is, only to face a horrifying reversal at the conclusion. The same is true of *Mourning Becomes Electra*'s Lavinia Mannon, who spends the vast majority of her trilogy trying to dictate her identity to those around her. Even when that identity changes—she spends the first two plays of the trilogy attempting to craft herself as fully Mannon, and then the final play as her mother's daughter only—she presumes for herself the ability to dictate who she is to her audience and to exist as such. She too has this illusion shattered moments before her dramatic conclusion, finding that she has been disastrously blind to the necessity of inviting other people into her journey of becoming. Harmond Wilks spends much of *Radio Golf* treading a similar path, but his reversal comes in the form of an awakening to the power and importance of black community. For Cabot and Lavinia, the overconfidence attendant upon their whiteness allows them to disguise loneliness as certainty, fooling even themselves. They presume a right to self-craft without the influence of other people, and ignoring the forces of the social precipitates their downfalls.

In O'Neill's late plays, dangerous loneliness evolves into a desperate attempt to foster contentment in alienation. In *The Iceman Cometh*, Larry Slade recognizes that his fellow denizens of Harry Hope's backroom are deluded in their pipe dreams, but he sees no point in disabusing them of their dreams because their preoccupation enables his own isolation. They do not need anything from him, so he can exist contentedly alone among the crowd in what he refers to as the grandstands of life. Mary Tyrone, by contrast, recognizes that the Tyrone men have lofty expectations of her that she cannot fulfill. As Judith E. Barlow argues, "Mary Tyrone is finally neither mother nor virgin [. . .] and in this lies much of the tragedy of the Tyrone family. The men demand that she be a mother in all senses of the word, but she cannot and will not fulfill that role."[3] Mary attempts to isolate herself from expectations she cannot meet, and the competing difficulties only exacerbate her crippling addiction. Both characters believe what turns out to be the great white myth of O'Neill: that they can happily isolate themselves from other people. Wilson created a few loners—Wining Boy, say, or Lyons—but they temper their isolation by regularly touching base with family. O'Neill's loners make no such effort, but the closing moments of *Iceman* and *Long Day's Journey* show clearly that although the drive for sociality is powerful in Slade and Mary, their long projects of engineered isolation have cost them valuable opportunities for productive engagement. The white myth is shattered by social desire as these two late plays underscore the tragic sense of existential and social alienation running throughout O'Neill.

All this gloom and tragedy is shot through with the playwright's whiteness. In Wilson, the willingness of the blues social sphere to contribute to a process of social becoming is always a precondition: when and if individuals seek an audience for the antiphonal process of identity crafting, the community will be ready to engage. The worldview of Wilson's *Cycle* throws into stark relief the grave difficulty of finding in O'Neill a common ground between characters and their dramatic societies of other people. Ultimately, O'Neill does not create a society like Wilson's that is supportive of collaborative projects of becoming, but he cannot exile from his dramatic world the powerful imperatives of social identity crafting that lie at the foundation of American drama. Through this neglect, O'Neill and many of his characters find tragedy.

From Dominance to Destruction: Brutus Jones and Yank

Brutus and Yank both establish themselves in positions of dominance within relatively small communities despite larger social disenfranchisement. Neither man receives much socially granted privilege, but that certainly does not stop them from presuming entitlement to power and leadership. At the openings of *The Emperor Jones* and *The Hairy Ape,* both men sit atop the highest rung of their particular social ladders. They have each gained this position by force, but an ethos of individualist whiteness motivates their rises to prominence, their defiant delusions of self-sufficiency, and their eventual downfalls. Both head specifically defined communities that are constitutive of their power, but both lose that power by failing to respond to changes in community dynamics. This failure reveals the presumed autonomy of individualism rooted in O'Neill's corrosive, tragic, white aesthetic. Neither character is in a position that could tenably be called "white privilege," but their playwright imbues them with a hubris of self-sustainment born out of the white American experience. Although both men rely on their communities to bolster their constructed identities, they believe fully in the promise of the self-made man, dangerously undervaluing the role of the antiphonal other.

O'Neill opens each play with a glimpse of the protagonist's position of power won through dominance. At the beginning of *The Emperor Jones,* for example, Brutus has secluded himself from the community, taking a leisurely midday nap confident that the island residents he has subdued will remain obedient. As Robert M. Dowling points out, Jones is able "to betray his race (hence the name 'Brutus') by adopting the role of a white colonist."[4] Jones does not adopt the strategy favored by Wilson's blues dramaturgy of approaching the black community in a good-faith antiphonal exchange in order to solicit its contribution to his identity; he manipulates and overpowers the community with lies and tricks. His blackness notwithstanding, Brutus's ethos of whiteness therefore emerges in both his oppressive conquest and his paternalistic attitude. In Jones's self-assessment, he is more powerful and more advanced than his black subjects, and although he knows that their patience for his rule will eventually run out, his confidence allows him to sleep easy for the time being.

And yet, audiences learn very quickly that this confidence is ill placed as the play begins to show the shortcomings of Jones's presumptions and the white individualist ethos that guides them. On stage, while the Emperor naps in the wings, his henchman Smithers dutifully stops a native woman attempting to steal away from the palace undetected. O'Neill eventually reveals that the woman is the last of Jones's servants to abandon him and that Smithers holds his boss in contempt, but the dramatic condition of the play's opening moments nonetheless shows that in the social sphere of this island, Jones has established a ruthless identity that acts even in his absence; this woman is frightened of punishment by Jones's authority which

Smithers, at least at first, enforces. But the rapidity with which that identity starts to crumble—as soon as Smithers hears that all the natives have abandoned the palace he loses interest in administering Jones's rule, lets the woman go, and unleashes a barrage of insults against the Emperor—reveals its shoddy construction. In this moment, Jones needs to be present in order to tend to the social construction of his identity, but fails to do so because of a hubristic confidence in that identity's viability.

This dangerous confidence even extends to Jones's strategy for an escape from his scheme, which he thinks will be simple because he has planned it so precisely. Revealing both keen self-awareness and cocky shortsightedness, he brags to Smithers: "I ain't no fool. I knows dis Emperor's time is sho't. Dat why I make hay when de sun shine. Was you thinkin' I'se aimin' to hold down dis job for life? No, suh! What good is gittin' money if you stays back in dis raggedy country? I wants action when I spends. And when I sees dese niggers gittin' up deir nerve to tu'n me out, and I'se got all de money in sight, I resigns on de spot and beats it quick." Upon hearing of the natives' revolt, Jones simply replies, "Reckon I overplays my hand dis once!" and decides on the spot to flee: "I cashes in and resigns de job of Emperor right dis minute."[5] Utterly convinced of his superiority to his adversaries, Jones pays no regard to the great complexities of his escape, while also ignoring the grievous error he has already made by attempting to overpower the influence of those around him. In a peculiar paradox, he is astute enough to recognize that his con can be undone by rebellion, showing a certain amount of awareness that his identity relies on the participation of other people, but not savvy enough to manage that reality effectively. From the opening moments of the play, therefore, Jones reveals his presumption that he controls his identity through management of himself and the responses of his social sphere. He believes that these abilities will allow him to create, sustain, and disembody the Emperor on his own terms.

Yank has similar commitments to his identity, but his are even more staunch because he believes in an unassailable right to respect growing out of his strength and virility. "I'm steel—steel—steel! I'm de muscles in steel, de punch behind it!" he insists to his loyal stokehole crew, extolling his central importance to the ship's operation.[6] Whereas Brutus has willfully created a fiction, Yank's conviction in his identity is more organic, nurtured out of the support he gets from the closed social sphere of his crewmates. O'Neill's stage direction says that Yank is *"more sure of himself than the rest. They respect his superior strength—the grudging respect of fear."*[7] He too begins his play in comfort and progresses through angry confusion to his death, but because Yank is more deluded about himself than Brutus is, it takes longer for him to crack. The play's first scene illustrates how effectively Yank has established himself in charge and how he brutishly maintains that position. When his fellow firemen displease him by getting rowdy, he restrains their exuberance with only his words and the threat of violence. After Long blusters about the Bible and the dangers of Capitalism, indiscriminate "Voices" try to shut him down before Yank, *"standing up and glaring at Long"* as if to attack before even opening his mouth, says, "Sit down before I knock yuh down!" whereupon *"Long makes haste to efface himself."*[8] After Yank retorts in a long speech about the value of brute, manly force, the indiscriminate "Voices" return in howls of approval and support. The community ratifies his leadership within a closed social sphere, but Yank believes their support to be a by-product of his rule, not its raison d'être. In Yank's mind, leadership and respect are what he deserves, and he has no need for community ratification. Wilson's Troy Maxson believes ardently that he deserves leadership and respect, but when he works for part of that respect by appealing to his boss, and instructs his son to be a good employee, Troy reveals a commitment to certain social structures for which Yank has very little patience. When Yank's bosses signal for more coal, he grows enraged, convinced that he is the man in charge. As in *The Emperor Jones,* O'Neill opens *The Hairy Ape* with a picture of his protagonist's unwavering commitment to a white American ethos of individual self-sustainment. Yank blindly feels entitled to the freedom of solitary self-crafting.

It does not take long for either of these virile figures to begin losing a stable sense of self, but by starting both plays this way O'Neill shows why their identities are so fragile: both men believe they have imposed their identities rather than having cultivated their selves in dialogue with the social sphere. Neither realizes the extent to which they rely on other people. By prizing their dominance, both men increase their isolation, rather than engaging in a functional social sphere. Their attitudes distance them from their communities, rendering them vulnerable; any change to how they have constructed their identities leaves them alone, without the support of a like-minded social sphere. O'Neill's openings in these plays marks these characters as committed deeply to the isolationist ideal of self-sustainment so distinctive of the playwright's white aesthetic. Both characters are from downtrodden communities, but rather than recognizing how those communities provide them strength (like Wilson's Solly Two Kings, for example), they presume the privilege of excluding themselves from extended social engagement. The isolation cultivated at each play's opening breeds the destruction at its conclusion.

The structure of these plays reveals how rapidly the destructive force of whiteness sets in. The first of *The Emperor Jones*'s eight scenes constitutes nearly half the play's length; there follow seven short glimpses of Jones growing more unsettled as he travels away from the constructed security of his palace. At the opening of the first scene, Jones brags that he dominates the natives—"I has dem eatin' out of my hand. I cracks de whip and dey jumps through"—and he brazenly admits the hollowness of his authority: "Sho', I talks large when I ain't got nothin' to back it up, but I ain't talkin' wild just de same. I knows I kin fool 'em—I *knows* it—and dat's backin' enough fo' my game."[9] In the Emperor's mind, he has the freedom and power to be in complete control of his destiny. He knows his audience's voice matters, but believes he can control that voice fully. His swift descent to death exposes the fatal errors in this strategy. The play's remaining seven scenes are all brief vignettes of Jones arriving at a new place in the forest, confronting a fear from his subconscious, and growing increasingly weaker as a result of the encounters. These fears—men he has murdered in the past, images of slavery—are all elements of his physical and spiritual past from which he fled in order to arrive at his temporary jungle respite where he established himself as Emperor. Once that constructed identity crumbles, he finds himself again among the fears he cannot ignore. Rather than turning to the community for help in engaging those fears like Wilson's Citizen Barlow does, he fled to the isolation of the jungle and his presumed self-sufficiency, so now he is ill equipped to engage them, and the natives quickly overcome and kill him. For Jones, a life of actively seeking and cultivating isolation has left him with no chance of sustaining himself through engagement.[10]

Yank desires nothing more than the voices of other people, but his story ends just as tragically. Yank spends much of the play in a variety of locales foreign to him: New York's Fifth Avenue, prison, a union meeting, and the zoo. None are the forecastle of an ocean liner, and none are populated solely by his colleagues, and so none are native territory for Yank. Nevertheless, in each new place he tries to establish connections with others. On Fifth Avenue, his socialist companion Long tells him, "This 'ere's their bleedin' private lane, as yer might say. (*bitterly*) We're trespassers 'ere," but Yank will hear none of it: "Yuh don't belong, get me!" he yells indiscriminately at the passing mob of high-class New Yorkers. "Look at me, why don't youse dare?

I belong, dat's me!"[11] To be sure, Yank has come to Fifth Avenue with nothing but malice. He does not want the fancy folks to accept him into their community; he wants them to look at him and to recognize a threat so that he can enjoy roughing them up.[12] To be a threat like he intends is by necessity to have a clear and recognizable identity to which the social sphere must respond. But Yank's efforts are for naught. After he *"deliberately lurches into a top-hatted gentleman"* trying to pick a fight, the man responds with the least possible engagement: "(*coldly and affectedly*) I beg your pardon (*He has not looked at Yank and passes on without a glance*)." The same happens moments later: Yank attempts to rouse anger by delivering a lewd pick-up line to a woman, but *"The lady stalks by without a look, without a change of pace."*[13] Yank goes to Fifth Avenue to demonstrate that he is a human with anger, strength, and consequence, but the high-class social sphere will grant him no acknowledgment until he actually effects change by preventing a man from making the bus and must be expelled by the police force. He is summarily dismissed from the society he intended to disrupt with his strong humanity.

From the moment Mildred Douglas calls Yank a filthy beast, O'Neill's protagonist sets off on a mission of self-crafting, but the sort of rejection he receives on Fifth Avenue is indicative of how each different community into which he enters himself refuses to recognize him as anything other than an outsider. Union members reject him as an interloping thug, and even when he tries to resign himself to a beastly existence at the zoo the actual ape rejects his companionship and kills him. At every turn beyond the stokehole, Yank faces rejection, and as a result, he never achieves a clear sense of selfhood that legitimizes or supports the identity he presumes the right of constructing below decks.

While it may seem as though Yank had that selfhood in the stokehole, the identity he achieves there is as hollow as Jones's Emperor construct. In both cases, a domineering man establishes a makeshift identity that becomes temporarily ratified through the fear of his audience and quickly dismantled when the dynamic of that audience changes. The calls of selfhood the men make initially do not trigger collaborative identity crafting, but are overpowering dictums. Thus, when they move into new territory they are ill equipped to perform the social process of identity crafting, and suffer as a result. When the natives around Jones revolt and when Yank leaves the stokehole, the two men find themselves alienated from any sense of selfhood. Stripped of their privileged aloofness, the danger of their individualist ethos emerges. Having imposed rather than received a ratification they do not believe is necessary, Jones and Yank are alienated from the start without ever having developed a productive identity.

The death of these two isolated characters does not simply suggest that alienation breeds destruction—a theme prevalent throughout both Wilson and O'Neill—but offers a broader critique of falsely imposed and poorly supported identity. Yank's biggest mistake, for example, is presuming that social spheres other than the stokehole function in the same manner as his below-deck comfort zone. On dry land Yank fails to adapt to social expectations, and society rejects him as a result. This is a failure of collaboration, with guilt shared by Yank and those around him. He does not meet them on their terms, and so they have little interest in engaging his performance of self. Although he desires a falsely collaborative performance that emulates the one by which he established his domineering identity in the stokehole, the people on land will not be his antiphonal audience, and he refuses (or is unable) to change his methods. *The Hairy Ape* thus shows a complete breakdown of social identity crafting; Yank travels through a variety of alienations, and ultimately finds his destruction, without ever entering into a productive call-and-response.

The fate of these characters undercuts any sense of stable, self-imposed, self-sustained identity, and their attitudes are indicative of their playwright's aesthetic of whiteness. Carrying themselves as independent of the community despite their reliance on its support, Jones and Yank isolate themselves in ways they believe are productive. Not to need communal support for identity crafting would indeed be a privileged position, but these two characters expose the untenability of that isolationist ideal. It is striking that the African American Jones has far more in common with Yank than he does with any of August Wilson's black characters besides perhaps Caesar Wilks, a man Wilson shows to have sold his African American soul for a shot at the power that comes with assimilation. But even Caesar is subservient to the type of legal social code that Jones tries to overpower. Jones is a black man with no place in Wilson's world, a distinction that illuminates how the domineering behavior of these early O'Neill characters is in service to their desperation for an identity independent of the social sphere. These characters feel entitled to overpower interlocutors rather than engage them antiphonally, but pay a great price as a result. Their attitude recalls Wilson's warriors, but O'Neill's characters do not fight for an identity like Boy Willie or Floyd Barton do; they believe themselves entitled to one. Lowly laborer and black man though they be, Yank and Jones fall prey to the corrosive ethos of whiteness.

Presumed Autonomy, Loss of Control: Ephraim Cabot and Lavinia Mannon

The danger of self-crafted identity grows only more devastating as O'Neill's career progresses. Even though Yank and Jones resist engagement with other people, they are nonetheless invested to a certain extent in the sociality of their existence. Yank demands recognition, and Jones knows that "Emperor" relies on the island people's complacency. This instinct for sociality wanes as O'Neill moves forward, producing characters like Ephraim Cabot in *Desire Under the Elms* and Lavinia Mannon in *Mourning Becomes Electra*, who presume for themselves the privilege of autonomous self-crafting, the ability to dictate who they are and ignore feedback. Although identity is a primary investment for Cabot and Lavinia, they neglect any sense of interpersonal collaboration in establishing or maintaining the self. Yank gets ratification for a time from his stokehole colleagues, and Jones from the island natives, and both are absolutely—albeit obliviously—invested in such ratification. Cabot and Lavinia show very little concern for how their imposed selves are received. O'Neill's aesthetic of whiteness grows stronger in them: not deigning to acknowledge any sense of social ratification, they presume autonomy over their selves and operate as though that autonomy is completely effective. Something similar emerges in Wilson: "Levee got to be Levee!" says Ma Rainey's trumpeter, and Boy Willie insists, "It don't matter to me what the law say. I take and look at it for myself"; both try to commit themselves to autonomous self-crafting like Cabot and Lavinia.[14] But Levee and Boy Willie undercut their autonomy by trying to generate power through business deals with white men on whom they rely, paradoxically, for the sort of self-sustainment that they crave. Whiteness is a factor in the development of these Wilsonian characters, but not an essential component of their selves. By contrast, the power of whiteness tells Cabot and Lavinia that they need rely on nobody for their privileged self-crafting. Wilson's lens, that is, demonstrates how deluded these two O'Neillian characters are about their relative social position.

Cabot, for example, is a paradigmatic, self-assured loner. Caring very little for his sons, wives, or neighbors, he puts his stake entirely in himself and his God, a deity of strict, unrelenting labor whom Diggins astutely calls "a Calvinist God."[15] Cabot is convinced that he knows what God wants out of humanity—hard work for little earthly reward—and that he is the type of person who can fulfill those demands. "God's hard, not easy!" he proclaims when explaining his New England rock farm to Abbie. "God's in the stone! Build my church on a rock—out o' stones an' I'll be in them! That's what He meant t' Peter! Stones. I picked 'em up an' piled 'em into walls."[16] By personifying a stoic Protestant work ethic, he considers himself growing into a more perfect embodiment of an elect man of God who labors in this world to earn reward in the next. As far as he is concerned, the easterners who migrate west for easy gold or black-dirt farming seek the sinner's way out, and he exists on a higher plane than them.

Cabot recognizes that he receives a dissonant response to this claim of identity from other people, but his ethos of white individualism is so ingrained that he is comfortable with such dissonance. By concentrating only on cultivating himself in his image of God's expectations, he tries to eschew any meaningful engagement with those around him. Of course, he cannot do so, and as a result, cacophonous feedback from his audience, which weakens the tenability of his identity, goes unheeded, leaving him to operate as a shell of his self-styled powerful, godly man. Indeed, while Cabot presumes himself to occupy an exempt sphere of godliness, those around him are mocking his presumptions. "Ye mustn't mind him. He's an old man," says Abbie to Eben behind the back of her new husband. "I calc'late I kin git him t' do most anythin' fur me" (338). After two months, Eben recognizes that Abbie has "made such a damned idjit out o' the old devil" (342). While Cabot convinces himself that he has complete autonomy over his identity, the play suggests that he has lost control of how his community perceives him. Abbie and Eben sneer behind his back, as do all the revelers who join him to celebrate the birth of the baby that everybody but Cabot realizes belongs to Eben. "Let's celebrate the old skunk gettin' fooled!" cries the Fiddler once Cabot exits (363). Nearly every character in the play has a different conception of Cabot's identity than he does of himself.

Even if Cabot understood others' assessment of him, it would likely not be bothersome. For him, the only audience that matters is the deity he considers "God o' the lonesome!" (340). This is a man who cannot find company in the space of other humans: "Will ye ever know me—'r will any man 'r woman?" he asks Abbie, mostly thinking aloud to himself. "No. I calc'late 't wa'n't t' be [it was not to be]" (348). Rather than working harder or differently to establish human connection, he excises himself from the space of that community: "I kin talk t' the cows," he tells Abbie in frustration that his life story finds no connection with her. "They know the farm an' me. They'll give me peace," and he heads to the barn for the night (350). Even when he is among other humans, he sees himself as different, better, and excluded from their tawdry concerns. He might occasionally give off an air of melancholy, perhaps wishing that there were more people who understood him, but he has no intention of soliciting understanding or approval. The cows know, and God knows, and that's good enough for Cabot.

Despite Cabot's stalwart conviction, this isolation is problematic because he lives in a society of other people, on whom he relies for sustainable social existence. He believes that he can exist as a respected hard man, but he fails to recognize that doing so requires the sort of social ratification that Yank gets below decks or Jones wins temporarily on the island or that fuels collective identity crafting throughout Wilson's plays. Cabot attempts constantly to craft himself as a singularly strong man: "I'd invite ye t' dance on my hundredth birthday," he tells the revelers at his house, "on'y ye'l all be dead by then. Ye're a sickly generation! Yer hearts air pink, not red! Yer veins is full o' mud an' water! I be the on'y man in the county!" (361). But these claims, like all his similar claims throughout the play, arouse only derision behind his back, damaging the identity he holds so precious. Refusing to participate in the process of social identity crafting from which he feels a privileged exclusion, he has removed himself from the act of making himself, allowing all those around him to construct his identity without his input.

For a brief few moments once tragedy hits, Cabot acts as though he realizes that his being exists entirely in the performative utterances of the other people who speak him into being. "God A'mighty, I be lonesomer'n ever!" he says shortly after realizing that Abbie has murdered the infant whom he learns to have been the product of betrayal by his son and wife (374). Family crumbles, and he realizes that much of his sense of self goes with it. It is a moment of traumatic reflection for Cabot, whose commitment to the mythic white ideal of self-sufficiency temporarily weakens as he recognizes that he could only come into being as a hard, godly man in relation to sons and wives who fear him. This trauma sends him to the barn to release the cows—previously his community of respite from the wilds of humanity—with the intention of "goin' to Californi-a—t' jine Simeon an' Peter," who he claims to be "true sons o' mine if they be dumb fools" (376). He quickly realizes to his horror that he cannot make the trip because the money he had stashed is gone, but the brief moments of desperation for Cabot reveal what seems like an innate desire for the sociality of family. He and his elder sons shared nothing but abuse earlier in the play, but his abrupt realization of radical loneliness drives him to seek some vestige of familial community. In the company of Simeon and Peter, he could again be a feared, hard-driving father figure, and not the cuckold he is among his current social sphere. Of course these hopes quickly pass once he realizes the money is gone and he must remain alone on his rock farm. Without a community of other people, he returns to the image of God he has crafted for himself: "It's a-goin' t' be lonesomer now than ever it war afore—an' I'm getting old, Lord—ripe on the bough. . . . (*then stiffening*) Waal—what d'ye want? God's lonesome, hain't He? God's hard an' lonesome!" (377). Within O'Neill's Nietzschean framework, *Desire Under the Elms* smiles on Abbie and Eben without forgiving them for their crimes: at least they will have a community in their suffering. The play condemns Cabot. Chained to his aloof construction of self, he has actively isolated himself for the foreseeable future without anybody on whom he can vent his frustrations.

Infected by an ethos of whiteness, Cabot conducts himself as autonomous from the other people that constitute his social sphere. Lavinia Mannon is in a similar predicament throughout *Mourning Becomes Electra*, but her situation is more nuanced and precarious. Cabot's error is failing to listen to other people, but Lavinia is happy to listen to others, as long as her whiteness allows her to select who those others are and how they will respond. Initially, Lavinia adores her father and her Mannon heritage, and so when she makes a call of Mannon identity and receives a ratifying response from her community, she is delighted to embrace this identity, broadcasting physically the identity she expects to be accepted. O'Neill's first description of the character says that she wears a plain black dress and that "[h]er *movements are stiff and she carries herself with a wooden, square-shouldered, military bearing*" (897), a description O'Neill will later recall when introducing her father, General Ezra Mannon. By contrast, Christine, Lavinia's mother, "*has a fine, voluptuous figure and she moves with a flowing animal grace*" (896). When Lavinia later attempts to reshape herself in her mother's image, she affects these features. Lavinia will presume the privilege in the first two plays to eschew the femininity of her body, and to revive it in the final play, attempting to self-craft and re-craft according to her own caprice. She is a product of the union of her mother and father, and her body contains elements of both, but her carriage throughout the trilogy is indicative of the identity she presumes her body will broadcast unambiguously to other people.

So whereas Cabot presumes autonomy to impose himself over his entire surroundings, Lavinia presumes the privilege of selecting which identity she will inhabit, a process that involves selectively ignoring half her ancestry. Nowhere in Wilson's *Cycle* is there evidence of such presumptions. The corrosive conditions of whiteness do not encroach into Wilson's black world, so even when characters like Troy Maxson try to seize control of their self-crafting, they do so through performance before an audience. Whiteness tells Lavinia she can handle matters on her own. The stage direction that introduces her in the trilogy's final play reveals the lengths to which she has gone to switch parental allegiance: "*One is at once aware of an extraordinary change in her. Her body, formerly so thin and undeveloped, has filled out. Her movements have lost their square-shouldered stiffness. She now bears a striking resemblance to her mother in every respect, even to being dressed in the green her mother had affected*" (1014). With both parents gone, Lavinia tries to step into the role of matriarch, following the only model she has ever had, but Christine had ardently defined herself in opposition to the Mannons, so for Lavinia to follow her mother's lead she must do the same. Backed into an existential corner but nonetheless bolstered by whiteness, she feels entitled to jettison Mannon lineage. "I'm mother's daughter," she declares defiantly to the dead eyes of Mannon portraits, "not one of you! I'll live in spite of you!" When a woman like Risa in Wilson's *Two Trains Running* feels isolated, she retreats inward; in distress, Mattie Campbell seeks out guidance and help; but Lavinia feels empowered to impose herself on ghosts. But as if to show how hopeless such a self-willed pronouncement of lineage is, O'Neill follows this assertion with a stage direction underscoring the irreducibility of Lavinia's Mannon blood: "*She squares her shoulders, with a return of the abrupt military movement copied from her father which she had of old—as if by the very act of disowning the Mannons she had returned to the fold—and marches stiffly from the room*" (1043–44). When pressed, her defiance does nothing to conceal the faltering of an identity baselessly created within a myth of privileged white autonomy, and the very elements she hoped to suppress emerge.

Like Cabot, Yank, and Jones, when whiteness's limits start to appear, Lavinia responds with aggression, betraying a desperation to protect privilege that was never hers. Early in the trilogy, Brant tells Lavinia, "You're so like your mother in some ways," and then goes on to innumerate physical characteristics like hair and eyes before Lavinia retorts *"harshly,"* "What do looks amount to? I'm not a bit like her! Everybody knows I take after Father!" (908). Her anger betrays desperation; she has worked hard to establish an identity as purely Mannon—"she's too Mannon to let anyone see what she feels" (952), says one of the choral characters of Lavinia, demonstrating Lavinia's longstanding commitment to Mannon austerity—and observations like Brant's threaten that construction. So she attempts to overpower any such idea, here by angrily rebuffing Brant, later by embodying a distinctively Mannon martial nature. "Orin!" she says *in a brusque commanding tone like her father's.* "Come and see Father!" To which her stunned brother responds, "Yes, sir," as if replying to his actual father (965). Throughout most of the trilogy's first two plays, Lavinia makes a call as a pure Mannon, and seems to receive a ratifying response from much of her social sphere.

But she runs painfully up against an existential limit during the trilogy's final play where she attempts to discard all the paternal Mannon lineage to which she previously dedicated herself so stridently, and to make herself entirely her mother's daughter. When she insists to Brant that everybody knows she is her father's daughter, she means to establish herself firmly within the Mannon line; her repeated emphases on duty and forbearance work in tandem with her physical appearance to cultivate as much Mannon in her as possible. But her attempts to make a complete switch from a Mannon identity to one in the mold of her mother are accompanied by presumptions of free social mobility. "That is all past and finished!" she tells Orin about the deaths of their parents. "The dead have forgotten us! We've forgotten them!" But the dead persist in their demands on Lavinia: "Why do you look at me like that?" she protests to the Mannon portraits. "I've done my duty by you! That's finished and forgotten!" (1015–16). She says the same later, as the Mannon portraits oppress with their gaze: "I've done my duty by them! They can't say I haven't!" (1023). This refrain from Lavinia betrays an awareness that she will never escape the pull of the Mannons that she wants so badly to break. "I'm only half Mannon," she tells Peter while standing among the portraits' gaze, but even this weakens her project of self-crafting into "Mother's daughter" because it is an acceptance of the portion of her identity that she has attempted to eschew (1023). Her decision at the trilogy's conclusion to wall herself up in the Mannon home with the portraits until she dies signals acceptance that the calls of identity she has made over the years are being returned through the Mannon lineage, and rather than plug her ears to that antiphony, she will embrace it, even if she is too far gone to effect any change.

Lavinia, that is, rushes toward one group identification at the expense of another, making any notion of identity in her partial and ill formed. Whereas Cabot's loneliness came from self-styled detachment, Lavinia's comes from an urge for inclusion in family communities as she has imagined them. She presumes the privilege to accept or deny the responses she receives from and about her familial legacies, and so, like Cabot, she puts herself in a position to be acted upon rather than actively engaging with her own identity crafting. In the trilogy's first two plays she ignores her mother's influence, as she does her father's in the final play, and ultimately the weight of all that unheeded response destroys any chance she has of existing productively in a world of other people. Over the course of the trilogy, her selective alienation grows increasingly out of her control, and she loses any potential agency she once had.

The motion in O'Neill's dramaturgy from characters like Jones and Yank to those like Cabot and Lavinia evinces a more all-encompassing aesthetic of white individualism as characters move away from the social sphere further toward an untenable self-contained realm of the self. Yank and Jones do not manage their relationships with their social spheres effectively, but they nonetheless show themselves to be concerned with engaging their audiences, however hollow those engagements turn out to be. But Cabot shows no such concern, and to whatever small degree Lavinia is interested in her audience, it is an audience she has selectively defined for herself. In this way, moving through O'Neill's career with a view to its divergence from Wilson's blues dramaturgy shows his characters becoming increasingly alienated from their societies and interior in their struggles. Yank and Jones suffer because the societies they had overpowered no longer submit, but little changes in the attitudes of other people regarding Cabot and Lavinia. Instead, these characters define the world around them as they see fit, and although unable to reshape their communities, they act in accordance with their own constructions. Whereas Yank and Jones force ratifying responses out of their audiences, Cabot and Lavinia simply presume those responses exist, rarely listening. Their worlds exist for the most part inside their own isolated white space, which provides for them a construction that they seem to think can withstand any empirical onslaught. Aloof and entitled, and certainly not committed to the type of blues antiphony running throughout Wilson's *Cycle,* Cabot and Lavinia care little for what the members of their social spheres have to say because they are self-assured and believe themselves to be self-contained, excused from any demand to engage the social other.

The Irrepressible Urge for Other People: Mary Tyrone and Larry Slade

Whereas the late portions of Wilson's career find him creating characters like Citizen Barlow and Harmond Wilks who make important strides toward sustainable, socially crafted identity, O'Neill, late in his career, explores new dimensions of alienated interiority, finding more profound despair than he had ever written. Tragedy is not a cataclysmic event in either *Long Day's Journey into Night* or *The Iceman Cometh;* instead it is deep, irreconcilable despair. As the fates of Cabot and Lavinia suggest, the greatest force of the tragic in O'Neill is the disastrous recognition of interminable suffering without the escape of death. Cabot finds himself alone on his rock farm with only his desperate hope for reward from God after death, and Lavinia resigns herself to suffering at the whims of the Mannon dead. But the struggles of Larry Slade and Mary Tyrone are more profound because these characters find despair by turning ever deeper inward. In the crowded back room of Harry Hope's bar and the claustrophobic Tyrone house, both characters are surrounded by a potentially antiphonal community but desperately try to avoid engaging with their social spheres. Slade wants to drink and be left alone, and Mary, ravaged by addiction and fear, only halfheartedly converses with her family. Both try desperately to remove themselves from any realm of linguistic, ethical, or interpersonal reference in favor of isolation. Unlike Citizen and Harmond, neither Slade nor Mary makes any progress toward a sustainable social identity, and—as seems to be their desire—they wither in loneliness.

It might seem, then, like there is little to pity in Slade and Mary: both achieve the alienation they desire. To call such a thing tragic might be to impose undue expectations of sociality on these characters. But shortly before their conclusions, both plays show painful glimmers of the drive for sociality that each character has been suppressing. Slade pities the death of Don Parritt, and Mary briefly reveals herself through the fog of morphine to lament her son's illness and her former marital happiness. These glimmers, however brief, demonstrate that these characters impose conditions of alienation on themselves in an effort to avoid confronting the difficulty of human engagement and embracing its inherent vulnerability. Both characters have been burned in the past by exposing themselves to other people, and as a result they attempt to protect themselves from harm by eschewing such relationships. This urge leads to suffering rather than liberation, as O'Neill's tragic dramaturgy finds only sorrow in the alienated self-crafting of isolation.

In these examples of late O'Neill, then, the scaffolding supporting white individualism crumbles most drastically. Jones, Yank, Cabot, and Lavinia are all to various degrees deluded about their relationships with other people, but Slade and Mary are not; they are hyperaware of and actively attempt to cultivate their desires for isolation. So their failures result, not from mismanagement of their isolation, but rather from miscalculating their entitlement to isolation. The ethos of whiteness that runs throughout O'Neill's work imbues these characters with the notion that they can choose not to rely on their social spheres for support of their identities and strength against their struggles, and more than earlier characters, Slade and Mary ignore any call of sociality. Their failures reveal the persistent, relentless demand of that call, even in the face of the most ardent denial. These characters attempt to dwell in a protected space to which whiteness tells them they have access, but their irrepressible urge for engagement with other people shows such a space to be a fiction, and that dedication to it engenders tragedy.

Slade and Mary in fact reveal the slow creep of corrosive whiteness, as both are older adults at cruxes in their lives: they have spent years trying to foster alienation but are hounded by the constant pull of the social. Both want to be alone with their demons, but Mary's family insists that she step into and embody the protective, caretaking role of wife and mother, while Slade cannot escape the scrutiny of Don Parritt and Hickey, both of whom ask him to be present to himself and others. But Slade sees himself as detached from the whole operation of daily existence. According to him, after abandoning the anarchist movement because he "saw that men didn't want to be saved from themselves," he "took a seat in the grandstand of philosophical detachment to fall asleep observing the cannibals do their death dance." But it is only moments later, when one of his companions in Hope's back room stirs fitfully, that Slade reveals a drive for interpersonal attachment: "Poor devil," he says before backtracking, "(*angry with himself*)

But to hell with pity! It does no good. I'm through with it!"[17] This is the tension that will rack Slade throughout the play: although he sees himself as a removed observer in the grandstands, his empathy, connecting him to other people, is too strong for him to shut down. For her part, Mary wants to be alone with morphine. She knows the drug has gotten hold of her and that her family would despise her relapse, so she attempts to manage her addiction on her own. She tries to laugh off her family's insinuations of morphine—"I won't listen when you're so silly! There's absolutely no reason to talk as if you expected something dreadful!"—but when her relapse becomes clear she takes the strategy of staunch denial:

> Mary—(*tensely*) Why do you stare like that?
> Jamie—You know. (He turns his back to the window)
> Mary—I don't know.
> Jamie—Oh, for God's sake, do you think you can fool me, Mama? I'm not blind.
> Mary—(looks directly at him now, her face set again in an expression of blank, stubborn denial) I don't know what you're talking about.[18]

Mary tries to conduct herself as though her drugged self is a covert, unseen interloper in the family space where her sober self holds forth. But like Slade's empathy, Mary's desire for personal connection consistently thwarts the isolation she prizes.[19]

Both characters consider interpersonal engagement anathema. For Mary, that engagement would be sharing her morphine struggles with her family, and she wants absolutely no part of such a thing. Her staunch denial to Jamie is only the first of several similar responses to the topic of morphine throughout the play. Shortly afterward she says to her husband, "I don't know what you're talking about" (754), and then in the following scene, "No, no. Whatever you mean, it isn't true, dear" (756), and soon she will say flatly to Edmund, "I don't know what you're talking about" (769). The trend continues throughout the play. In *Iceman,* Slade's call for engagement is embodied most directly in Parritt, who asks Slade to wrestle with his former dedication to the anarchist movement. But Slade avoids such memories ardently: "I'm telling you I don't know anything and I don't want to know," he says regarding the arrest of Rosa Parritt that has occasioned Don's tracking him down. "To hell with the Movement and all connected with it! I'm out of it, and everything else, and damned glad to be" (575). "I've refused to become a useful member of society," he says later. "I've been a philosophical drunken bum, and proud of it" (581). Whether it is the State, the Movement, or the promised salvation of Hickey, he will throughout the play renounce any structure that threatens to include him in an interpersonal collective. Both characters have gone to great lengths to define themselves as interior and self-sustained, and both attempt to dig their heels in against any lure into the social sphere.

Of course, such temptation is minimal, since both characters exist in closed environments that enable their drives for isolation. The ideals of white individualism in fact define most of the relationships in Harry Hope's saloon and the Tyrone house. Slade has buried himself in "No Chance Saloon," "Bedrock Bar, The End of the Line Café, The Bottom of the Sea Rathskeller!" where for the most part he can be left alone to drink away his remaining days; the hounding of Parritt and Hickey upsets this comfortable accord (577). And each of the Tyrone men would much rather support a fantasy of family cohesion than entertain the idea of morphine. Whenever the subject comes up throughout the final three acts of *Long Day's Journey* it is because the men as if by impulse press Mary on her behavior, but knowing well enough why she seems erratic, they always catch themselves before pressing further. After Jamie tells his mother to examine her eyes in the mirror, for example, and she says to Edmund, "Your brother ought to be ashamed of himself. He's been insinuating I don't know what," Jamie characteristically *"turns his back with a shrug and looks out the window"* (750). As all the Tyrone men frequently do, Jamie has the opportunity to press the issue further, but he demurs with a shrug, opting to leave Mary her delusions of isolation. All the Tyrones seem to prefer the option of a healthily functioning family life, but since each is well aware of the challenges to that ideal, they make due trying to keep to themselves without upsetting the shared charade of Tyrone domesticity.[20] So although there are elements of these characters' social spheres that pull them toward sociality—Parritt reminding Slade of the psychological struggle involved with the Movement, Edmund's sickness reminding Mary of love for family—they could for the most part exist in the isolation their societies offer them. Their colleagues in O'Neill's plays are as committed to the fiction of white individualism as are these two characters, so it would seem that the conditions are ideal for Slade and Mary to succeed in their projects of isolation.

The problem for Slade and Mary, however, is that their desires for alienation struggle mightily against powerful urges for sociality. Despite Slade's repeatedly professed desire to remain in the grandstand watching the action of life from a distance, he constantly betrays an urge for investment and engagement. "How is it they didn't pick you up when they got your mother and the rest?" he asks Parritt (579). Here and elsewhere he shows that he cannot absent himself from the everyday to the extent that he wishes.[21] By asking Parritt for more details even after he has professed a fundamental lack of concern for his troubles, he gives the young man space for performative unburdening and gives himself the opportunity to engage the action of the Movement; even if that engagement is secondhand, Slade shows a greater investment in other people than his rhetoric would suggest. This same push and pull racks Slade throughout the play. His attunement to other people causes him to explode at Parritt's string of excuses—"You stinking rotten liar! Do you think you can fool me with such hypocrite's cant!"—but he quickly catches himself and returns to his own cant of disengagement: "I don't give a damn what you did! [. . .] All I know is I'm sick of life! I'm through! I've forgotten myself! I'm drowned and contented on the bottom of a bottle" (636). To be at the bottom of a bottle as Larry professes to be would be to be alone with himself, his self-loathing, and his misery, but the consistent flaw in this self-stylization is his concern for others. "May the Chair bring him peace at last," he says of Hickey after the police drag him out of Hope's bar, "the poor tortured bastard." O'Neill's stage direction marks this speech as *in a whisper, aloud to himself,* as if Larry is attempting to suppress the sentiment that he wishes he did not feel (703).

Mary is much less certain than Larry of what she wants. She seems at times to desire at least somewhat the role of wife and mother that the Tyrone men impose on her, but she also knows that embodying that caretaker role exposes her to the pain of Edmund's illness and her own lingering Catholic guilt for abandoning the convent. And so morphine serves a similar alienating function for her as alcohol does for Larry, although her intoxication is far less willful; it is an addiction that pains her in the process of providing her the comfort of removal from engagement with personal and familial problems. While on morphine, especially when alone in the spare room, she can absent herself from engaging with the painful realities of her family life. When not in the haze of the drug, she has only language and denial to protect her, as throughout the first act when she repeatedly and staunchly refuses to entertain any notion that Edmund is seriously ill: "It *is* just a cold! Anyone can tell that!" (727). Her instinct is for the self-preservation of isolation, but she knows well enough that isolation leads her to relapse. Strikingly, she is at peace in the play for a very brief few moments, after all three men leave the house; once alone, "*She appears to relax. She sinks down in one of the wicker armchairs at rear of table and leans her head back, closing her eyes.*" Alone and unencumbered by the demands placed on her by her family, she can be at ease. "*But suddenly she grows terribly tense again,*" says O'Neill, indicating that her solitude has drifted into thoughts of morphine. "*Her eyes open and she strains forward, seized by a fit of nervous panic. She begins a desperate battle with herself*" (742). This battle epitomizes Mary's plight: she cannot meet the unfair demands placed on her by her family, so she seeks the solitude that breeds destructive drug use aimed at further assuaging her fears and self-loathing. This brief moment of peace is indicative of Mary's desired condition of isolation—away from the gaze of her family, out of the grip of morphine—but it is a condition she cannot sustain. The conflict between her desire for isolation and her drive for sociality leads her into morphine and back into the charade of family life, a performance of normality so hollow that it only pushes her farther away from the other people in her life.

In the end, self-sustaining isolation underwritten by O'Neill's white aesthetic proves just a destructive pipe dream for these two. "Poor devil!" says Larry. "*In a whisper of horrified pity*" upon hearing Parritt crash to his death, "God rest his soul in peace." These utterances cause a moment of terrible recognition for Slade, realizing that he is invested in the plight of Parritt and the other people that populate his social sphere far more than he would like or can effectively manage. "I'll never be a success in the grandstand—or anywhere else!" he blurts out ruefully to himself. "Life is too much for me!" (710). He goes on to suggest that what he means is that he is damned always to see both sides of all issues, but what is ultimately at stake is the pull of an active, engaged life being too great for him to withstand. Mary has similar problems, all of which mirror her earliest crisis of identity that pulled her in the conflicting directions of life as a nun or wife to James Tyrone. That choice, like those she will make throughout her life and on the long day that occasions her play, is one of absenting herself from society versus engaging in its process, and she is never comfortable with the choices she makes. Much of her susceptibility to morphine addiction comes from an urge to access the peaceful happiness of her past. "It kills the pain," she tells the servant Cathleen of morphine. "You go back until at last you are beyond its reach. Only the past when you were happy is real" (777). But despite this desire to exist in a morphine-induced past, she drifts constantly toward interpersonal connection with her family, most especially Edmund. His illness is the same that killed her father, but she constantly tries to avoid that painful reality by explaining it away. Her morphine use is in part a desperate attempt to support this strained denial. It is only when Edmund tries to make her face the reality that her extreme intoxication of the play's final scene shows any cracks. "Mama! It isn't a summer cold! I've got consumption!" he says in a desperate plea for connection, whereupon O'Neill's stage direction says that *"For a second he seems to have broken through to her,"* but her drugged self overpowers the maternal self as she asserts, "No!" *"as if giving a command to herself"* and drifts back into her haze (826).

The tragedy for both these characters is that they cannot shut down the desire to make a call of identity to their social spheres, even while telling themselves that they want nothing more than isolation. The individualist fiction of whiteness tells them that they are able to retreat into their alienation, but despite professing little care for the thoughts or opinions of the other people around them, that alienated existence proves untenable. "It's lonely here," Mary says to herself after the men leave the house to head into town, but she catches herself bitterly: "You're lying to yourself again. You wanted to get rid of them. Their contempt and disgust aren't pleasant company. You're glad they're gone. (*She gives a little despairing laugh.*) Then Mother of God, why do I feel so lonely?" (771). She feels lonely because there exists in her a bitter conflict between isolation and community that will leave her unsettled at all times. Slade reveals the same conflict by constantly praying for death and isolation while perpetuating the ersatz community of Hope's bar. Both make calls of identity to their social spheres in spite of themselves, but cultivate sorrow by ignoring any responses, ratifying or otherwise. The conclusions of *Gem of the Ocean* and *Radio Golf* find Citizen Barlow and Harmond Wilks rushing eagerly offstage to go join a community with which they will engage in a collaborative process of identity crafting. The comparison is stark in O'Neill. Slade and Mary have convinced themselves almost entirely that they are able to exist on existential islands—they do not seek ratification like Yank and Jones, and they do not even bother to presume it like Cabot and Lavinia—but their needs for other people overwhelm the faulty sort of self-crafting so paradigmatic of O'Neill's white aesthetic.

Community's Stubborn Imperative

On one hand, the imperative of community underwriting August Wilson's black dramatic world helps illuminate the stark lack of community in O'Neill's predominantly white plays, but in another regard, examining O'Neill vis-à-vis Wilson reveals as if by palimpsest how that imperative runs throughout the earlier playwright's work, despite his characters' frequent obliviousness to it. O'Neill's characters regularly consider themselves self-sustaining individuals who are able to craft their identities in isolation, but the tragic gloom that attends these presumptions throughout O'Neill's work consistently proves this notion false, as characters pay a significant price for ignoring the call of the social. Wilson's black blues community is always prepared to engage individual processes of becoming, but O'Neill's communities, shot through with whiteness, are dedicated to isolation, individualism, and self-sufficiency. Redemptive community seems unattainable. "I've got the blues," says Larry Slade ruefully twice in *Iceman* (571, 597), but his tortured existence in a liminal space between isolation and community prevents him from engaging productively in any antiphonal process of becoming. He might feel blue, but he certainly does not deploy blues performativity like many of Wilson's characters. Still, his suffering suggests that there exists an expectation of social engagement within O'Neill's tragic metaphysics.

Ubiquitous though whiteness is in O'Neill's plays, therefore, it does not succeed in constructing an isolationist world evacuated of the need for a functioning social sphere. Characters throughout the playwright's work regularly believe themselves excused from calls of sociality, but find tragedy as a result. This dialectic between self and community reflects the complicated dynamic of O'Neill's life and art. As emotionally and philosophically isolated as he was throughout his life, his outlet was consistently the social art of theater, a form that relies fundamentally on other people. For him to ignore the call of the other would have been to have folded into himself, eschewing what was an important mode of expression. Stephen A. Black has categorized O'Neill's artistic output as mourning not only for his immediate family members, who all died within the span of just over three years, but also for his own tumultuous life. Like his characters, O'Neill often struggled to find and understand his place in a society of other people. Black influentially argues that O'Neill wrote as a method of psychoanalyzing himself in order to work through his grief, something that is true of many artists, including Wilson. That O'Neill's self-analysis happened in plays for the theater, though, reveals its reliance at all times on other people. A paradox therefore exists at the heart of O'Neill's work. He was a man and an artist concerned principally with individualism, and yet from his time with the Provincetown Players forward, he constantly relied on the contributions of other people—directors, actors, set builders, audience members, critics, and so on. Regardless of how badly and frequently he desired to write a novel, his artistic home was the social space of the theater. *Strange Interlude* demonstrates this most clearly: even at his most novelistic, O'Neill revealed his urge for sociality by writing what Dowling dubs "a novel for the stage."[22]

The paradox of needing other people for a project of self-crafting that is conceptualized as interior leads O'Neill's characters to tragedy, but the playwright considered this fate something more noble than rueful. "What I am after," he wrote, "is to get an audience leaving the theater with an exultant feeling from seeing somebody on stage facing life, fighting against the eternal odds, not conquering, but perhaps inevitably being conquered. The individual life is made significant just by this struggle."[23] Like Wilson's great respect for the doomed fighting spirit of his warrior characters, O'Neill found honor in the plights at the center of his tragedies, praising the wandering, ultimately unproductive search for stability. "Faced with this modern human condition that threatens our sovereignty," argues Diggins, O'Neill's work "may help us understand how difficult it is to come to know ourselves and become who we are."[24] This sentiment is most true, and the process is most difficult, if one refuses like many of O'Neill's characters to permit other people access to one's self. As an important pioneer of modern American drama, O'Neill presages what will come to be one of the form's primary concerns: the dialectic of identity between self and other. That O'Neill's characters suffer so frequently as a result of being dismissive of other people evinces the obstinate pervasiveness of community's call. The nobility that O'Neill sees in tragic suffering arises from an individual ignoring the influence of others, something that American drama punishes consistently.

Of course, all this was the case in the work of O'Neill long before the life and career of August Wilson, but allowing for a gaze on O'Neill refracted backward through Wilson drastically increases the visibility of O'Neill's operative whiteness. Race is a powerful motivator of the action throughout O'Neill's plays, but the critical tendency to universalize and neutralize whiteness occludes its force. Recognizing how the experience of O'Neill's characters differs so drastically from that of Wilson's when they encounter similar challenges of crafting a sustainable identity reveals layers of whiteness's influence and its corrosive effects in O'Neill's work. Wilson's lens therefore helps conceptualize O'Neill's plays as indicative of their creator's privileged white American experience and suggests a link between that experience and the plays' regular gloom. The characters discussed in this chapter and others like them do not participate in the sort of social identity crafting present in Wilson largely because they feel entitled to define themselves on their own terms, aloof from those with whom they engage in everyday social spheres. This presumed entitlement smacks of the same sort of white American individualism so central to O'Neill's life.

5

"Laws of Silence Don't Work"
Tennessee Williams and the Problem of Sexualized Masculinity

DIALOGUE BETWEEN THE WORKS of Tennessee Williams and August Wilson seems in many ways natural. Both playwrights wrote lyrical prose, were fascinated with the social legacy of the postbellum American south, and were deeply concerned with their characters' search for clear and sustainable identity. Moreover, both worked in a style of tenuous realism, making the predominantly realist strands of their plays always susceptible to rupture, as when Wilson sends Citizen Barlow on a mystical voyage to the City of Bones in *Gem of the Ocean* or when Williams sets *The Glass Menagerie* in the space of foggy, not-so-reliable memory.

These and other similarities notwithstanding, rarely do critics consider Williams and Wilson closely related in the field of American drama. Williams regularly evokes comparisons to his midcentury contemporaries and predecessors like Miller and O'Neill, while discussions of Wilson most often approach his work only in the context of other African American playwrights like Lorraine Hansberry, Amiri Baraka, and Ed Bullins, or his successors like Suzan-Lori Parks.[1] One exception is a valuable essay by Sandra G. Shannon dubbing both playwrights "sons of the South," and arguing that "Wilson-Williams resemblances command attention on several levels that include both playwrights' challenge to traditional notions of realism onstage; their tendencies as poets toward lyrical expression, cadenced rhythms, and the use of metaphor; their love-hate relationship with the South as central metaphor and site of memory; and a parade of restless and tortured men and women choosing between primal needs and individual quests to find meaning in their existence." For Shannon, "efforts to juxtapose these two Titans of twentieth-century American theatre, yield fascinating new dimensions that are far from inconsequential." Shannon demonstrates persuasively how each playwright was compelled by similar motivations—like a "bittersweet ambiguity" in their relationship to the South—and suggests that examination of these themes in discussions of American drama would benefit from a robust juxtaposition of the two.[2]

Shannon's important insights on similarities in plot, theme, and characterization invite an expansion into consideration of dramaturgy, of how two influential American playwrights utilize similar dramatic strategies for approaching comparable conflicts. Scholars often relate Wilson to Baraka because they both deal very directly with blackness in America, but other than sharing this theme, they are very different playwrights. Williams too is quite distinct from his midcentury contemporaries, with whom he shares little other than epoch and genre. Following Shannon's lead and focusing on how these playwrights use theater as a mode of social critique open fruitful avenues of analysis.

Williams and Wilson in fact belong in direct conversation as playwrights invested in exploring the harrowing process of social identity crafting for their characters and for themselves. Both playwrights' work is deeply concerned with the process of coming to know one's self in a society that has expectations for, makes demands on, and contributes to the construction of that self. The tension between characters' self-assessment and how those characters' social spheres treat them is a master theme for both writers. As with Wilson's warriors, for example, often a great chasm between self and social assessments fosters crises of identity. Ultimately, putting Williams and Wilson in conversation reveals more clearly how both approach the unique challenges of American identity crafting.

Reading Williams after Wilson shows the earlier playwright to be deeply invested in the performative potential of drama and theater to contribute to the nascent midcentury social process of male sexual identity crafting, a topic rarely broached before Williams. As James Fisher puts it, "Williams was the theatre's angel of sexuality—the dramatist most responsible for forcefully introducing sexual issues, both gay and straight, to the American stage."[3] Williams opened this new terrain in American drama at a time in the United States when concepts of masculinity were growing unstable and, as a desperate result, would become increasingly rigid. Factors like the Great Depression challenging men's abilities to provide economic support for a family, increased industrialization demoting manual labor, and a steady increase in women in the workplace combined to weaken a formally stalwart paradigm of American masculinity. With opportunities to perform masculinity perceived to be dwindling, mainstream American culture redoubled its investments in male identity, constructing and vigorously supporting heteronormative conceptions of manhood defined by father-knows-best patriarchy, idealistic patriotism, and pronounced homophobia as a means of performing one's own resolute heterosexuality. In short, the middle of the twentieth century in America found masculinity in ontological crisis and turned in response to the security of conservative heteronormativity.[4] One powerful result of the frantic effort to establish clear expectations of masculine behavior was suspicion of anybody who did not meet those standards, solidifying one's own identity by marginalizing others.[5]

This was the environment surrounding Williams's examinations of masculine sexuality, the most prominent component of identity at stake in his work. His plays regularly feature men whose fraught sexual identities foment the psychological and social turmoil that forms the crux of his drama. Whereas pressure on masculinity in Wilson often leads to characters' forceful assertions of conservative gender roles, like Avery telling Berniece "I need a woman that fits in my hand" or Herald Loomis beginning to unbutton his pants to assert masculine dominance over God, Williams's plays are fascinated by the men who diverge from norms of midcentury expectations for masculinity and male sexuality.[6] Men in Williams's plays are queer, hypermasculine, ambiguously confused, or even clearly heterosexual in ways that would seem to satisfy conservative norms but for a variety of reasons do not. Very few of his men are comfortable in their sexuality, because they seem to have internalized normative expectations of masculinity. They look at themselves and recognize that they contradict those norms, and they can find no satisfactory method of exploring or cultivating their own identities.

Williams returns constantly to the tension of his men struggling to reconcile their self-reflexive notions of sexuality with those imposed by society. His men do not quite understand who they are or how they relate to the other people in their worlds, and their method of responding to this ambiguity is usually to turn inward. Williams writes neither warriors nor griots, and any community his men develop is regularly deficient and stifling. David Savran has argued that "the primal scene of Williams's drama" can be productively theorized as "the closet." Savran deploys the term as an existential cocoon shielding undisclosed homosexual identity, but he also uses it in its literal denotation of an enclosed, limited space: "In *Cat on a Hot Tin Roof,* the closet is represented by the bed-sitting-room; in *The Glass Menagerie,* by the movie theater to which Tom makes his nightly pilgrimage; in *A Streetcar Named Desire,* by that chamber that Blanche discovers inadvertently." Savran points out how the closet in Williams is far from private; rather, like the frequently disturbed bedroom of Brick and Maggie, the closet is eminently permeable, where any fleeting privacy is subject always to capricious intrusion. Ultimately, for Savran the closet is "the culturally (rather than individually) produced inner sanctum usually relegated to an offstage position, the empty/not empty room in which the homosexual subject is constituted."[7] Savran's notion of the closet conceptualizes a psychological space that Williams's characters seek in an attempt to define themselves sexually through the desired privacy of a closet. Consistently, though, they find that privacy ruptured by cultural forces that are intrusive and regulatory. Even though these spaces are often offstage, little can be done by Williams's men to use them as sanctuary.

Thus the blues impulse for community and sociality residing in many of August Wilson's characters is largely absent in Williams's men: Brick wants nothing more than to drink alone, for example, and Tom rushes away from the sociality of his family whenever possible. The closet for them and others is an idealized place of existential freedom that never comes to fruition. Wilson's blues dramaturgy underscores the radical lack of community in Williams's work, and the constant struggle of his characters to reconcile their negotiation of sexualized selves with this lack. Wilson's African American characters stand in constant reference to a black community ready to engage in productive performances of identity crafting; those like Levee or Roosevelt Hicks who desire commerce with the white community, contributing to what Shannon calls "Wilson's theme of cultural fragmentation," are clearly seeking forces external to their play's community.[8] Often the inverse is true for Williams's men. They struggle to understand their sexual identity, but are isolated among a community that is either not representative of them or simply unwilling to support exploratory identity crafting. Usually, the central men attempt to excise themselves from the play's community, sometimes driven by a search for sociality elsewhere and sometimes simply seeking privacy, but neither is available to them.

Williams's men exist along a broad and diverse spectrum of sexuality; hermeneutics of determining their homo- or heterosexuality often obscures the complexity of their sexual identity. Audiences often search for answers about the sexuality of characters like Tom and Brick, but Williams's plays are far more concerned with exploring these characters' struggles than in developing some definitive answer. It is clear that they diverge in some way from heteronormativity, but their plays cultivate ambiguity, examining in the process the effects of rigid social expectations for sexuality.[9] Williams also writes men who seem to conform to social expectations for heterosexuality but who nonetheless disrupt their plays through the exertion of sexuality. These are the hypermasculine like Stanley Kowalski and hypersexualized like Val Xavier, whose exuding sexuality drives the conflict of their plays. Savran calls characters like Stanley and Val in Williams's oeuvre the "phallic male," and argues that they are "(hetero)sexually vital young men who epitomize what Kazan describes as 'the virility that will rejuvenate,' the force that can suddenly and almost magically awaken sexual desire and transform a woman . . . from a state of real or feigned innocence to a wary yet vigorous adulthood."[10] If the phallus is the idealized embodiment of masculinity with which men strive to identify and which society expects them to embody, then Williams's virile phallic men would seem to suit fully the expectations of midcentury American masculinity. And yet, their disruptions of their plays' social spheres catalyze the dramas' central conflict. Ultimately, Williams's plays struggle to accommodate the phallic male, who fails as a result to find community ratification for identity.

While Williams's introverted queer characters and his phallic males may seem quite distinct expressions of masculinity, they actually exist on the same plane of social expression in Williams's drama. Looking closely at Williams after Wilson, that is, shows Williams's characters engaged in the quintessential task of American drama: seeking a social means for expressing the oppressed self. Williams's most central characters frequently find themselves beset by an existential angst that at once bewilders and drives them to seek some form of communal engagement for the purposes of social identity crafting. As the queer characters turn inward, unable to locate a discursive community, the phallic males strike outward, overbearing their discursive communities.

In both cases, social identity crafting fails because of a dissonance between self and community: the individual struggles to identify the self, the community has rigid expectations for that self, and no supportive common ground emerges. When Williams crafted the experience of men in mid-century America, he did so with an eye turned specifically toward the varied experience of masculinity. All his men live under rigid expectations for masculinity, most of the central characters occupy an existential space askew from normative expectations, and none of these characters are comfortable in that identity. How they struggle to respond to this condition reveals in Williams's work a clear distrust of normative masculinity. This is of course clear enough from the consistently flawed characterization of his men, but what becomes most clear when reading Williams after Wilson and as part of an American dramatic tradition invested in social identity crafting is his critique of the society that refuses to take part in such a process. Wilson's black characters for the most part have a like-minded African American community that they can engage should they choose to do so; Williams's men have a society offering only rigid demands and cacophonous feedback to any deviation. Wilson's warriors frequently suffer because they try to overpower the antiphonal community, but in Williams, men suffer because they can find no dialectical community to engage them in antiphonal identity crafting. Comfortable sexual identity in Williams's work is elusive because the social sphere is far more regulatory than collaborative.

Lacking a Dialectical Queer Community: *The Glass Menagerie*

Tom Wingfield, Williams's semiautobiographical narrator of *The Glass Menagerie,* is at all times unsure about himself and his place in the world. With his father having abandoned the family, Tom's mother has very clear expectations for Tom to be a provider. This is a paternal role, carrying with it the expectation of normative heterosexual masculinity. Tom fills his role in part, but it is never natural for him; he can work in the shoe factory and dutifully bring home his paycheck, but he will not attempt to fulfill the heteronormative expectations his mother foists on him. Instead he will flee to the movie theater, the likely site of homoerotic liaisons. For Tom, there exists a distinct fissure between his murky understanding of self and his imposed social function, one that gapes along lines of masculinity and sexuality. C. W. E. Bigsby suggests that if Tom "had settled for what he had got, if he had offered his mother and sister the security they needed, he would have destroyed himself as a poet."[11] Certainly this is true, but Tom places his aspirations of selfhood above even his poetry; staying in the apartment where his identity was dictated by his mother would have destroyed him as a person on a journey of becoming.

The opacity of Williams's dramaturgy reflects Tom's uncertainty. Although the implications of Tom's trips to the movies seem clear, especially when considered in light of the motif of the movie theater balcony as a site of homoeroticism in several of Williams's short stories, the playwright never grants audiences access to Tom's activities in the movie theater.[12] Leaving the life of Tom outside the Wingfield apartment foggy, a life that contains the entirety of his sexual identity, Williams creates a character who is at once immediate and distant. This paradox grows when we consider the fact that Tom so frequently speaks directly to the play's audience. His most important actions remain cloaked even during these seemingly intimate speeches. This distinction illustrates Tom's hesitant search for a community of identity crafting as well as the play's critique of the absence of such a social sphere for a queer like Tom. Even when he engages in performances of self-disclosure, the sexuality that underwrites much of who he is remains absent from his speech, and so opportunities for full social becoming dissipate.

The play limns the potential of identity crafting for Tom by granting him the privilege of greeting the play's audience and setting the stage for himself: "the play is memory" he says at the opening.[13] The memory in question is his own, as he will perform the recent events that engendered his abandonment of mother and sister in favor of the life of a wanderer. Over the course of the play, Tom speaks four monologues directly to the audience, including the play's introduction and conclusion. But he is not quite the active conversant of identity that he might seem. Given the number of lines the actor playing Tom must deliver, it is easy to mistake him as fundamentally loquacious. But without the monologues, in just the interpersonal communication with other characters in the play, Tom appears as laconic as Brick Pollitt, interested primarily in avoiding conversation at all costs.

This juxtaposition most clearly shows Tom's urge for performative identity crafting. This memory play is after all entirely his memory, and the moments of dialogue are therefore always filtered through his consciousness. He is talking to the audience even when he is talking to other characters. In this sense, the most immediate speech of the play is its conclusion, when Tom admits that his constant traveling is driven in part by his desire to escape the guilt of abandoning his sister: "Oh, Laura, Laura, I tried to leave you behind me, but I am more faithful than I intended to be! I reach for a cigarette, I cross the street, I run into the movies or a bar, I buy a drink, I speak to the nearest stranger—anything that can blow your candles out!" (465). The tone of this speech is exploratory bewilderment: he is talking himself and his audience through his travels, but he is uncertain how best to understand them. This is why he needs the audience; this is what gives occasion to the play. He claims in his opening monologue to give the audience "truth in the pleasant disguise of illusion," but "truth" is misleading (400). The term presumes veracity, but Tom well knows that this is not the case. He is providing memory, not truth, and memory by necessity forfeits claims to veracity. Instead, memory—especially when told orally—is a process of exploration and creation. To recount a memory is to take a trip along a winding path through a foggy wood, searching for the best recollection possible.

Tom's memory is a voyage toward self-understanding. In his opening monologue, he references his absentee father, calling him a "fifth character" (401), and thereby identifying him as a force with which Tom will struggle throughout the play. Doing so reveals his consistent challenge in understanding how he relates to the man perpetually smiling on the wall. He calls himself "the bastard son of a bastard" (441), but if that were really the case his sister's memory would not be constantly creeping up behind him on the dark roads he travels. The mythology of Tom's father is that he abandoned the family and never looked back, but Tom has come to recognize that the identity of a remorseless drifter does not suit him. He does not understand why he cannot forget his mother and sister, and so he turns to a social audience in the theater, searching for some sort of recognition. He makes a call as a knowable person and seeks a response that ratifies his presence.

Conspicuous in its absence from that call is any clear discussion of his sexuality. This identity is something that Tom relegates to the wings of the play, never engaging it directly either in the action of his memory or in the language of his monologues. Besides his repeated references to movie theater excursions, the most explicit Tom ever gets about his queer identity is his claim that most of his coworkers "regarded me with suspicious hostility" before they began to warm up and smile at him "as people smile at an oddly fashioned dog that trots across their path at some distance." Some critics read Jim O'Conner's surprise at Tom's domesticity—"You know, Shakespeare, I never thought of you as having folks!"—to indicate a clear if tacit queerness attending upon Tom, but even if so, the play never makes Tom's sexual identity explicit (432).

Wilson's blues dramaturgy helps illuminate the social critique latent in Williams's almost complete silence about Tom's sexuality. For the social expectation of blues is that a performer presents him or herself before a potentially like-minded community in the hopes of receiving a response of recognition. But within the dramatic framework of *The Glass Menagerie*, Tom does not have that community. His sister clearly cares for him, but Tom never opens up to Laura. Instead he turns to the play's audience, obliquely and tentatively, searching for a sense of identity recognition to which he has no access in the space of his memories populated by other people. But even when he does, he remains guarded and incomplete in his disclosures. Wilson's blues dramaturgy helps reveal Tom's fraught internalization of his identity crafting and highlights Williams's censure of the society that refuses Tom an audience. Wilson fortifies his imperative of sociality by providing his fraught characters with a space for antiphonal performance—Seth Holly's boardinghouse, Doaker's kitchen, Memphis Lee's diner—but Williams shows Tom feeling at a loss for a willing audience within the claustrophobic space of his family apartment. Wilson's methods underscore Tom's solitude.

Tom's ill-formed audience leaves him on a stunted and incomplete journey of self-discovery. He performs before his social sphere, but that performance is one-sided and guarded. But Tom shares with his broader society some responsibility for the dissonance, as both his methods and convictions are flawed. He says in the play's closing monologue that after abandoning his family he "followed, from then on, in my father's footsteps, attempting to find in motion what was lost in space" (464–65). There are two important facets to this assertion. The first is his claim to be following in footsteps that are inevitably imperceptible to him. He does not know where his father is or—more importantly—how his father conducted his travels after leaving the family. But Tom's claim is definitive—he says he *followed* his father's footsteps, not *attempted to follow* them—revealing a sense of certainty in a fabricated reality he has no evidence to support. This questionable certainty also attends upon the second fascinating aspect here: his lyrical claim to search in motion for what was lost in space. His search is for identity: nowhere in the cramped space of his apartment or the shoe warehouse could he find a means to explore his identity, and his hope is that in the motion of his travels he will find that identity. Again though, there is slippage between Tom's desires and his methods: for in the space of the play, he is not traveling. He is instead standing before an audience and telling his story. He fled space in favor of motion, but he has returned to space that is distinctly theatrical, communal, and in the terms through which he defines it, testimonial.

In his closing monologue, that is, Tom reveals that he has run up against a limit in his search for identity and is trying a new tack. The family apartment is not productive, and he has no band room, backyard, or cabstand in which to express himself, like Wilson's characters do. The space of St. Louis failed him, as did nomadic motion, and so he turns to the performative space of theater. In this space, he makes a call of crafting his identity through performative memory and seeks out a response ratifying his murky, ill-defined humanity. But the incompleteness of that call emphasizes Williams's suggestion that midcentury queer masculinity has no clear community for social becoming. Tom's ideas about his sexuality remain as ostracized in the play as any sense of a queer community is in Williams's society. In the face of a society that rejects him at every turn, he looks to the performative community to help construct his makeshift identity, and even there he is guarded and silenced. The fact that he must keep moving, stalking off down an alley even before the final curtain falls, suggests that there is no community that will embrace and welcome him. His linguistic, performative attempts at social becoming are stunted and therefore cannot succeed.

Internalized Demands of Masculinity: *Cat on a Hot Tin Roof*

Cat on a Hot Tin Roof's Brick Pollitt adopts a strategy quite different from Tom's search for a linguistic community; Brick would prefer nobody talk to him at all. Such discussion might force him into active negotiation of his sexual identity, a process of which he wants no part. Tom abandons his mother and sister for the life of a wanderer, but his monologues betray a desire for antiphonal sociality that he fails to find. Brick, on the other hand, tries his hardest to shun linguistic community. Aside from a couple of long speeches in the closing moments of act 2, he in fact hardly has much to say at all. He may be the character in American drama with the greatest chasm between the degree of significance to the play and number of lines delivered. The actor playing Brick faces significant performance demands, but learning a great many lines is not one of them.

Brick's reticence for linguistic engagement, especially when juxtaposed with Tom's eagerness for the same and the consistent garrulousness of Wilson's characters, elaborates Williams's critique of queer masculine identity crafting. Rather than looking to the social sphere which offers no audience for Tom, *Cat* looks more directly at the self, at Brick's psychological struggle to reconcile himself with his own internalized expectations for masculinity. Devoted to heteronormative ideals, Brick is in no way eager to explore any aspect of queer identity. Maggie and Big Daddy offer him chances for personal linguistic engagement, but Brick consistently refuses, favoring an agonizing interiority that can only be soothed with alcohol. The only times he takes an active role in the discussion with either Big Daddy or Maggie are his defensively desperate attempts to shut down discussion of his relationship with Skipper. His interiority is of such paramount importance to Brick that he has made a deal with Maggie barring her from even attempting to access it. Brick's longest speech in the play's first act is dedicated to reminding Maggie of that very fact: "I don't have to do anything I don't want to do. You keep forgetting the conditions on which I agreed to stay on living with you" (895). Throughout the scene, Williams's stage directions mark Brick's speeches with adverbs like "*absently,*" "*dreamily,*" and "*coolly,*" while his lines are little more than variations on "Did you say something?" (889–90). But when there is the slightest hint of Brick being coerced into doing something against his will—all Maggie wants at this point is for him to sign a birthday card—he unleashes what for him is a veritable tirade: twenty-six words in two complete sentences. For this character to expend that amount of energy marks this as a moment of the utmost importance. Brick is determined that any identity will come on his own severely limited personal terms.

Brick considers his right to protect his prerogatives so important because acting on other people's expectations threatens to make him engage a complex identity that he has no interest in developing. Sex with Maggie, or even the simple task of giving in to a request that is at odds with his desires, illuminates the gulf between his self and social expectations for him. The play never discloses the precise conditions underwriting Brick and Maggie's sham relationship, but a lack of sex seems paramount. Establishing this condition is self-protection for Brick: if he can prevent the situation of sex with Maggie he can prevent the occasion of facing his lack of desire for sex with this beautiful woman. Brick goes to great lengths in attempting to arrange his social sphere so that he can be left alone with his psychological torment, turning consistently to booze rather than other people for respite.

Nonetheless, Brick harbors deep anxieties about the possibility of his identity developing out of his control. For him, the most frightening prospect seems to be the social sphere around him drawing conclusions about his relationship with Skipper and, in turn, his sexual identity. Brick's most loquacious scene results from Big Daddy pointing out that Brick's drinking began after Skipper's death, an observation that Brick takes as an implication of homosexuality. He raises his long-reserved voice for the express purpose of not allowing his identity to be crafted in reference to Skipper without his input. In fact, whenever Skipper's name arises, Brick attempts to shut down the conversation. Initially, he does not even engage Maggie's urge to discuss Skipper. "It was just beginning to soften up Skipper when—" she says in reference to alcohol's effect on the body, but Williams's em dash cuts off her line and leads into the stage direction *"She stops short,"* followed by an apology: "I'm sorry. I never could keep my fingers off a sore." Shortly thereafter, with no lines from Brick mitigating Maggie's long pontifications about their dormant love life, she mentions Skipper again: "What were you thinking of when I caught you looking at me like that? Were you thinking of Skipper?" Brick has nothing to say in response, but he does react: *"Brick takes up his crutch, rises"*; Maggie immediately apologizes: "Oh, excuse me, forgive me." During this page and a half of the script when Maggie cannot seem to avoid repeatedly fingering the jagged sore of Skipper in connection with her ruminations on the couple's lack of sex, Brick adopts a complete silence that is only broken by the necessity of asking for help: "I've dropped my crutch," he says by way of asking Maggie to pick it up for him (891–93). Here in the relative privacy of their bedroom, Brick seems to believe that letting Maggie vent her anxieties about Skipper will do little harm to his own identity, so his defense is nonengagement.

The situation changes when Maggie's reference to Skipper becomes more sexually explicit. Initially, she vaguely alludes to Skipper as a person from the past that may retain some influence on present circumstances, but later she raises his name as a sexual being. The former Brick can allow to float by unremarked upon; the latter he tries to shut down violently. "Yes, I made my mistake when I told you the truth about that thing with Skipper," says Maggie in reference to her ill-fated sexual encounter. "Never should have confessed it, a fatal error, tellin' you about that thing with Skipper." By referencing a sex act with Skipper—however unsuccessful it was—Maggie enters him into the discourse of sexuality, and Brick clearly feels implicated in this discourse because he again starts to string together complete sentences: "Maggie, shut up about Skipper. I mean it, Maggie; you got to shut up about Skipper." After she refuses to relent, Brick tries to impress on her the seriousness of the situation, but he is vague and struggles for words: "Look, Maggie. What you're doing is a dangerous thing to do. You're—you're—you're—foolin' with something that—nobody ought to fool with." Brick is toeing a delicate line: he wants to shut the conversation down, but tries not to do so by meeting Maggie on her terms of dialogue about her sexual encounter with Skipper and its implications. Desperate, he "(*turns suddenly out upon the gallery and calls:*) Little girl! Hey, little girl! [. . .] Tell the folks to come up!—Bring everybody upstairs!" Throughout the play Brick yearns for privacy, but his determination to terminate this conversation drives him to the extreme length of inviting his entire family into his bedroom. Maggie will not relent, and Brick's instinct is for violence: "Maggie, you want me to hit you with this crutch? Don't you know I could kill you with this crutch?" (908–10). From avoidance to deferral to distraction to violence, Brick runs the gamut in his desperation not to entertain any discussion of Skipper as a sexual being.

    The conflict in this scene exists between Maggie's desire to voice her conviction about Brick and Skipper, and Brick's stalwart determination to avoid any such vocalization. "It was one of those beautiful, ideal things they tell about in Greek legends," Maggie says, attempting to validate the attraction between Brick and Skipper. "[I]t couldn't be anything else, you being you, and that's what made it so sad, that's what made it so awful, because it was love that never could be carried through to anything satisfying or even talked about plainly." She is attempting frank and open discussion, making it plain that she understands and accepts now what was formerly so wrenching. But Brick will hear none of it. Before turning to ineffectual violence, he offers one brief response engaging with Maggie's story: "One man has one great good and true thing in his life. One great good thing which is true!—I had friendship with Skipper.—You are naming it dirty!" He cannot embrace Maggie's acceptance because to do so would be to enter into a discursive social performance that would begin to give shape to a queer identity, something that Brick cannot risk. "I married you, Maggie," he says in a last-ditch effort to abort the identity crafting to which he seems to be contributing against his will. "Why would I marry you, Maggie, if I was—?" (909–10). Later, in act 2, he supplies the word "queer" for the thought he cannot bring himself to finish here, but at this point he breaks off and resorts only to swinging his crutch at Maggie in an effort to quiet her. He speaks up briefly to contribute to the image of himself that the scene is crafting, but he quickly removes himself from the linguistic environment by turning toward violence. Maggie offers Brick the chance at a dialectical performance of identity crafting, but he balks hard.

Brick's anger with Maggie betrays an obstinate determination to keep any discussion of his relationship with Skipper out of the Pollitt home's performative environment. The prospect seems too risky for Brick to allow: should his relationship with Skipper become a topic of discussion, its characteristics and Brick's identity would become subject to that very discussion. But during his conversation with Big Daddy, Brick finds that any control he thought he retained over his identity vis-à-vis Skipper might be lost. After raising the taboo name, Big Daddy quickly expands for Brick the community of people with concerns about the relationship: "Gooper an' Mae suggested that there was something not right exactly in your—." Brick briefly asks for a clarification he does not need, but he is mostly concerned with the apparently surprising fact that more people than he thought believe in the homoeroticism of his relationship with Skipper: "They suggested that, too? I thought that was Maggie's suggestion." Williams makes clear that this information vexes Brick greatly: "*Brick's detachment is at last broken through. His heart is accelerated; his forehead sweat-beaded; his breath becomes more rapid and his voice hoarse.*" Brick continues with his attention focused squarely on the extent of people believing the suggestions about him and Skipper: "Who else's suggestion is it, is it *yours*? How many others thought that Skipper and I were—." And after Big Daddy tries to defuse his son's growing anger, Brick returns directly to this point: "Whose suggestion, who else's suggestion is it?" (944–45). At the core of Brick's anger is the fear that belief in his queer identity is spreading beyond his control to more people than he would be able to silence with the swing of a crutch.

Brick's manner throughout the vast majority of *Cat* is one of detachment; only the suggestion that judgments about his identity are spreading provokes his active presence. When he becomes convinced that Big Daddy believes in his queer identity, Williams's stage direction relates that "*Brick is transformed, as if a quiet mountain blew suddenly up in volcanic flame*" (947); only here does Brick become an animated, loquacious character. He actively defines himself as detached from the social sphere swirling around him, but when his sexual identity is at stake he will clearly enter the fray to defend himself against what he considers salacious charges. In his defense, he tells the story of his and Skipper's fraternity chasing out a member suspected of homosexuality, and he directly attacks the queer couple of Jack Straw and Peter Ochello, the former owners of the Pollitt plantation for whom Brick knows Big Daddy holds affection. Backed into a corner, he goes on the attack, making specific efforts to foreground homophobic prejudices that would support his heteronormative self.

In his angry responses, Brick betrays a strong commitment to social identity crafting. Conversing with Big Daddy, Brick is most concerned with performing a hypermasculine, queer-hating male who had a great friendship with a man and has lost sexual interest in his wife for reasons other than homosexuality. Like many of Wilson's warriors, Brick wants nothing more than to receive a response from Big Daddy and the rest of the family ratifying his masculine identity, but he does not get it, so he drinks and yells some more. He in fact seems to recognize the antiphonal process of identity crafting so acutely that he refused to provide Skipper with a ratifying response for his call of queerness. Brick confesses to Big Daddy that the last conversation he had with Skipper was a long-distance phone call "in which he made a drunken confession to me and on which I hung up!" (951). The implication is that Maggie's encounter with Skipper made him more aware of his homoerotic attraction to Brick, which he confessed on the phone. Brick realizes that to respond to Skipper's call is to legitimize his claims and implicate himself in a homoerotic affair. Ever aware of the power of performative identity crafting, Brick will take no part in risking his hypermasculinity by joining this antiphonal performance.

Brick therefore exists always on the edge of a social existence he tries to ignore but which he cannot stop himself from attending to. He hopes through alcohol to escape the world of other people who disgust him, but he cannot shake off the need for community ratification of his identity. That need is far too fundamental to his understanding of self. When raging to his father, Brick focuses much of his anger on what he perceives as the social shortsightedness about male friendship:

> Brick: Why can't exceptional friendship, *real, real, deep, deep friendship!* between two men be respected as something clean and decent without being thought of as—
> Big Daddy: It can, it is, for God's sake.
> Brick: —*Fairies*.... (948)

Brick does not provide a subject for his verb *thought of,* but his suggestion here and elsewhere in the play is that the agent of these thoughts is society at large. "Don't you know how people *feel* about things like that?" he says, accusing Big Daddy of tossing around the subject of homosexuality too easily. This social taboo has infected Brick fully. Williams follows Brick's use of the word *"Fairies"* with a stage direction illuminating an important element of Brick's psyche: *"In his utterance of this word, we gauge the wide and profound reach of the conventional mores he got from the world that crowned him with early laurel"* (948). He earned such laurel through the conventional masculinity of athletics and radiant sexuality, both of which have recently been challenged. In his youth, he made a call to the world as a phallic male and received an enthusiastic ratifying response, but he seems never to have realized how strongly he depends on that response to constitute his identity. He wants to withdraw into the bottle, but his unflappable psychological programming tells him that the voice of the social sphere is fundamental to his identity.

Brick's psychological turmoil has its roots less in a confused sexual identity than in a strenuous push and pull between solitary exclusion and participatory inclusion. Tom can find no linguistic social sphere with which to engage, so he turns to the theatrical audience, but Brick has the opportunity to examine his self with both Maggie and Big Daddy, both of whom are willing participants in his social becoming. As Mark Royden Winchell recognizes, "One of the ironies of Williams's play is that its two most overtly heterosexual characters—Maggie and Big Daddy—are also the most tolerant of the latent erotic ties between Brick and Skipper."[14] It is this tolerance that offers Brick the opportunity to explore his self, but although Big Daddy can be no clearer in telling Brick that his friendship with Skipper can be and is considered decent, Brick's wrestling with his own demons causes him to gloss right over this assurance. Savran argues that in *Cat* "Williams radically redefines both the self and the Other . . . and cunningly destabilizes normative constructions of sexuality."[15] For Brick, the Other would seem to be his interlocutors, but the play reveals that Brick's Other is in fact internalized social expectations. He is stuck in a feedback loop as both self and Other, a process so all-consuming that he cannot help but project his self-crafted Other onto Maggie and Big Daddy. He attempts to define himself as a stalwart defender of normative sexuality, but as Savran and others point out, he exists in a social genealogy stretching through the homosexual couple of Straw and Ochello, something that Big Daddy embraced as he moved into the plantation's line of succession. Within the play, normative restrictions on sexuality come from Brick. He is the one who frets about potential queerness, and he is the one who condemns himself for it. Savran suggests that in this play, "as throughout Williams's work, genders and sexualities are not set in opposition but are dispersed and plural, constantly in circulation."[16] Although this plurality surrounds Brick, he cannot see it or embrace it; he is anguished because he imposes rigidity on a social sphere defined by plurality.

Brick's struggle to articulate where he locates mendacity ("The whole, the whole—thing . . ." is all he can muster in response to Big Daddy's demand for specifics about lies and liars) underscores his constant struggle to understand both himself and the process of social becoming (941). He cannot identify specific mendacity because the lies of his world are at once too vast and too localized within his self. The world has told him that he is a hypermasculine ideal—a "superior creature" and "godlike being," as Maggie articulates it (909)—but he cannot even jump hurdles or desire his beautiful wife any longer. Worse still, he tells himself that he upholds the rigid normative ideals of sexuality and masculinity, but his mind cannot help but ponder the inherent complexities thereof, so he drinks until he has reached a level of inebriation that frees him from such concerns. Brick can understand neither why he deviates from the norm by which he has been defined nor why he is driven so strongly to engage with the social sphere. He is, at bottom, stranded on an island between the self and the social, intimidated by the horizons in both directions.

Cat on a Hot Tin Roof, then, looks more directly than *The Glass Menagerie* at the psychological turmoil exacted by heteronormative demands of masculine sexual identity. To a greater degree than Tom, Brick has little sense of who he is or how he fits into his social sphere, a lack of understanding exasperated by a hubristic sense of certainty: he feels damn sure he knows himself and that it is others who are mistaken. Williams writes in his famous bird-in-the-net stage direction that rather than exploring "*the solution of one man's psychological problem,*" he seeks "*the true quality of experience in a group of people, that cloudy, flickering, evanescent—fiercely charged!—interplay of live human beings in the thundercloud of a common crisis*" (945). The play certainly does not solve Brick's psychological problem, using it instead as a vehicle for examining a larger social experience, but Brick's tumult helpfully illuminates the thundercloud of opaque, ill-defined sexuality beset by social expectations. His most immediate social sphere constituted by Maggie and Big Daddy resembles the performative spaces of Wilson's *Cycle* because it is willing to join his antiphonal process of becoming, but like many of the fiercely charged about whom Williams writes, Brick cannot effectively release his charge of self because he cannot reconcile self and other. If *The Glass Menagerie* teases the facile conclusion that all Tom needs is somebody to talk to, *Cat* warns that the success of such a solution is not so guaranteed.

A Dangerous Surplus of Heterosexuality: *Orpheus Descending*

The sexual identity of Val Xavier in *Orpheus Descending* is not opaque. Val exudes heterosexual energy, and this powerful force is the source of his troubles. He claims to have the ability to "burn down a woman [. . .] any two-footed woman" (37), bravado that the action of the play supports. The women in the Torrance Mercantile Store stare at him lecherously as soon as he walks on stage, and over the course of the play Val as a sexualized object of attraction—"the sexual free agent," in John M. Clum's apt phrase—will engender much of the drama's conflict.[17] Val's claim to be able to "burn down a woman" suggests an active seduction on his part, but Williams shows very little of that in *Orpheus Descending;* instead, Val exists as the embodiment of sexual attraction, drawing women like Lady Torrance and Carol Cutrere to him gravitationally. This is a character fulfilling almost entirely the social expectations for a sexualized, phallic male.

Missing, however, is eagerness to embody the role his social sphere has assigned him. He has been a sexually marked man for most of his life, but he confesses a desire to shed that identity. What alternative exists for him is unclear. Throughout the play, he repeatedly objects to being treated like a stud horse, but never does he articulate his preference for an alternative other than taking his guitar and wandering, and he ultimately does fulfill Lady's sexual desires by impregnating her; he quite literally functions as Lady's stud horse. So whereas Tom and Brick act very much at odds with the expectations of their respective social spheres, Val plays his part. The heterosexual phallic male exerts profound sexual influence on his play and forces the rest of the characters to respond to that influence.

This of course does not work out well for Val. After the revelation that he had been acting on his sexual energy with Lady offstage, the phallic, heterosexual male reaps the reward of a torturous death. Even though his sexual identity is quite different from Tom's and Brick's, Val remains out of sync with the regulatory powers of his social sphere and is rejected. What unites these men in Williams's dramatic world, then, is ostracization founded in sexual identity. Brick excludes himself from a social sphere that is at least in part willing to embrace him, and Tom actively runs away from a family and society that simply do not understand his identity, but Val cannot escape before his society exacts murderous discipline as recompense for his identity and the actions it engenders. Strikingly, of the three characters, Val acts most in line with heteronormative expectations for masculinity, and he pays the most violent price.

But as normative as Val's heterosexual identity might seem, he remains a character always on the outskirts of the play's social sphere; he does not seek entrance into the community, and the community does not seek to include him. Savran points out that *Orpheus Descending* deploys what he calls "perhaps the most durable characterological pattern in Williams's work," which is the triangle "figured as a sexual conquest over a woman between a virile young man and a weak or effete older man." For Savran, this virile phallic man becomes most influential by transforming a woman "from a state of real or feigned innocence to a wary yet vigorous adulthood," and this central drama "appears to (re)construct masculinity." So, for example, Val revives the normative masculinity that was so deconstructed in *The Glass Menagerie* and *Cat on a Hot Tin Roof*. Importantly, though, Savran does not argue that Williams simply appropriates and redeploys narratives of normative masculinity; rather, he suggests that Williams's phallic male is "distinctively and unmistakably *Other*."[18] The paternalistic Jabe Torrance, relegated mostly to an offstage deathbed, is a suitable member of the play's community, but the virile Val, often at center stage, remains always a mysterious and disruptive force at odds with normative domesticity.

Val and characters in Williams like him (Savran groups him with Stanley Kowalski, Jim O'Connor, and others) stand in for the paradigm of heteronormative masculinity but remain perpetually othered and problematic in Williams's oeuvre. They seem uninterested in social identity crafting because either like Stanley they are delighted to embrace the role of phallic male, or like Val they are at least partially invested in rejecting it. Val is particularly instructive of Williams's critique of social expectations for the phallic male because he is a character that rejects his socially imposed identity through language but supports it through action. With his sexualized body he makes a call, and while seeming to reject the ratifying response, he nonetheless fulfills the sexual expectations of that body. Val therefore demonstrates how pervasive and restrictive heteronormative sexual identity can be in Williams. Even the character who seems genuinely invested in rejecting the "stud" role prescribed for him cannot manage to escape it.

The fundamental problem defining Val's experience in this play is that he is an outsider in the hermetic, conservative Two River County which allows little space for change or disruption. But Val cannot help but personify rupture. Although the play provides a realistic story of car troubles to explain Val's arrival in town, like most elements of *Orpheus Descending*, that arrival also has a nonrealist, spiritual component. Once Carol convinces the "Negro Conjure Man" to perform the primal "Choctaw cry," Williams's stage direction says that "*Just then, as though the cry had brought him, Val enters the store*" (19). The implication is that the primal power of the Conjure Man's performance summons Val as if from an immaterial and unknowable realm beyond the quotidian, earthbound environment of Two River County. Williams therefore introduces Val as not simply a geographic or social outsider, but as one from an entirely different plane of existence, fundamentally not of the world demarcated by the Torrance Mercantile Store.

This allegorical context in which Williams introduces Val bespeaks the challenge of identity for both him and the Two River social sphere. The play marks him from the very beginning as in no way a member of the community, and so much of *Orpheus Descending*'s tension lies in the rigidity of identity between Val and Two River that shows no signs of softening. His first awkward interaction with Carol Cutrere demonstrates the vast gulf between him and his new environment; not even with the branded outsider does he find common ground. As Val busies himself trying to ignore Carol, her long story tries to convince him that they have met previously in New Orleans, but in the process it attempts to define Val in Carol's terms. She has a likely enough story of Val making some money in New Orleans by playing his guitar in bars on New Year's Eve, one that she supports with seemingly concrete details, but Val will take no part in her attempt to define him. "Why are you so anxious to prove I know you?" is his only response to her story. He refuses to ratify her crafting of his identity with a response. He actively engages shortly thereafter, however, when she tells him she wants to take him "jooking," a nighttime ritual of drinking, dancing, and eventual sex. He tells her, "I don't go that route," and explains that the reason he does not is because he is getting older: "Heavy drinking and smoking the weed and shaking with strangers is okay for kids in their twenties but this is my thirtieth birthday and I'm all through with that route" (23–24). Carol tries to tell Val who he is and then engage him in the activities that such a person would enjoy, but Val resists.

He resists because he is attempting to capitalize on his mystical appearance in foreign territory by using the opportunity to redefine himself. The play does not reveal whether or not Carol's story of her New Orleans encounter with Val is entirely truthful, but the implication is that the story and her impression of Val's history have elements of truth; he is clearly attempting to pivot himself away from a riotous history. Like Herald Loomis and Citizen Barlow, Val shows up in a new space in search of a clearer understanding of himself, but whereas Wilson's characters find a willing community, the Two River community is only and consistently regulatory to Val. Although defined in large part by his sexuality, he claims to Lady in the next scene that he denied Carol's sexual advances because "[s]he made a mistake about me":

> Lady: What mistake?
> Val: She thought I had a sign "Male at Stud" hung on me.

And he bristles shortly thereafter when Lady presumes to understand him:

> Lady: Well, what in God's name are you lookin' for around here?
> Val: —Work.
> Lady: Boys like you don't work.
> Val: What d'you mean by boys like me?
> Lady: Ones that play th' guitar and go around talkin' about how warm they are . . .

As Val recognizes, Lady says more here in her ellipsis than in her words, suggesting that sexy traveling musicians seek means of pleasure rather than work. But as he did with Carol earlier, he refuses to ratify her identity crafting of him, responding with his own claim: "Lady, I'm thirty today and I'm through with the life that I've been leading. I lived in corruption but I'm not corrupted" (33–34). In just the first two scenes, Carol and Lady serve as voices of the community, making clear the presumptions made about Val in Two River County, but in both cases Val objects. While in the county, he is invested in redefining his social self, but as the utterances of Carol and Lady reveal, his body carries expectations of self that are not so easily shaken.

In this case, Val's body rather than his voice makes a call, one that the antiphonal community is eager to ratify by placing clear expectations on him. Two River County expects Val to be a phallic male with all the sexual activity that that identity entails, but Val constantly repudiates these expectations. He tells Lady that he refused Carol because he is no stud; he claims to have given up the life of parties and sex; he plays dumb when Lady insists, "Ev'rything you do is suggestive!"; and when he tries to abandon Lady, he tells her, "I was disappointed in you," because he is convinced that she planted the cot in the store's alcove so that he could sleep there and potentially be a sexual liaison for her (41, 67). Repeatedly Val makes a call of identity as a nonphallic male—a heterosexual male not defined primarily by his sexuality—but he never receives a ratifying response to that identity. The social sphere of Two River County is unwilling to accept him as anything other than the personification of sexuality. Their initial reading of him brands him as such, and there seems to be little Val or anybody else can do to alter that.

When community feedback eventually overwhelms Val and he begins to perform the identity demanded of him, he steps into the role of sacrificial victim that county residents always wanted him to play. Val chastises Lady for what he sees as her manipulation of him, asserting that she "hired a man off the highway to do double duty without paying him overtime for it. . . . I mean a store clerk days and a stud nights," and attempts to leave without ever stepping into the role of stud about which he has spoken with such disdain. But Lady desperately protests his leaving, throwing herself in front of the store's door, and Williams's stage direction says, "*The true passion of her outcry touches him then, and he turns about and crosses to the alcove. . . . As he draws the curtain across it he looks back at her*" (68). Now Val finally sees fit to step into the role of phallic male by having sex with Lady. She joins him in the alcove to inaugurate their sexual relationship, at which point Val embodies all that the Two River County social sphere had presumed of him. Val has offered a reluctant performance of identity, but he has presented and confirmed a social identity nonetheless. With that confirmation, he marks himself as the element for which this hermetic society has no room, and the men of the county violently murder him and Lady to preserve their closed system.

Val shows up in Two River County as an outsider seeking an opportunity to change his identity. That opportunity is denied him, and fulfilling his socially prescribed identity gets him tortured and destroyed. The social sphere of the county needs a sacrificial victim in order to preserve its own collective identity that it is unwilling to alter in collaborative performance; as it destroyed Lady's father and attempts constantly to eradicate Carol Cutrere, so too does it impose a definition on Val and then destroy him. The county society is invested in preserving its paternalistic notions of power and sexuality, and in the process it reveals a destructive force of heteronormativity. Like Brick, who was crowned with the early laurel of masculinity because of his athletic prowess, Val's masculine identity is foisted upon him at an early age because of his eminent sexuality. Both men find themselves at odds with their socially imposed identities later in life, but what distinguishes Val from Brick is that he attempts to thrust off the socially constructed ideal of phallic masculinity. Any variance from that ideal on Brick's part causes him great distress, but Val tries to wander from an identity he considers tainted. The problem is that he is in a social sphere that will brook no self-styling or participate in any communal identity crafting that deviates from its imposed conservative norm.

For a variety of reasons both within and beyond his control, Val is a bluesman manqué. He tells lady that his guitar is his "life's companion" that "washes me clean like water when anything unclean has touched me," and shows her inscribed on it the names of great musicians. These include such foundational blues, jazz, and folk figures as Lead Belly, Bessie Smith, King Oliver, Fats Waller, Jelly Roll Morton, and Woody Guthrie. These names provide for Val a spiritual community through which he finds emotional or psychological solace, but they do little to constitute a physical, antiphonal community. Val says that the names are people he has "run into here and there," emphasizing the solitariness of his journey (34–35). Lead Belly, Bessie Smith, and the rest do not accompany him through Two River County, and since he has defined himself so fundamentally by his guitar, he leaves himself with little recourse to engage antiphonally with the community. He attempts to deploy performative blues tactics on an audience unwilling to participate in open-minded antiphonal performance.

Instead of a receptive antiphonal audience, Val meets a regulatory force of imposition. This is the same regulation that Brick internalizes, rendering him deaf to Maggie's and Big Daddy's open-minded responses, regulation that Tom understands well enough to send him into darkened movie theaters and secluded alleyways. Val tries to resist regulatory force, ultimately succumbs to it, and meets his violent death after fulfilling what is expected of him only too well. More so than *The Glass Menagerie* and *Cat on a Hot Tin Roof*, *Orpheus Descending*—the play that Kimball King suggests "may be the most eloquent indicator of Williams's particular contribution to modern drama"—holds heteronormativity up to harsh scrutiny.[19] In part, Williams does this by altering the myth that is his source. Critics regularly read Two River County as the Hades from which Val/Orpheus must rescue Lady/Eurydice from the clutches of Jabe/Pluto. But in the myth's most influential telling, Ovid's Orpheus returns from the underworld having failed to rescue Eurydice. In his sorrow, Orpheus sings a long narrative song that constitutes a frame story in *Metamorphoses* book 10 consisting of a wide variety of sexual encounters that stray from heteronormative, procreative expectations. Among these stories, Orpheus sings of Ganymede, a young boy who becomes the object of Jove's lust; of Hyacinthus, a male object of Apollo's lust; of Pygmalion, who lusts after a statue; and of Myrrha, a young girl who tricks her father into incest. At the end of Orpheus's performance, having earlier written that

> scores of women
> were burning to sleep with the bard and suffered the pain of rejection.
> Orpheus even started the practice among Thracian
> tribes of turning for love to immature males,

Ovid writes that the bard is torn asunder by a group of Maenads who cry, "Look! Look there! The man who rejects us!" before murdering him by dismemberment.[20] Orpheus rejects heteronormativity and is punished, but Val faces similarly severe destruction for embodying heterosexual masculinity to the utmost.

By altering his source material, Williams underscores the destructive force of regulatory heteronormativity and suggests that the most dangerous aspect of sexual identity is that which is imposed by the social sphere.

Ovid's poetry was subversive enough to get him exiled from Rome, but ultimately his sexual politics are quite conservative: Orpheus rejects the sexual company of women and is destroyed as a result. But Val plays his sexualized masculine role fully. In the most practical sense, his crime is an active contribution to Lady's adultery, but the play makes clear from the beginning that Lady is more prisoner than wife to Jabe. Ultimately, both Lady and Val are destroyed for being *too* heterosexual and *too* desirous of acting on that sexuality within a social sphere that has little patience for such things.

While it might seem that in *Orpheus Descending* Williams swings his dramatic pendulum to the opposite end of the sexuality spectrum as *The Glass Menagerie*—there a queer character trying to reconcile his queer masculinity, here a heterosexual character trying to reconcile his heteronormativity—the critique of socially crafted sexual identity remains consistent. For Val is a character defined in large part by his struggle to self-craft his sexual identity within the limited social sphere. Early in the play, he makes a call to a social sphere that is contentious and adversarial to his endeavors. He insists that he is "not corrupted" and done with the life of a sexual wanderer, but his audience is unprepared to accept and ratify those claims. The only way this social sphere will participate in Val's performance of self is if that performance aligns with their expectations; he resists participating with these expectations for a time, but eventually accepts the identity that society allows for him. By destroying the very thing that they insisted must exist, the people of Two River County make the phallic male a sacrificial victim in support of their conservative, paternalistic sexual politics. Val and Lady are made examples of the type of sexual vibrancy that will not be tolerated. The Conjure Man summons for the county a scapegoat on whom they can place all their sexual anxieties, and they eagerly expunge themselves of any guilt through his murder.

So, like Tom and any number of Williams's other men, Val's sexual identity exists at odds with his social sphere. Like Brick, there exists a disconnect between how Val responds to the social expectations he has internalized and those that are newly upon him. Val reveals, however, that while the existential and social forces of homosexuality, queerness, and homophobia are powerful antagonists in Williams's work, the most pressing challenge is the struggle for sustainable sexual identity. Frequently, that identity seems to be queer, but Val and other phallic men (like Stanley Kowalski, whose sexuality, though less a problem for him than it is for Blanche, is nonetheless responsible in large part for the drama of *Streetcar*) cause problems for themselves and their plays through seeming to embody socially idealized heteronormativity. The root problem is the challenge in Williams of developing one's sexual identity within a social sphere. This is equally true for many of the playwright's women as it is for Tom, Brick, and Val. Characters find themselves in some way sexually at odds with what their social spheres expect of them, and they struggle to find productive means of developing an identity within that society.

Williams and the Theater of Social Critique

Like O'Neill, Williams often inspires hermeneutic readings intent on identifying how the author wrote his life into his plays. Certainly the plot and characters of *The Glass Menagerie* track very closely to Williams's own life, and critics often point out how some aspect of the playwright's beloved sister Rose can be identified in most of his plays; John Lahr calls him "the most autobiographical of American playwrights."[21] But although Williams's plays are certainly personal and often find source material in his life, Williams was more socially and politically minded in his work than an autobiographical or psychological reading might suggest. Although critics like Thomas P. Adler occasionally recognize that for Williams "the concepts of 'artist' and 'revolutionary' are virtually synonymous," this element of his drama is under-remarked upon.[22] Quoting Williams's own self-commentary, Lahr points out that "despite his increasing interest in progressive politics, he was also avowedly 'not a person dedicated primarily to bettering social conditions.' He was too oblique and allusive a writer for polemical drama."[23] Indeed, as Lahr demonstrates, Williams's tendency for opacity and obliqueness in his politics often frustrated "some zealous members of the gay liberation movement" who late in the playwright's career urged him to be the sort of vocal public advocate of gay rights for whom they yearned.[24] Perhaps this frustration as well as the critical tendency to overlook Williams's political critique emerges because the playwright's social commentary is less topical engagement with contemporaneous affairs than it is a politicized critique of social structures. Savran, pointing out an apparent disconnect between Williams's repeated claims of political activism and the seeming lack of overt political content in his plays, argues that the playwright shows himself to be socially subversive most clearly in his "enunciation of a decentered and fragmented subject," one that emerges in Williams's "conflicted relationship with the dominant and the 'deviant' notions of sexuality during the 1940s and 1950s."[25] As Savran suggests, Williams's social activism exists most clearly in the crafting of characters at odds with dominant, normative ideologies of sexual self.

Thinking through August Wilson's blues dramaturgy allows a more vivid and robust theorization of Williams's dramaturgy of social critique. For it is clear enough that sexuality provides the pivotal drama to many of Williams's plays, and that very often the crux of that drama is a disconnect between self and society in terms of sexual identity. But much less clear is how that disconnect manifests itself. Wilson's blues dramaturgy shows how many of Williams's men exist in dysfunctional antiphonal communities. The community establishes conditions for performative self-crafting, but falters in such a way that counteracts or disallows the performance of self to function felicitously. Abortive performances of sexual self therefore exist throughout Williams. For this reason among others, Williams's characters struggle to use their communities productively for a collective establishment of their own social identities.

In this way, Williams appears far more pessimistic about the potential of a sustainable sexual identity for midcentury men than Wilson was about the experience of black Americans. For Wilson, through blues, there is at least the potential of identity resolution. Citizen Barlow and Harmond Wilks take important steps toward social self-crafting at the close of *Gem of the Ocean* and *Radio Golf,* for example. Especially since these are the final two plays that Wilson wrote in the *Cycle*, these characters augur well for Wilson's outlook on the journey of his contemporary community of blues people. By communing actively with their ancestors and those around them who embrace their heritage, these two characters begin to come into their own as sustainable black men. Little similar success exists in Williams's plays. Men comfortable with their own sexual identity are those like Stanley Kowalski and Jim O'Connor, whose plays use that sexuality to contribute to heart-wrenching conclusions. Even these seeming exceptions follow the trend in Williams whereby the form of masculine sexuality that emerges in the play proves problematic.

Certainly Wilson is far more explicit in his social critique than is Williams, whose aesthetic can best be described as one of opacity. As narrator of *The Glass Menagerie*, Tom highlights the nonrealist elements of his play, as Williams himself often does in stage directions. But what may seem stylistically apolitical betrays social critique in its very form. For in relegating masculine sexuality largely to the shadowy corners of his plays—even the heterosexual encounter between Lady and Val happens behind a highly stylized curtain in the alcove, that play's "closet"—but nonetheless pivoting his plays' drama on that sexuality, Williams demonstrates the danger of a taboo on communal sexual becoming. Williams's plays, that is, expose the problematics of midcentury masculine sexuality. Wilson's characters get into trouble by ignoring their blues community; Williams's characters face difficulty because such a community is either lacking or impossible to embrace.

Consistently, the social sphere of Williams's plays renders the social becoming of his men nearly impossible. Savran argues that during the middle of the twentieth century, at a time when the United States was particularly concerned with its national identity among growing international influence, Williams's work "vividly illuminated the pressures and anxieties circulating around the normative constructions of masculinity and femininity," offering "subtly subversive models of gender and sexuality that, I believe, suggest a way beyond those 'sex roles' that continue to exercise a powerful hold of the American domestic *imaginaire*." For Savran, Williams's progressive politics exists where his work and his life converge, "simultaneously articulating a potentially revolutionary site of resistance and reducing the language of homophobia to a barely comprehensible babble."[26] Savran locates a subversive power in Williams's representation of fraught manhood, but a more prominent argument emanating from his representation of men is a critique of the society that fails to support their social becoming. Certainly Williams's own life became increasingly difficult as he grew into a queer masculinity that lacked a receptive audience from his father on through his professional critics, making him, in Philip Kolin's phrase, "a character in his own drama of self."[27] August Wilson argues in his *Cycle* that black American blues people must embrace a performative community to develop their senses of identity more fully, but Williams suggests that American men who are in any way out of sync with regulatory expectations of sexuality lack community. Theater offered a potential community, but Williams found that theater remained mired by the same regulatory social expectations as society at large. Like Tom, Williams and other midcentury American men who did not fulfill rigid heteronormative frameworks could turn to the performative social sphere only to a limited extent. It is telling that homosexuality figures so much more prominently in Williams's fiction than in his drama: for Williams, the social space of theater was, like the broader performative social sphere of which it was a part, insufficient for examining the sexualized masculine self.

6

August Wilson's Legacy and Its Limits

Worrying the Line in Katori Hall
and Tarell Alvin McCraney

IN ITS PREVIOUS TWO chapters, this book has concerned itself with the potential of August Wilson's legacy to reshape how critics, scholars, and audiences think about the modern American dramatic tradition that preceded him. Certainly, however, Wilson's influence extends forward, shaping how contemporary playwrights conceive, harness, and deploy the social operation of theater. Wilson's work shows theater's potential to engender and participate in a dialogue of social humanization, and allows for playwrights following his career to adopt, revise, and expand this model by repeating and revising—worrying the line of—his blues dramaturgy.

Wilson's influence shows its greatest impact in the work of African American dramatists whose plays seek a constant reassessment of black life and history in America. Strong Wilsonian echoes appear throughout Dominique Morisseau's three-play cycle *The Detroit Project,* for example, which uses small settings—a basement, a breakroom, a small jazz club—as crucibles to examine individual lives as microcosms of much broader communities and histories. Morisseau's *Paradise Blue* (2015) in particular teems with thematic elements familiar from Wilson, including the arrival of a mysterious stranger in black, the danger of a volatile musician determined to make it big, and the threat of urban renewal to uproot a black community in the name of progress. Wilson's lead allows Morisseau to examine questions about black community, history, struggle, and joy within her own dynamic register. Similarly, in part because of Wilson's precedent, Suzan-Lori Parks in *The America Play* and *Topdog/Underdog* is able to treat the fraught racial experience surrounding Abraham Lincoln and African American identity as at once problematic and productive without offering simplistic answers. Rather, she opens questions about the narrative of black life's relationship to Lincoln as a call, inviting active response from her audience and community. This is a blues impulse that bears distinctive markers of Parks's influence from Wilson dwelling within her own distinctive dramaturgy.

Similar evidence for Wilson's influence exists throughout much contemporary drama, but two playwrights who take Wilson's techniques in important new directions are Katori Hall and Tarell Alvin McCraney. Both show clear signs of a Wilsonian influence throughout their work, as in their productive use of location and space. Hall treats Memphis not unlike Wilson treats Pittsburgh; the city where she sets several plays is for her a microcosm of black life in America through which she can examine both local communities and broader social concerns. By setting her 2008 play *Saturday Night/Sunday Morning* entirely within a local beauty parlor, for example, Hall is able to introduce the vibrant and complicated individual denizens of the salon while also tackling broader issues of gender, religion, and sex, all underscored by race. In her introductory note to the script, Hall makes clear that although the play is set in a very specific time and place, its actions and concerns are far more universal to the community: "The text is delivered in the roaring, heightened music of black beauty-shop banter. These women use words like tennis balls—insults are served fast and they are skilled at the verbal volley."[1] For this play, Miss Mary's beauty shop acts like Vera's backyard in *Seven Guitars*, Seth Holly's boardinghouse in *Joe Turner*, or Memphis's diner in *Two Trains Running*: it is the central stopping place of the community where concerns find voice, conflicts flare, shared joy emerges, and identity might find expression. Hall uses a similar technique in her other Memphis plays, and even in her later work set in Africa like *Our Lady of Kibeho* and *Children of Killers*, she shows clear traces of Wilson, who establishes the notion that black drama grows directly and powerfully out of localized black community.

McCraney works similarly with this technique, particularly in his 2009 trilogy, *The Brother/Sister Plays*. These plays move through a variety of specific locations—several houses, a high school track, a block party, a mechanic's garage, a school, among others—but all take place in the fictional location of San Pere, Louisiana. The characters in McCraney's trilogy are spread over several families and generations, but they all share the distinctive markings of their bayou town. This shows up in dialect and custom, but most distinctively in the characters' collective responses to trauma. Division within the small society is frequent and strong, but such strife is handled through and by the community. The playwright returns to the bayou in 2013's *Head of Passes*, where he finds one family in turmoil, and examines that strife through the distinctive vernacular and customs he has established for his dramatic community. Yet, like Hall and Wilson, McCraney's local attention has broad implications. As the playwright shows through near constant references to spirituality, the plights of his characters stretch beyond the spatial and temporal confines of their plays into the more universal and timeless experience of black life.

More generally, the work of both these playwrights shows Wilsonian influence by focusing on the processes of identity exploration and tentative identity creation. Like Wilson and Pittsburgh, both these writers hail from or close to the setting of their plays, and so there is at least some element of self-examination in the process of setting their plays close to home. But also like Wilson, Hall and McCraney create large communities—their plays usually have big casts, and each play is in dialogue at least referentially with all the others—so their plays expand from self to family to local community and, by implication, to the broader African American community. They both paint distinctive and unique portraits of localized communities, but in doing so both are asking their audiences to recognize general qualities of black American life so that their plays might contribute to the ongoing dialogue so prevalent in Wilson's work about the experience of finding a sustainable identity while being black in America.

And yet, what is most compelling about any case of influence is how the successor carves out room for distinction from the predecessor. Hall and McCraney both take the examination of identity into fertile territory that Wilson either only broaches or does not explore at all. This is for Hall the complex realm of women, and for McCraney that of queer men. As Cheryl A. Wall argues, a thorough examination of the black American experience must attune itself to a vast field of social intricacies: "The cultural identity that the history of African Americans in the United States informs is necessarily multidimensional. Its complexities mitigate against the formation of a unitary identity." Being black in America is a precondition for Hall's and

McCraney's characters, but from there the playwrights resist a unified racial portrait in favor of close examinations of groups of people who do not garner much attention from Wilson. Wall goes on to aver that "the existence of an African American literary tradition inevitably derives from a racial identity that its authors are presumed to share. Too often that common racial classification has veiled differences of gender, class, ethnicity, and sexual preference."[2] What is true of authors is also true of black characters, but Hall and McCraney are two playwrights who work to remove this veil, exploring uniquely defined plights that are particularly arduous because they go further than race into the realms of gender and sexuality.

Hall's dramaturgy defines itself in contrast to Wilson's first by placing women at center stage, and secondly by focusing particularly on loci of failure in women's continuing blues journeys. Consistently, Hall creates women who face awful situations despite the assertion of unique strength of identity. In *Hoodoo Love* (2007), for example, the main character, Toulou, attempts to take charge of her domestic situation by casting a spell on the object of her desire, while also keeping her deadbeat brother in line. After both efforts fail, Toulou is left at the play's conclusion with the harrowing task of recovering from several crushing defeats in order to begin a new performance of self. In *Hurt Village* (2012), the situation is similar for Cookie, a young, precocious, independent girl who lives in a dangerous housing project. Cookie opens the play by claiming to be a "grown ass woman" at thirteen years old, and carries herself as one with the ability to rise above the danger of the projects, but she suffers under the conditions of her environment nonetheless.[3] Like Toulou, Cookie ends the play at the outset of a new journey, one that will force her to search for a definition of self in the wake of defeat. As Angela Davis, Hazel Carby, and others have shown, often the female expressiveness of blues is assertively defiant, and Hall's work is particularly concerned with examining how that attitude might redress failure.

Critics have long taken Wilson to task for what many argue are flat, simplistic portraits of women, but no similar criticism of his representation of queer men is possible because they are entirely absent from the *American Century Cycle*. McCraney worked closely with Wilson while a student at the Yale School of Drama, and he is perhaps Wilson's most significant successor, but he departs from and expands his predecessor's work in two important directions.[4] First, McCraney's examination of queer characters struggling to find interlocutors for journeys of self-crafting at once echoes the work of Tennessee Williams while also challenging the comprehensiveness of

Wilson's blues dramaturgy. McCraney refuses to respect any blues taboo on male homosexuality, and does important work in expanding the sphere of blues drama to the identity-crafting performances of queer black men. Secondly, in part because male homoeroticism is such a derided subject, the search for an antiphonal audience must broaden its scope, causing McCraney to push out past the quotidian world into the spiritual realm of West African religious and folk traditions. In Wilson, most references to black life in a time before America stretch only to the Middle Passage. McCraney's blues community expands through time and myth in order to engage the full depth and complexity of the black American experience. For him, the present, the local, and the real are insufficient confines within which to craft a fully actualized self, so he must turn to the spiritual and mystical. His plays are hyperaware that contemporary, realist audiences will not be enough to find the interlocutors his characters and community require, so he strikes out beyond the predominantly realist bounds of Wilson in the hopes of engendering the fullest, most effective becoming.

Both Hall and McCraney employ Wilson's distinctive blues strategy of offering their characters unsentimental empathy. Their characters regularly cause strife or are victims of attacks, all of which contributes directly to the downtrodden condition of their communities. But Hall and McCraney neither condemn nor forgive their antagonists, and they do not offer the plays' victimized characters pity. Instead, they look with understanding on the conditions engendering their characters' situations and offer them an empathy that recognizes the complexity underlying struggle without attempting to assuage that struggle artificially. By doing so, they continue Wilson's examination of black American life as a community of suffering, perseverance, and shared senses of strength and joy in the active search for sustainable identity.

Katori Hall: A Blues Aesthetic of Failure and Empathy

The work of Katori Hall is at once fascinated by the challenge of establishing black female identity and skeptical of convenient outlets for such identity. Hall's drama is about the hollowness of the surface and the daunting task of plunging the depths of social existence in search of complex, sustainable identity. Sandra Adell aptly frames the plight of Hall's women: "Katori Hall delves deep into the lives of her characters and their relationships with each other. What she reveals is bound to make audiences uncomfortable."[5] Audiences may grow uncomfortable because they wish for these beleaguered women to overcome their circumstances, but Hall's plays routinely deny such a result, calling into question the opportunity for female self-actualization within a masculine social framework. For many of Hall's women, identity must be forged in new, uncharted terrain.

Often that journey only comes by way of a failure. Hall's plays regularly feature women who attempt to define themselves as strong and self-sufficient but face reprisal from the social sphere. While recognizing an important trend in African American literature "of celebrating black survival by overcoming racial obstacles," Claudia Tate points out a prominent mode of black literature dominated by female authors whereby "writers give their attention to those who fall in battle, insisting that their fight, though unsuccessful, is valiant and therefore merits artistic attention." Tate argues that black women writers "acknowledge defeat, not for the purpose of reinforcing a sense of defeat or victimization but to ensure that we all learn to recognize what constitutes vulnerability in order to avoid its consequences in the future."[6] Although Hall fits into this tradition which Tate finds in the work of Toni Morrison, Gwendolyn Brooks, Gayle Jones, Ntozake Shange, and others, she does not stop her examination of her characters' failures at the moment of defeat. Instead, she treats failure as a moment of potential productivity, wondering if her black female characters can muster enough strength to move into new paths of self-crafting. In Hall's plays the consequences of racist misogyny are harsh and for the most part unmitigated by the playwright, but she distinctively allows for the process of responding to and moving on from failure.

Her plays, that is, are most interested in the response to failure, the attempt at recovery through a redirection of self-crafting performances. Before the play's opening, Camae in *The Mountaintop* had attempted to craft herself as a nurturing prostitute; Toulou in *Hoodoo Love* tries to make herself into a wife and homemaker; and *Hurt Village*'s Cookie tries to self-craft a defiantly intelligent young woman who can rise above ghetto violence. For various reasons, all three fail, but their playwright does not condemn their stories to tragedy. In these three plays, Hall examines women at various points in their journeys of becoming. Camae spends her entire play in the first stages of a new performance; *Hoodoo Love* is a slow, gradual failure for Toulou before she redirects herself in the epilogue; and *Hurt Village* shows a great deal of concern for the uncertainty surrounding young Cookie's self-crafting project. This sampling of plays reveals how the unsentimental empathy that lies at the heart of Hall's blues dramaturgy consistently refuses easy salvation for her characters, offering instead clear-eyed assessment of the difficulty attendant upon female self-crafting.

Camae in *The Mountaintop,* for instance, must be murdered before she can begin to define herself. Set in Memphis's Lorraine Motel on the eve of Martin Luther King Jr.'s assassination, the play features only King and Camae, a woman King meets as a motel maid before discovering her to be an angel of death personally sent by God to escort him to Heaven. But Camae is by no means a conventional angelic figure; after spending some time with her, King calls her a "cussin', fussin' dranking' angel," characteristics Camae retains from her life as a Memphis prostitute, which ended only one night earlier.[7] Camae also retains depths of self-loathing. "I've hated. Hated myself," she says in a long speech disclosing her life before death as a prostitute: "I thought it was my duty. All that I had to offer this world. What else was a poor black woman, the mule of the world, here for? Last night, in the back of a alley I breathed my last breath. A man clasped his hands like a necklace 'round my throat" (241). Throughout the play, Hall defines Camae largely by her sass, determination, and sex appeal—after she first arrives with coffee for King, a stage direction says, "She sets the tray on the downstage table, bending slightly at the waist. King appreciates his view" (193)—consistently denying any expectations for some conventional "angelic" figure.

By doing so, Hall subverts masculinized notions of female virtue, allowing Camae to carve out space for herself as a reluctant, unsure angel at the very beginning of her process of becoming. Insisting that "*The Mountaintop* is most forceful when it is Camae's play," Soyica Diggs Colbert argues that Camae's centrality in the play helpfully decenters King as a dominant paradigm of the civil rights movement and "draws attention to the essential role of women in the movement and the particular gender violence they suffer."[8] Colbert finds the central conceit of the play to be its insistence that King is but one particularly important runner in the long relay race of civil rights, and that Hall works toward this claim by putting Camae in a place of prominence. She says that Camae's role "calls for a reconsideration of the way we understand the history of a great man."[9] On the one hand, the play does this simply by making King rely in his final hours on two women, Camae and the offstage God whom Hall casts as a woman. But the play takes the additional step of insisting on this angel's sexuality. Colbert argues that

"*The Mountaintop* casts Camae as a sexually exploited and overtly sexual character that ushers King through his final hours in order to reframe him as a man in relationship to women activists from all walks of life."[10] For Colbert, as for Hall, Camae's sexuality and sexual history are constitutive of her angelic identity because they underscore the abused and exploited femininity at the heart of racial oppression, appropriating it as a mode of resistance. Camae is not so much an angel that shows her scars as an angel because of her scars.

By embracing those scars, Camae develops a strong-willed sense of self-crafting. She confesses reluctance to take up the job of escorting King to death as her first angelic duty, but once she commits herself to it there is nothing that a resistant King can do to alter her mission or her persona. Thus, it may seem that Camae shows no interest in social identity crafting because she is acting like the angel that God tells her she is, and making no concessions to the expectations of or responses from her one-man audience. This argument makes her sound like one of O'Neill's identity ideologues—Yank, say, or Ephraim Cabot—and such a claim would not be entirely off base. Camae has little interest in feedback on who she is, proceeding throughout the play more or less undeterred, if often frustrated. For Colbert, this determination stands in for the necessity of history remembering and respecting the invaluable contribution of women to the civil rights movement, a task from which Camae should not be deterred.

But what is perhaps easy to forget about Camae is that in order to become the angel she is during the play, she first had to die brutally. Her death is the completion of her previous project of identity crafting, one whereby she would be a sexual nurturer, allowing others to assuage their pain through the pleasure of sex with her. After describing her calling to prostitution as altruistic, saying that she "[s]acrificed my flesh so that others might feel whole again," she goes on to describe the particular emptiness she recognized in her murderer: "I stared into his big blue eyes, as my breath got ragged and raw, and I saw the hell this old world had put him through. The time he saw his father hang a man. The time he saw his mother raped. I felt so sorry for him. I saw what the world had done to him." But although this recognition may provide some context to the brutality of her murder, it does nothing to stop her John from killing her. In the moments before her death, Camae's altruism dwindles: "I still couldn't forgive. I hated him for stealing my breath" (241). Camae here fails to perform the identity of understanding nurturer while the community simultaneously rejects it;

and so that identity collapses. Before she appears within the space of *The Mountaintop,* that is, Camae has already suffered through a failed journey of self-crafting.

Thus, Camae's actions in the play begin a newly conceived performance of self, one that grows out of the necessity created by a social rejection of her former performance. Camae is not eager—"Believe you me I ain't want this job," she confesses. "First day? Bring over you? The Kang? I ain't wanna do it"—but she takes the job because it is the option God gives her for reinvention (224). She says that when she met God after death, "I was just a' cryin', weepin' at her feet. Beggin' her not to throw me down. All that sinnin'. All that grime on my soul. All that hatred in my heart. But then I looked up and saw that She was smilin' down at me. She opened her mouth, and silence came out. But I heard her loud and clear. 'I got a special task for you and if you complete it, all your sins will be washed away'" (241). Ultimately, God sends Camae back into the land of the living not much changed; she has greater understanding of history and the future, and can grow flowers from carpet with her tears, but in her desires, emotions, and frustrations she remains more human than angelic. Success for Camae is soothing King and convincing him that the long narrative of civil rights has progressed and will continue to progress after his death. To do so she must convince him to accept her as the humanized angel presented to him. She must receive a ratifying response to her newly formed performance of self from her audience.

Camae embodies well the unromantic empathy that Hall offers characters, especially black women downtrodden by an unrelenting society. Camae is an extreme example because her defeat is death and Hall's intercession is supernatural, but the playwright does not outright save and forgive her character. Doing so might be a process of simply resurrecting Camae the prostitute, writing off her mistaken belief that she could nurturer away others' pain, and giving her another shot at establishing a sustainable social identity. But such a course of action would betray the clear-eyed sense of defeat and reappraisal that runs throughout Hall's plays. In Wilson, characters engage constantly in the call-and-response process of gradual identity crafting, slowly and meticulously making strides toward a recognizable and sustainable identity. In Hall, black female characters consistently fail in that process. But failure is not the end of their journey, because their playwright shows more concern for the next step, asking what active steps a character can take to begin redefining herself in the wake of failure. Camae dies, but she has the opportunity to satisfy God as long as she can establish a functional rapport with King. The defeat is irredeemable, and the new direction is by no means guaranteed, but out of failure Camae gains access to a potentially productive new path forward, one that will require diligence and dedication.

Camae's defeat comes before the play's opening, and the audience sees her from the outset of a new journey of becoming, but the situation is strikingly different in *Hoodoo Love,* a long, sad tale of defeat on several fronts for its main character, Toulou. A young woman living alone in Depression-era Memphis after fleeing an abusive home in Mississippi, Toulou is in love with an itinerate bluesman named Ace of Spades, who has no qualms about telling her of the other lovers he visits when traveling. Early in the play Toulou receives an unexpected visit from her brother Jib, who comes to town and spends his time carousing on Beale Street. Toulou's neighbor Candylady— "the Hoodoo madame of Beale Street" (4)—helps her cast a successful spell on Ace in order to secure his love, but on the evening they are to run away together, a drunken Jib rapes his sister as he suggests he used to do when they were younger, and Toulou misses her train with Ace. Act 2 finds Toulou pregnant, the identity of the father uncertain, and the hoodoo spell on Ace quickly broken. Toulou's attempt to poison her brother winds up killing Ace instead, who dies in her arms calling another woman's name. The play ends with an epilogue during which Toulou leaves her infant with Candylady before taking her guitar and catching the train to go play blues clubs as a solo act.

This is a play about blues people and music, but it veers away from Wilson's brand of blues drama and even from *The Mountaintop* because it is almost entirely about victimization rather than agency. It is a play about the failure of hoodoo, feminine agency, resistance, and love. Only once these constructs crumble does Toulou turn to blues, and even then it seems less like a mode of response than a last-ditch effort to salvage a voice for herself. Shortly before the play's conclusion, Toulou, whose nickname was given to her by her father as an elision of "too little," claims she will "Name myself for once," suggesting that this moment, with guitar in hand and departure imminent, is a progression into a world of agency, where she can finally claim her voice as her own (85). The situation was just the opposite for the entirety of the play, and seemingly for all Toulou's life, so the epilogue shows a radical change for this woman. Blues has not to this point been her mode of response to a world of oppression, and only at her lowest does she adopt a blues ethos.

There is however no denying that Toulou finds personal strength in blues during the play's epilogue. In part, this vigor comes from embracing her entrance into a community of suffering. Wall argues that blues in literature can connect "individual pain to the history of Africans in America,"[11] a condition that is similar for Toulou, who has suffered alone throughout the play but turns to blues at its close as a way of inserting herself into a long historical community. Before pledging herself to blues, Toulou is a wanderer with no apparent ethos other than an ill-placed hope that Ace will be true to her. She tries to adopt a hoodoo life, but that fails her. Ultimately, then, this play is a prequel to blues, showing a decision to turn to blues once promises of love and hoodoo prove ineffective. Yet, Hall denies audiences access to the long extent of Toulou's blues journey. *The Mountaintop* asks audiences to bear witness to the process of Camae's reinvention. In *Hoodoo Love* the focus shifts, showing Toulou die a social death, but staging only the initial call of her process of reinvention.

Hoodoo Love thus reinforces the notion that Hall treats her female characters with distinctive unromantic empathy in their troubled and challenging processes of defining the self. Toulou fails, and although her playwright does not invoke some deus ex machina to save her, Hall does give her character a bold epilogue in which she makes an assertive claim over her right to self-sufficiency (echoes of Loomis abound). Still, the conclusion of *Hoodoo Love* comes with a troubling detail. In the closing moments of the play, Toulou sings, "Gotta catch that train / Ride it like a maine," and then repeats that line at the end of the song (*maine* is *man* rendered with a southern draw). Moments later, when Candylady gives Toulou one last opportunity to reconsider her decision, the reborn blueswoman again casts her decision in gendered terms: "They say, 'When a woman heart broke, she break down and cries. When a man heart broke, he take a train and rides.' I'ma catch that train" (85). In Toulou's mind, there is the womanly option of sorrow and wallowing or the manly option of travel and expression, and she will shake off her womanly constraints for the masculine paradigm. This does not sound either like the women's blues of artists like Ma Rainey and Bessie Smith, whose songs are marked consistently by gendered defiance, or like Camae's reclamation of female sexuality.

Yet, in Toulou's limited social sphere, she has no other paradigm of strength and agency than the masculine one. Candylady is the only strong woman in her life, and Toulou's earlier attempt to follow her precipitated greater heartbreak. If she is to find some space for herself where she can take active strides toward defining her identity, she can either create it entirely from scratch, or follow the example of a man like Ace, somebody who broke her heart repeatedly and consistently. Her decision to follow a fraught masculine roadmap emphasizes the degree to which Toulou prioritizes her agency by the end of the play. Ace moved about with a high degree of freedom and autonomy, and although Toulou became a victim of that autonomy, she nonetheless admires its power and aspires to a similar position.

This is not to claim that Toulou's future success is predicated on her abandoning femininity in favor of Ace's brand of masculinity. Rather, like all protégés of blues, Toulou must both repeat and revise, finding room for her own expression within the paradigm shaped by her predecessor. Her determination to become a musician is by no means a guarantor of success. "The blues and black vernacular tradition in general both inspire and silence women," argues Wall, "they authorize articulation of self yet too often demean the individual woman who finds the courage to speak." Toulou is making a perilous choice that could very well engender rejection and humiliation. But, continues Wall, "Black women who draw on this wellspring write through and beyond the blues."[12] For Wall, black women writers like Alice Walker and Toni Morrison at once appropriate and depart from the blues tradition, desiring its liberatory power without gendered subjugation. This is the strategy that Hall's play suggests is necessary for Toulou's future success; following the path of Ace too strictly is dangerous, and so she must worry the line by repeating with a difference. This concept plays out over the course of Wilson's *American Century Cycle* as he repeats characters and dramatic situations with important and telling differences. Blues is repetitive, but its artistry lies in difference. The blues future of Toulou will therefore be determined by the space she carves for herself outside the paradigm of Ace. By the end of the play she knows only the notes Ace taught her, but in the future blues will call on her to improvise and create on her own, to find her unique blues voice.

Hoodoo Love is about a woman who makes herself into a blues performer as the first step in a performative presentation of self. In this way it carves out space for itself as women's blues drama. For Hall will allow her protagonist neither to wallow in her sorrow nor to find some miraculous method of recovery: Toulou must dust herself off and strike out to find some sense of identity in a world beyond her shack. Adam Gussow says that "a central element of the blues ethos—and I can't stress this enough—is never, ever give up. Even when you give up, don't give up. Give up if you got to, but don't get hardened, don't spend one more moment in that given-up state than you have to. Because there is a kind of spiritual unwiseness in that, because what you're doing is you are reifying your present moment," and this helpfully captures Toulou's position.[13] She is at her lowest with perhaps one clear path in front of her—stay in her shack and scrape by with more housecleaning jobs to try to feed herself and her baby—and one less than clear. To stay as a struggling mother would be the path determined for her, and Toulou rejects that proscription. Instead, she chooses a journey of active self-discovery. The play does not concoct an excuse to assuage her of the guilt for abandoning her infant, but Hall shows clearly that her decision is based on a powerful desire for realization of her self. This is the complex blues matrix into which Hall enters her play, neither forgiving nor condemning her characters, but acting as a willing blues audience, bearing witness to the outset of Toulou's blues journey.

In *Hurt Village,* the playwright moves from exploring the effects of identity-crafting projects that fail to one that remains almost entirely in stasis. The scene shifts from Depression-era Memphis to the twenty-first century (an era Hall dubs the "Second Bush Dynasty"), and the musical expression of the character on the search for identity shifts to rap (252). "Thirteen-year-old flat-chested woman-child" Cookie opens and closes the play with rapped odes to the dilapidated housing projects that give the play its title (253).

> This be war
> ungh
> this be war
> ungh

is her refrain to verses like

> They makin' niggahs extinct
> Too many drugs in the jail meat
> Chickenheads ain't comin' home to roost
> And Welfare man stopped sellin' Juicy Juice. (254)

Within the dramatic world of the play, Cookie struggles to garner any respect, but in the theater she enjoys the privileged positions of prologue and epilogue that allow her to speak to the audience and contribute directly to its perception of the play's events. "I mean Hurt Village always been bad," she says in the play's opening moments, "but it done got bad-bad, like you-betta-move-yo-Big Mama-out-these-muthafuckin-projects-fo-she-get-gang-raped-robbed-and-murdered-by-her-gangsta-disciple-crackhead-son bad" (255). She is also able to address the audience in order to talk about herself. She claims, for instance, to have been "the queen of muthafuckin' curb-ball" (255), a game the neighborhood children used to play before violence became too pervasive, and in her rap she insists,

> I'm precocious
> most here know this and they know I spit the illest shit
> I spin ghetto tales that'll make you weep
> My lyrical lullabyes'll knock yo' ass to sleep
> 'Cause I be the street storyteller. (254)

Over the course of the play, she attempts to support this claim to precociousness by trying to show intelligence, wit, attitude, and a powerful independence streak.

But little of this action garners her either respect or the sustainable identity she seeks as an intelligent, keen social critic and fiercely independent young woman. Instead, she gets treated like a child by her family and like a sexualized body by the community. Her calls are not returned with much of what could tenably be called ratifying responses at any point in the play. Nor, for that matter, does the play do much to support her claims to intelligent independence. The hypothesis for her science experiment proves to be wrong, and she completely misunderstands human reproduction: "I know all about it. A boy put his wee-wee in a girl mouth. She swallow his seeds and it go down into her belly and then nine months later she blowed up bigger than a house" (348). Thus, *Hurt Village* introduces Cookie in the position of a wise, assertive chorus figure in the prologue, but then spends much of the play demonstrating how she has little ability to establish her own identity among her social sphere.

The play's epilogue shows that like Camae and Toulou before her, Cookie is going to be in the position of having to return from a defeat and find a new way of approaching the task of defining herself. She reveals in the epilogue that she and Big Mama are moving out of the projects to Raleigh, despite the earlier news that they were rejected from the relocation list. But she looks at her time in Hurt Village with a sentimental nostalgia. "Some say it take a village to raise a chile," she muses. "Some time the child gotsta raise they goddamn self. I believes that. But no matter how the Hurt was, I'ma be a Hurt Village Hustler, for life, for life." This claim presages a future in Raleigh attempting to establish her identity as a hard transplant from Hurt Village, one who may have relocated to the government-assisted suburbs but retains the attitude honed in the projects. The play gives no indication of how that project will go, as the final curtain comes after Cookie says she will keep all her former Hurt Village compatriots "in my rhyme and in my heart and in my mind" before reprising the "This be war" refrain that opened the play (351–52).

The play's bookended structure suggests a lack of growth and development in Cookie. She raps the same refrain about war, but there is nothing indicating an advance in or any evolution of the war; Cookie is right back where she started, trying to define herself through performance in front of the play's audience. The process of defining herself in opposition to the various ways that Hurt Village society wants to brand her is paramount to Cookie, but Hall undercuts those efforts. Cookie getting her first period during the middle of the play becomes an ironic commentary on the character's social existence: although she matures and changes physically, little about her social position shows evidence of change. Cookie's mother, Crank, suggests at one point that Cookie "need to go to school and get her lesson. She don't need to be kicked out, 'cause she gone be somebody" (344), but this expression of belief in her daughter's future comes amid drugged-out efforts to strip Cookie naked so she can beat her with an extension cord. Earlier, drug lord Tony C asks Cookie if she can add and subtract and then inquires lecherously, "You wanna be my lil' friend?" (309). The implication is that if Cookie could be useful to his business operation she could also be useful sexually. Both Crank and Tony C recognize potential fostered by intelligence in Cookie, but neither is prepared to treat her any differently from how Hurt Village treats all young girls. In the space of *Hurt Village*, Cookie is unfulfilled potential.

This sounds like pessimism bordering on fatalism: a young girl wants to make something of herself and escape the projects through education and art, but Hall's play denies her that escape. The play's conclusion sees Cookie moving out of Hurt Village, but that is only because her grandmother fights hard to remain on a government relocation list; it has nothing to do with who Cookie is as a person. Rather than pessimism, though, it would be more accurate to call the play's treatment of Cookie as the sort of tough love that is distinctive of Hall's blues. This playwright does nothing to stop Camae's murder or Toulou's rape and betrayal because her work is primarily interested in the process of recovery from a fall in the hopes of reinvention. Her plays are neither tragedies nor sappy melodramas. Rather, they are attempts at undiluted examination of the struggle of black life, with a particular awareness of the compounded difficulty facing black women. There is no getting around the fact that Cookie's social existence is going to be very arduous, and Hall makes no efforts to reduce the impediments to her character's social becoming.

But the playwright does reveal her distinctive empathy by putting Cookie in the privileged position of addressing the audience, conscripting audience members into her performance of self much more directly than any of the other characters. Since other characters are not prepared to participate in Cookie's evolution into an intelligent woman with a sustainable identity beyond the prescriptions of Hurt Village, the play's audience is asked to take on that role. Cookie is not murdered like Camae nor raped and betrayed like Toulou, but the play suggests that her resistance against the oppressive forces of her society is a constant failure; she does not evolve because she is in the steady stream of a losing battle. The play therefore intimates that in a self-contained society like Hurt Village, hope of defining one's self beyond preordained expectations must be to find another social sphere with which to engage. Hall's empathy shows an understanding of the drastically limited options for Cookie's journey of becoming, and although the play makes no promises of success, it provides the character with an outlet for possible success. Hall's theater is much less about redemption than it is about the arduous beginning of a new project of becoming.

In Camae, Toulou, and Cookie, then, Hall reveals a fascination with black women's arrested attempts at establishing identity and the steps they take in response to the trauma of their social spheres rejecting their performances of selves. Certainly this is not a universal trend for Hall's women; Cookie's mother, Crank, for example, begins *Hurt Village* as a reformed crack addict, but returns to the drug before the play's conclusion. Crank attempts a performance as soberly maternal, but she cannot sustain the identity. Even here, though, Hall's dramaturgical sense of empathy emerges. The play does not forgive or make excuses for Crank's remission, but as she slips back into addiction, Hall gives her character a poetic soliloquy expressing her love, regret, and pained humanity:

> Dear Cookie, I hope you find this letter
> You won't be able to because I can't write it
> I can only spin the memories
> Unwind the facts in my mind
> As this rock makes my thoughts implode
> Onto one another and hide behind
> Prison walls of project cement
> Stone the house we call home
> If you only knew I thought in poetic slants, diatribes
> That my mind held more words
> Than the largest dictionary could ever find
> That often I cannot heave my brain into my mouth
> To impress redress the mask I die behind.
> These are the thoughts of a druggie's
> Coked-out choked-out wired mind
> I can't seem to crack the safe I've hid my heart in
> As I think about how I've never hugged you Cookie
> My Cookie monster. I don't know how to begin
> How to open my arms wide
> Stretch my neck to a caving sky
> Say those words my dictionary hearts
> But my mouth fail to
> "I love you."
> Never heard those words said.

The play will offer no happy ending for Crank, nor will there be any sugar-coating the fact that she has "a druggie's coked-out choked-out wired mind," but in this mystical moment—the stage direction preceding the poem says that as Crank begins to smoke "*she rises high in the air as if she's levitating*"— Hall gives her audience a glimpse behind the shroud of addiction, as if to say that this lyrical, Shakespeare-alluding, love-starved, vulnerable, and worrisome woman is the complex human that the Hurt Village social sphere will never be able to access beyond the drug addict on the surface (342–43). With Camae, Toulou, and Cookie, Hall's investigation of struggling black female subjectivity goes further because each of these characters is in a position to begin a new project of becoming; they have the opportunity to reveal their complex humanity from behind socially imposed shrouds.

As Toulou pronounces, an old blues adage claims that when a woman gets the blues she breaks down and cries, which suggests that women's blues is marked mostly by sorrowful, powerless weeping. This makes for a pithy axiom, but it is hardly true, not least because blues' fundamental performativity means that a woman with the blues is performing rather than wallowing. More importantly, though, these performances are not full of self-pitying sorrow, but an often-defiant search for selfhood in the face of woe. As Bessie Smith, Zora Neal Hurston, and others demonstrate, blues women are interested in the process of working through trauma. Hall adds her work to this collective of women's blues by crafting female characters who neither hang their heads and cry nor rise up in some sort of conquering triumph. Most distinctive about women's blues is its acknowledgment of oppressive gender strictures, and Hall does nothing to spare her women such injustice. But she does set them to action responding to oppression in the uncertain hope of locating sustainable identity in its wake. Certainly they may face conditions that make them cry, but Hall's blues will not allow them to hang their heads and give up.

Thus Hall takes Wilson's blues dramaturgy into new terrain by examining how the project of performing one's self before an audience in the uncertain hope of receiving a ratifying response is far more daunting for women than it is for the men at the center of Wilson's plays. To be sure, Wilson's women struggle against odds similar to those in Hall's plays, but his female characters are immersed in their social performances, calling and responding as they move through the challenging worlds of their plays. Hall's most complex women are those who fail, underscoring the playwright's unromantic gaze. A number of Wilson's women—Mattie Campbell, Rose Maxson, Risa, Mame Wilks among them—face resistance from their patriarchal social spheres in their attempts to establish a self, but each continues the performance, adjusting based on trials and responses and perhaps employing different tactics, but nonetheless soldiering forward. Hall's women face radical defeat and must begin a new performance, because Hall's work is not interested in preserving the defeated identities of her women. Her plays face the harsh reality of those defeats in an attempt to make the next step in the journey more fortified. Hall repeats and revises Wilson's dramaturgy: in her work, black personhood relies on a shared social commitment, but garnering a useful and effective response from the social sphere is much more precarious. Hall's blues are deftly attuned to an aesthetics of failure.

Tarell Alvin McCraney: Expanding Horizons of Queerness

The difficulty of community incorporating queerness is a prominent theme in the work of Tarell Alvin McCraney. The playwright sets *Choir Boy* (2012), for example, at the fictional Charles R. Drew Prep School for Boys, examining how Pharus, the virtuoso leader of the school's renowned choir, balances his position in the community while also being the target of homophobia. Late in the play, after getting punched because of a classmate's sexual anxiety, Pharus explains that throughout his young life he felt like an outsider

> Until I got to Drew.
> Everybody didn't like me but
> I had . . . I had space to let me be. That was what was
> Good about being here.[14]

One of the play's last images shows Pharus being comforted by his friend and roommate AJ, but his black eye from the punch precludes him from performing at graduation. The community that allowed him to be himself for four years rejects him once the open secret of his sexuality becomes manifest. There are far fewer secrets in *Wig Out!* (2008), which focuses on the predominantly queer community of a drag house, a makeshift family of drag queens that compete at balls with other houses for glory. In his author's note to the script, McCraney argues that drag houses serve as alternative communities for "people who are transgender gay and 'other'" and are harshly rejected from society: "During the day, one might get stared at, called a name on the street corner or, worse, accosted by someone outside the circle, but for that night at the ball one could be literally the *queen of it all*. The next day, it's back to being 'queer.'"[15] Over the course of the play there is tension among members of the house, and one gay man not part of the drag community is ultimately rejected, but the social conditions of the house are such that the complex identities of drag queens—which one character calls "two souls in one"—are supported and sustained by members of the closed community.[16] The house is certainly not some compassionate utopia, but the social structures are in place there for felicitously antiphonal performances that recognize the unique identity of drag queen.

Throughout his work, McCraney examines what sort of social and community conditions are necessary for the performance of black male queerness. In *Choir Boy* and *Wig Out!* black men perform their queerness before a limited social sphere in the uncertain hope of receiving responses that ratify and accept those identities; and they have mixed results. In Wilson, this subject is a gap whose depths McCraney anxiously probes in his own plays. In McCraney's work, queerness is at once a personal and a communal challenge, one that adds dimension to and places stress on the black community that structures Wilson's *Cycle*.

This stress is particularly pronounced in McCraney's most complex community, the fictional bayou town of San Pere, Louisiana, where he sets *The Brother/Sister Plays* trilogy. Young black people with names like Shango, Oya, Elegba, Shun, Ogun, and Oshoosi populate San Pere, a contemporary community beset by many of the same oppressive forces apparent in Wilson and Hall. McCraney's characters are poor, contentious, and downtrodden, and as a result the sense of community in the plays is constantly strained. McCraney's characters recall Wilson in their construction, habits, prejudices, and even occasionally directly in their language: "How come you never like me," Elegba asks Ogun in *The Brothers Size*, almost directly quoting Cory Maxson's famous question from *Fences:* "How come you ain't never liked me?"[17] Elegba's use of the term "bone people" when he talks about a dream of walking on the bottom of the ocean points directly to both *Joe Turner's Come and Gone* and *Gem of the Ocean*.[18] When in *Head of Passes*, the central family's matriarch, Shelah, tells the story of her husband long ago bringing her a child he had with another woman to raise, clear echoes sound of Troy's same affront to Rose in *Fences*. Wilson is a particularly bright star by which McCraney steers his dramaturgical ship through an examination of black community.

But the plays reveal how McCraney's strategy of actively operating in the wake of Wilson allows him to guide his examination of black life into new terrain. The blues motif of repetition with revision emerges again as McCraney carves out space for himself in the gaps of Wilson's tradition. Hall works similarly by homing in on black women, but McCraney's introduction of queer black men pushes further afield of Wilson, because the *American Century Cycle* excludes these characters entirely. Homoeroticism shows up briefly in *Ma Rainey's Black Bottom*, as the title character keeps among her entourage a young female lover whom Toledo warns Levee against pursuing because "don't you know that's Ma's gal?" but it is an element of the play ancillary to its primary themes.[19] Nowhere in Wilson is the potential of male homosexuality even broached. Indeed, as if to instantiate heteronormative masculinity, nearly every man in the *Cycle* has at least a few lines expressing some sort of romantic or sexual desire for women.

Like *Choir Boy* and *Wig Out!*, *The Brother/Sister Plays* are interested in the social construction of black male queer homosexual identity, but they are by no means some sort of utopian safe space where same-sex desire can flourish unencumbered. Rather, San Pere proves deeply conservative in its heteronormative expectations, as characters in the trilogy do their best to shun and ostracize queer characters without much overt engagement. Consistently, McCraney's queer male characters face the same sort of predicament that besets many of Tennessee Williams's men: they lack a willingly antiphonal community who will receive their calls of identity and respond in good faith. In Williams, the social sphere usually offers only regulatory responses in the apparent hope of restricting sexual identity to accepted social standards, but in *The Brother/Sister Plays,* characters attempt not to engage, as if by ignoring calls of queer identity its performances will fail and dissipate. McCraney paints a picture of a community actively attempting to cut off and discard one of its parts.

The examination of queer identity in the trilogy finds root in the character Elegba during the trilogy's opening play, *In the Red and Brown Water;* becomes more pronounced in an older version of the same character in *The Brothers Size;* and passes to Elegba's son, the title character in the trilogy's final play, *Marcus: Or the Secret of Sweet*. *In the Red and Brown Water* relegates "Lil Legba" mostly to the periphery of the play, stealing candy and slipping in and out of shadows, only revealing his homosexual proclivities privately to a close friend late in the play (having already gone so far as to father a child in order to hide them). Adult Elegba in *The Brothers Size* underhandedly pursues Oshoosi in an attempt to continue the sexual relationship the men shared in prison. After Elegba's death between the trilogy's final two plays, *Marcus: Or the Secret of the Sweet* follows his son's confused search for identity, uncomfortable with his own sexual desires and desperate to learn if the rumors of his father's homosexuality are true.

Throughout the first two plays, homosexuality simmers below the surface, threatening to emerge and disrupt social order as it does in *Marcus,* where characters do their best to suppress Marcus's quest for clarification of his past and understanding of his present. The first reaction to Elegba in the trilogy is Mama Moja's aside after he enters and calls her name; exasperated before their interaction even begins, she says, "Not today Lord. . . ."[20] Shortly thereafter, once Elegba begs Moja to allow him to tell her about a dream he's had, Moja says, in one of McCraney's distinctive voiced stage directions, "Moja sighs. Giving into the lil fucker . . . / What your dreams say

Lil Legba?" (23). Immediately, the play marks Elegba as a bothersome presence in his social sphere, one other characters begrudgingly accept as part of the community but would rather avoid if possible. Later, when he comes weeping to Moja's daughter Oya after Moja has died, Oya's first reaction is "Why is he so loud?" and moments later, after conversing briefly with and trying to console him, she announces herself as "Not wanting to deal." (41–42). Lil Legba is at once within and without this community.

He is therefore treated as queer—outside the bounds of regulatory society—and at least partially shunned well before he reveals his sexuality late in the play. On the surface, it seems like others' avoidance of him results from Elegba's aggravating personality, and certainly this is partially true, but McCraney signals his sexuality from the beginning by planting a seed that will slowly germinate over the course of the trilogy. Before Elegba asks Moja to read his dream, he says, "I come to beg some candy or some money to get some," and when she denies him he claims, "I know it's bad for me, I know it but Mama Moja / I have to have it, I need it in my life" (20). Later in the play his need for sweetness emerges again when he gets himself into trouble by stealing candy. Over the course of *Marcus: Or the Secret of Sweet* McCraney reveals that *sweet* is bayou code for homosexual. In that play, a woman named Shun angrily pulls her daughter Shaunta Iyun out of Marcus's company, calling him "sweet Marcus" and "Candy Marcus" who is "just / Like his dead damn daddy, Legba." Moments later Shaunta Iyun asks Marcus about his sexuality directly: "Are you sweet, Marcus Eshu?" (254–56). Elegba's constant desire for candy in the trilogy's first play therefore signals his queer identity. Thus, from the very beginning of the trilogy, McCraney locates queerness in subtext, below layers of metaphor, code, and indirection, signaling a social world resistant to overt queer desire.

Since Elegba does not have a willingly antiphonal audience for his sexual identity, his call of that identity is cloaked in layers of misdirection, imagery, and ultimately spiritual mythology. In the trilogy's first two plays he is constantly sneaking, lurking, appearing unannounced, and existing among shadows; this legacy continues in *Marcus*, where no truth of Elegba's identity emerges outright. Elegba and his sexuality are peripheral presences in *The Brother/Sister Plays*, placing his identity in direct conversation with the character's namesake, the potent Yoruba trickster deity who is the guardian of the crossroads and who slips furtively between the realms of gods and humans. In Yoruba cosmology, Elegba is an orisha (variously called Eshu, Elegua, Legba), one of a vast pantheon of divinities with different worldly associations.[21] Yoruba orisha have dominion over elements, features of the natural world, vocations, and customs. Elegba, Oya, Shango, Ogun, Oshoosi, among other characters in McCraney's trilogy, take their names and characteristics from Yoruba orisha. According to J. Omosade Awolalu, "The Yoruba attach great importance to names. Nearly every name given by the Yoruba depicts a significant character as well as the circumstance of the birth of the bearer of that name."[22] Awolalu gives examples of names that signal children having been long desired by their parents, or children that were in the womb when their fathers died. Benjamin C. Ray adds that "on the psychological level, the orisha also serve as images of the self, integrating and completing unrealized dimensions of the personality."[23] McCraney incorporates this notion of names signaling important characteristics by linking his characters to the nature of their orisha namesakes. Orisha Oya is associated with wind, and McCraney's character is a track star who runs like the wind; orisha Ogun has domain over iron, tools, and vehicles, which helps emphasize the craftsman in McCraney's auto mechanic character.[24] As several critics point out, McCraney does not simply impose orisha traits on his characters; instead, he refracts his stories through the lens of Yoruba myth in order to broaden the context of his characters' struggles. The association of McCraney's queer character with the orisha Elegba speaks loudest in announcing the character's social conditions.

In Yoruba stories, Elegba has a variety of duties, but his most distinctive characteristic is his complicated inclination toward both benevolence and malevolence. Orisha, whom Wole Soyinka calls "profoundly humanist," interact with humans in ways similar to Christian patron saints (in whose guise many diasporic Africans were able to continue worshipping their Yoruba deities); they may not necessarily respond to all invocations, but when they do they are there to help.[25] Elegba is an exception. The most unpredictable and humanlike orisha, he is neither wholly generous nor wholly malicious, and so it is a challenge for humans interacting with this orisha to determine if following him in any particular instance will lead to profit or trouble. This is a difficult concept for a New World Christian mind to accept. As Jon Michael Spencer demonstrates, what he calls the trickster orisha's "synchronic duplicity," his nature as "both malevolent and benevolent, disruptive and reconciliatory, profane and sacred," has been "from the Victorian or Eurocentric perspective, interpreted as demonic rather than holistic. These qualities have been perceived as causing anarchy rather than as functioning to open up social and psychological boundaries, to enlarge the scope of the human and to turn repressive dead-ends into liberative crossroads." Spencer argues that Elegba's "synchronous duplicity was bifurcated by Christian dualism" leaving the character who is associated in any way with malevolence to develop into a devil figure.[26]

In similar ways, the community of *The Brother/Sister Plays* struggles in the face of Elegba's complicated nature: not comfortable accepting him into their community entirely lest he usher in danger, they are constantly tempted by the simpler answer of deeming him evil and rejecting him. Keenly self-aware, McCraney's character embraces his trickster identity, allowing him to thrive in the liminal space between the community and its outskirts, as his orisha namesake thrives at the crossroads between the realm of gods and humans. To various degrees, each of the other major characters in the trilogy seeks connection to, acceptance within, and development among the bayou community, but Elegba is content on the periphery. *In the Red and Brown Water*, for example, finds him only rarely out of the shadows, and in *The Brothers Size* he shows up with the express purpose of luring Oshoosi back out of the community. If a consistent ethic of self-crafting is a desire for community and audience, then Elegba complicates this, just as his orisha namesake complicates notions of divine benevolence.

Elegba's characteristics underscore the trilogy's critique of the challenges attendant upon queer identity crafting. San Pere does not constitute a supportive antiphonal community to which Elegba might perform his sexual identity, and so he must cultivate himself as an outsider. Even when he intimates his sexuality to his trusted friend Oya in *In the Red and Brown Water*, he does so by performing intimacy with a man in front of her rather than through words:

Egungun: Eh my man Legba!
Elegba: They pull close.
Egungun: Too close to be just friends.
Elegba and Egungun: Just friends.
Oya: Oya sees it how could she not. (112)

Oya recognizes what Elegba is communicating, something he makes more clear by inviting her to join the two of them in a threesome, but she is reticent to engage Elegba's queerness.[27] "You . . . you got any kids?" she asks Egungun, implying a question about his sexuality, and after his negative response she announces, "Oya moves to . . ." trying to extricate herself from the situation. Her retreat is denied, but shortly thereafter, once Elegba becomes more specific about his desires, she tries again: "Oya walking back./Turns" (113). Here the tension is broken by the entrance of Aunt Elegua, but soon Oya proves briefly—but only briefly—ready to engage Elegba's performance of queerness:

> Oya: You a gray boy?
> Elegba: I got a son.
> Oya: Gray boys have sons.
> Elegba: I came to tell you . . .
> Oya: Don't . . .
>   I don't feel. . . . (117)

The news Elegba has come to tell is about Shango's return to the bayou rather than a revelation of his sexuality, but that only becomes apparent after Oya attempts to shut down what she believes will be an assertion of queer identity, one that will call upon her as audience to respond. She attempts to terminate the performance before she is implicated.

Oya demonstrates the community's resistance to Elegba's performance of identity; she knows what she sees, but tries her hardest to avoid engaging it. Elegba fades into a choral role for the short remainder of *In the Red and Brown Water*, and by the time the story reaches *The Brothers Size* he is a convicted criminal and master manipulator. He will be dead before the opening of the trilogy's final play, where he has faded to only a memory that the community would rather forget. "Some things are better buried" is the response Marcus gets about his father's sexuality from his mother, Oba, after she tries desperately to avoid his interrogation: "Some things left better/Unsaid. Ain't nothing sweet about a soft son" (263).[28] The playwright's enjambment here is powerful, showing how Oba would much rather just let the line of dialogue dissipate before curtly dismissing the prospect of voicing the sexuality of Marcus's family history and thereby admitting queerness into the linguistic social sphere. Like Oya does with Elegba years earlier, Oba's strategy with Marcus is to disengage and avoid the topic at all costs.

Elegba's interaction with Oya is just one of several failed opportunities to develop a functional antiphonal community, highlighting the sort of social existence that engenders his slip to the periphery. As both Colbert and Kevin J. Wetmore point out, McCraney at once invokes and disrupts the Yoruba image of Elegba by splitting his divine roles between two characters. *Elegua* is another name for this orisha and is the name that McCraney gives to an older woman in the community. "Whereas Elegba primarily represents the trickster aspect of Eshu," says Wetmore, "Aunt Elegua represents the messenger, the divine opener, the one who bridges the worlds of the human and the divine."[29] The orisha antecedent to McCraney's two characters is multifarious and complex, and so the playwright signifies on the tradition by dispersing its functions between two characters, allowing him to accentuate certain characteristics in each. McCraney's Elegba does not need to be the messenger or psychopomp because Aunt Elegua fills those roles; and so Elegba can simply be the trickster with a voracious sexual appetite. This is important because Elegba needs all the cunningness he can get: community resistance to his queer sexuality necessitates skirting social expectations through tricks. McCraney's concentration of queerness and trickery in this character underscores how onerous a development of queer identity is in this social sphere. Without a willingly antiphonal audience, Elegba must signify on social expectations.

Similarly, stressing the profound difficulty his characters like Elegba face in performing the self before an audience, McCraney signifies on dramatic realism. *The Brother/Sister Plays* trilogy is spiritual in subject and ritualistic in dramaturgy. The plays actively destabilize the walls between the real and the mystical. Only in rare cases must Wilson's characters escape the quotidian for the mystical in order to facilitate their journeys of becoming; McCraney's characters have little hope but to embrace the mystical constantly. Colbert argues that "in McCraney's plays ritual allows the characters to craft liberatory dreams."[30] Liberation in this case would not necessarily be escape from the bayou but full self-actualization, something the plays suggest cannot come simply within the bounds of the earthly. Ritual enters *In the Red and Brown Water,* for example, from a variety of avenues, one of which is song or, more frequently, humming. This ritualistic duty falls most often to Elegba, who punctuates significant action with an underscore of hums, or comments on Oya's suffering with a refrain he sings three times over the course of the play:

> Come down peace
> Come down night
> Cover over Oya girl
> Make her world all right. (66)[31]

Colbert also insists that "moments of ritualized rupture in the play," like these songs from Elegba or other nonrealist spiritual elements like Oya floating, "fill black freedom practices with ancient and yet unborn power."[32] This refrain sounds very much like a liberatory dream that Elegba is crafting for Oya—a world free of her desire for Shango and her shame of infertility where she can understand herself as a person disentangled from those scars would certainly be liberatory for her—and because it is coming from Elegba, whose name suggests he is to a certain degree a conduit to the spiritual world, the song invokes an ancient power. And so Colbert is insightful in suggesting that moments like this throughout the trilogy incite greater communion between the real world of the theater and the spiritual world of Yoruba cosmology. Wetmore argues something similar, suggesting that McCraney's dramaturgy allows him to "mythologize the lives of rural African Americans and link them to a much larger global culture."[33] McCraney's invocation of the orisha and their stories, as well as his ritualistic dramaturgy, put his plays and his characters in dialogue with a community far vaster than that defined by the plays' dramatis personae or theatrical audience.

From this technique emerges a critique of realist social structures that fail to support individual projects of performative becoming. Elegba retreats to the shadows; Oya's hopelessness provokes self-mutilation; Oshoosi's restlessness makes him susceptible to manipulation; Marcus can find nobody willing to engage his search for understanding. The Yoruba overlay in these plays suggests that the quotidian world is insufficient for sustainable identity and that any search for an empathetic antiphonal audience must include the ancient, eternal spiritual realm. "If one of the roles of the orisha is to make community," argues Wetmore, "McCraney's plays expand the idea of community from small American town to the African diaspora and indeed the entire cosmos."[34] As Wetmore suggests, the invocation of a deity like Ogun in southern Louisiana points as much to Western Africa as it does to the cosmos, suggesting that these characters are in dialogue with their genealogical ancestors and their spiritual forebears. Doing so emphasizes the problematic limitations of closed, physical, realist community. Oya does not satisfy the procreative demands of her society, and the combination of social scorn and her self-loathing from having internalized those demands leave her lost and alone. Her only solace is to commune with the wind, the domain of her namesake orisha. Elegba's sexuality is beyond the pale of his bayou community, and so in order to embody his identity, he must follow the sly example of his patron orisha. Marcus's task is therefore the most arduous. Soyinka says that "orisa is community. Community is the basic unit, the common denominator and definition of humanity—this is the lesson of the orisa."[35] But Marcus has no clearly identified patron orisha to guide him into community; shunned by his community and lacking a clear association with an orisha, he must forge his own path.

McCraney's work is therefore critical of the limits for communal engagement in queer identity crafting. Shaunta Iyun in *Marcus* claims that the prejudice, which she calls "BlackMoPhobia," that hinders Marcus's social development has been "[p]assed down since slavery," when owners violently discouraged homosexuality in fear of diminishing returns on their investment in human chattel (267). She insists that the slave owners' self-serving bigotry infused itself into black life through the generations, leaving contemporary black culture ingrained with heteronormativity. McCraney gives no indication of supporting this etiology, but he does create closed societies resistant and hostile to queer identity, leaving his queer characters with little hope of self-actualization unless they broaden the audience of their performance. The greatest import of McCraney's invocation of Yoruba cosmology emerges here. If contemporary realist culture proves insufficient for identity crafting, then he will invoke the cosmic world of spirits and deities to contribute more effectively to this process. "What McCraney does," says Wetmore, "is link the African-American experience into an archetypal and divine past from the Motherland and then use the orisha to create room in black masculinity for black homosexuality."[36] Ultimately, the orisha appear in *The Brother/Sister Plays* through the force of necessity. The human characters have very little interest in engaging notions of queerness or female infertility, so if the playwright wants to work through the nature and effects of those identities he must expand the social sphere of the plays. He must make these characters part of something larger than their bayou home.

The invocation of the orisha proves to be one method of doing so, but another important tactic is exploring the world of dreams. Prophetic dreams are a consistent motif in the trilogy, but it is only characters associated with queerness who dream. This includes Elegba and Marcus, but also Oshoosi, the object of Elegba's amorous pursuits after developing a physical relationship in prison, and Ogun, who kisses Marcus during a moment of mutual grief. These dreams broaden the plays' social and spiritual dimensions. Young Elegba dreams about Oya's infertility, for example, well before her affliction becomes apparent. In the first part of his dream, Elegba walks along the floor of the ocean, where, like Citizen Barlow and Herald Loomis, he meets "bone people" mired in the Middle Passage. Then the dreaming

Elegba ascends to the muddy surface, where he sees Oya naked, bleeding from her vagina but not in pain as she floats on top of the water. The young boy does not understand that the dream reveals Oya's infertility, and he wakes up having ejaculated, responding only to his dream's sexuality. Late in the trilogy, Marcus tells Ogun of a dream that confirms Oshoosi's death. These two dreams bookend the trilogy, and in between them dreams of queer characters reveal a variety of other important matters. Aunt Elegua tells Marcus about a legend that "[s]ay sweet boys got a secret of sight," but Marcus later refines the concept while soliloquizing, "more like the secret of the sweet" (294, 299). As Marcus here recognizes, queerness in this trilogy grants characters unique insight (not to say understanding) into themselves, their communities, their histories, and their spiritual realm. It is nonetheless telling that McCraney's dreamers constantly seek out others to help them interpret dreams. Their playwright grants them unique insight, but the characters are still reliant on the social sphere in order to make sense of who they are and what they can do. Even with the greater context of the dream world, these characters must turn to the social sphere for guidance.

McCraney's use of dreams works in concert with his voiced stage directions, the musical and mystical interludes, and the overarching invocation of Yoruba cosmology to create what Colbert calls "a twenty-first-century ritual theater." Colbert argues that "the choric breaks and Elegba's dreamy prophetic monologues" in *In the Red and Brown Water* "integrate the metaphysical into the quotidian and the future into the present."[37] This is an important insight that need not stop at one character in the trilogy's opening play. In fact, the many distinctive features of McCraney's dramaturgy, including the naturalistic setting, the frequent and often ribald humor, and the overt intertextuality, contribute to his construction of a dynamic ritual theater. The mingling of metaphysical and quotidian, future and present (as well as past and some sort of eternal time-out-of-time not unlike Soyinka's concept of "the fourth stage"), suggests that these characters are at once members of their closed bayou community and also of a much more expansive community that extends across dreams, history, myth, and spirituality.[38] McCraney's plays foment a performative realm populated by the eternal spiritual as much as it is by the temporal material. A ritualistic dramaturgy becomes necessary in order to create and sustain such a world, one the plays suggests is imperative for the characters to have any hope of establishing some sense of identity.

McCraney's work therefore shows much influence from Wilson, but out of necessity, he revises Wilson's predominantly naturalistic world. Wilson's is not a world concerned with black male queerness; his men are beset by many social forces and personal demons, but struggles with sexual identity are not among them. Thus, McCraney retains and reexamines afresh Wilson's concerns for black masculinity, social identity, and community, insisting that queerness is not a force that can be ignored. But McCraney does not simply add queer characters to a world that looks like Wilson's. Instead, he emphatically asserts that the spirituality Wilson flirts with in scenes like the City of Bones ritual must be more central in black life in order to facilitate identity crafting more effectively. This is similarly true in *Wig Out!, Choir Boy,* and *Head of Passes,* each of which forces the limitations of naturalistic theater to expand. *Wig Out!* frequently breaks the fourth wall in order to make clear that its audience is a very real part of the drag queens' performances of identity; *Choir Boy* features regular musical interludes that invoke the force of ritual; and nearly the entire second half of *Head of Passes* finds Shelah raging at an offstage God. McCraney's is a theater deeply concerned with its characters' fledgling attempts at discovering and constructing the self, but they struggle in these projects because any realist dramatic world of their plays proves insufficient to develop an antiphonal community for performances of self. For his queer characters especially, McCraney insists that the performative world must expand beyond restrictive realist bounds in order to reconcile their complexity.

The Brother/Sister Plays follow Wilson in treating identity as social and performative, but they drastically expand the participants in the performance of identity. Not only are characters performing the self, but in many cases they are also performing some sort of dialogue with an orisha, and because of the terms through which McCraney defines the dramatic space of the plays, all characters are constantly performing a long genealogical lineage. Wetmore insists that "the plays propose a complex and fluid identity, therefore, in terms of African diasporan identity, in terms of sexual orientation, and in terms of dramaturgy. . . . McCraney mythologizes experience but also links African-American history with African culture."[39] This is a move that Wilson, who insisted repeatedly that his history began when the first African slaves set foot on American soil, resisted. Citizen and Loomis make brief contact with the Middle Passage, but black history stretching back into Africa is not a pronounced presence in Wilson's work. As Wetmore recognizes, Africa for McCraney is perpetually present. Recognizing the limitations of identity crafting within the everyday world beyond restrictive social paradigms, McCraney opens his characters' performative space by summoning the spiritual and the past.

McCraney also follows Wilson in implicating the audience of his theater in his characters' performances of identity, but again he repeats and revises, making his turn to the audience more overt, direct, and therefore more imperative than his predecessor. Wilson's blues dramaturgy is always performative and communal, but nowhere in the *American Century Cycle* do characters address the audience like the playwright's own character in *How I Learned What I Learned,* or Tom in *The Glass Menagerie,* or Cookie in *Hurt Village.* Wilson implicates his audience in the performance through unique dramaturgical strategies rather than direct address. McCraney demands audience engagement through his spoken stage directions. Sometimes the spoken stage directions announce a character's entrance or exit: "Shango: Enter Shango dressed in his Army Fatigues" (103); sometimes they contextualize a character's mood: "Marcus: Marcus apologetic" (269); sometimes they narrate action:

> Elegba: Elegba offers his hand to Oshoosi
> Oshoosi: Oshoosi takes it, how could he not. (159)

In these and many other examples throughout the trilogy, McCraney's characters break their plays' dramatic flow in order to communicate important context directly to the audience. Sometimes such scene directions provide helpful context—like when Ogun announces that his calls to Oshoosi are coming "From outside" (145), which is clear neither in the script nor on a mostly bare stage—but sometimes they are more superfluous: costume design could allow a theatrical audience to see Shango entering in fatigues clearly enough, and readers could easily be supplied with a parenthetical, unvoiced stage direction. By speaking these stage directions, characters specifically request audiences to embrace all layers of the play's crafted world. That the practice happens so frequently, regardless of dramatic necessity, demonstrates how instrumental it is to the drama of these plays. It shows, ultimately, that speaking to the audience in order to invoke their agency in crafting the dramatic world of the play is fundamental to the operation of the trilogy. These characters and their world self-consciously need an audience for full actualization.

By conscripting the audience into their identity-crafting community, *The Brother/Sister Plays* underscore the playwright's critique of social space for queer identity crafting. For it is in the always ephemeral domain of theater that McCraney creates a space for the physical audience to join the ritual performance of his plays. This space is functional, but neither lasting nor concrete. Set in a fictional town at a time McCraney calls "Distant Present" (10), the plays define a space and time for themselves that are recognizable but that nonetheless resist being wholly knowable. It is as though this particular bayou town is just out of arm's reach, defined only by the false potential of accessibility. The trilogy suggests that only in a mystical space of potentiality like this, one that is wholly created and sustained through ritual performance, can black male queer identity find room to examine and performatively construct the self. In response to the community's resistance to the identity crafting of Elegba and Marcus, the plays call on the orisha, social and aesthetic black history, and especially the audience to witness for these characters, contributing to the constitution of a performative space for their becoming by taking up the role of a willingly antiphonal audience. Where realist drama reaches a limit, McCraney moves to the spiritual and the self-consciously performative.

Early blues artists turned to relatively safe spaces defined by juke joints and rent parties in order to perform their contested humanity in front of willingly antiphonal audiences, and Wilson does important work deploying these performative conditions for American theater. McCraney follows the lead of his predecessor by activating theater in the struggle for sustainable black identity, but finds that Wilson's blues dramaturgy is less capacious than it may seem in supporting a project of black queer masculine identity crafting. Thus McCraney's work forces blues, like realist drama, to expand. McCraney invests himself throughout his plays in exploring what tenable conditions for performative queer community might be. Although he does not distinguish the identity of the sneering, potentially violent oppressors "outside the circle" he references in his author's note to *Wig Out!*, the clear implication is that they are members of so-called mainstream society who are so deeply committed to heteronormativity that they cannot brook any transgression of its rigid protocols by queer bodies. In turning to a performative space defined largely in opposition to such people and oppression, the drag community of *Wig Out!* emulates the southern blues community under Jim Crow, and in examining this community in drama, the playwright steers Wilson's blues dramaturgy into functional uncharted terrain.

McCraney's characters are blues people, but they are performers uncertain of who defines their audience. Yoruba myth suggests that humans select their guardian orisha before birth, but forget that selection upon entering the human world; unless humans can determine their patron orisha through successful Ifá divination, they spend their lives ignorant of their closest spiritual relationship.[40] In giving his characters orisha names and characteristics, McCraney reduces that gap, but does not close it. His characters do not demonstrate any awareness that they have a special association with a particular orisha or with the long history of that deity's cultic worship. The work to help characters' Ifá is left to the theatrical audience, and it is in this regard that McCraney deploys a revised blues dramaturgy most clearly and powerfully. For his characters are much more lost than Wilson's, and require much more active participation from their theatrical audience. Wilson's characters have a sense of who they are and who they would like to be, and to varying degrees they realize that they need a ratifying response from a social sphere in order to achieve that identity. McCraney's characters wander more than they search. And so their creator initiates rites of performance, ushering to their aid a complex audience that transgresses bounds of narrative, temporality, theatricality, and naturalism. McCraney's dramaturgy demonstrates that blues is an effective method of addressing the important community concerns while also leaving open the question of precisely how that can or should happen. This is a blues dramaturgy revised into contemplative uncertainty, reliant on community not simply for participation in its performance but much more so for contribution to its dynamics. McCraney's work suggests that blues must adapt to fit the needs of an evolving contemporary black community while retaining its fundamental reliance on a performative social sphere as a path toward clarity.

Evolving the Scope of Blues Dramaturgy

Hall and McCraney thus prove fruitful case studies in examining how Wilson's influence guides contemporary black theater while also giving way to new, innovative techniques and avenues. Certainly other contemporary playwrights have embraced and deployed the influence of Wilson, but Hall and McCraney do so in ways that encourage examination of the lasting importance and necessary evolution of Wilson's blues dramaturgy. By turning their attention to women and queers, Hall and McCraney extend the scope of Wilson's project in a way that can more capaciously serve the contemporary project of black identity crafting, demonstrating the evolving dynamics of a blues dramaturgy. At its core, this is still a performative process that invokes an antiphonal community in the hopes of productive and sustainable identity crafting. But in the *American Century Cycle*, the practice does not serve well the needs of women or queers, two groups often particularly in need of asserting their human identity against callous oppression.

But as blues music was able to adapt from the rural Mississippi plantation to the urban Chicago nightclub in order to respond to expressive needs of an evolving population, so too is a blues dramaturgy capable of adapting to the needs of a broader population. Adaptation demands change, and as Hall shows that there must be room for an aesthetic of failure and McCraney demonstrates the need for a more broadly defined antiphonal audience, the blues dramaturgy pioneered by Wilson expands and evolves. Consistently, however, black dramatists follow the lead of Wilson by cultivating a socially responsive theater, one that evokes communal participation in order to advance the humanity of characters, actors, playwrights, and community members. Wilson suggested that his genealogy as a socially aware artist consisted of mingling between giants of Western drama and racial activism, and he claimed that that legacy placed him on "the ground of the affirmation of the value of one's being, an affirmation of his worth in the face of the society's urgent and sometimes profound denial."[41] He dedicated his career to countering such denial for black Americans, but Hall and McCraney demonstrate how theater can be at the ready to respond to new and mounting affronts to humanity and dignity. As the twenty-first century moves forward, Wilson's blues dramaturgy therefore proves a valuable tool for the continuing project of turning to theater as a collaborative means of working productively against the grain of contested humanity.

Notes

Introduction

1. The 1996 *Jitney* is a revision of 1982's *Jitney!*, which also focused on father-son tension, so it would be equally legitimate to argue that *Fences* reinvestigates the theme that emerges first in *Jitney!*
2. Portions of this discussion on The Greene Space series were previously published in Maley, "August Wilson Takes New York."
3. Wilson, "How to Write a Play."
4. Livingston, "Cool August," 58; Sheppard, "August Wilson," 111, 110.
5. Harrison, "August Wilson's Blues Poetics," 299.
6. McClinton, "Foreword," viii.
7. Jones, *Blues People*, 153.
8. Shannon, "Framing African American Cultural Identity," 29.
9. Gadamer, *Truth and Method*, 85.
10. Colbert, *African American Theatrical Body*, 203.
11. Colbert, *African American Theatrical Body*, 271.
12. Baker, *Blues, Ideology, and Afro-American Literature*, 3, 7.

1. Blues and the Social Human

1. Sheppard, "August Wilson," 110.
2. Moyers, "August Wilson," 63.
3. Wilson, *Three Plays*, x; Moyers, "August Wilson," 63.
4. Shannon, *Dramatic Vision*, 16.
5. Salaam, *What Is Life?*, 7, 10.
6. Salaam, *What Is Life?*, 7. Some scholars disagree, citing African roots as foundational to blues. See especially Kubik, *Africa and the Blues*.
7. A. Davis, *Blues Legacies*, 5.
8. Jones, *Blues People*, 11.
9. See Lawson, *Jim Crow's Counterculture*. Lawson offers a broader notion of blues' geographical homeland, which he names the Lower Mississippi Valley. "During the Jim Crow era," he argues, "the blues world is best conceived as having been a great three-channeled pipeline moving material, people, ideas, and sounds from New Orleans and the plantation districts of the Lower Mississippi Valley in the South to Chicago and other industrial, urban communities in the North. The three channels were the Illinois Central Railroad, Highways 51 and 61, and the Mississippi River" (3).
10. Comentale, *Sweet Air*, 35, 41.
11. Gussow, *Beyond the Crossroads*, 5.
12. Comentale, *Sweet Air*, 35.
13. Cobb, *Most Southern Place*; Woods, *Development Arrested*, 2.
14. Salaam, *What Is Life?*, 7; Gussow, *Seems Like Murder Here*, 15; Lawson, *Jim Crow's Counterculture*, 2.
15. Harrison, "August Wilson's Blues Poetics," 299.
16. Wald, *Escaping the Delta*, 3, 4.
17. McGinley, *Staging the Blues*, 91.
18. Miller, *Segregating Sound*, 2.
19. Jones, *Blues People*, 7, 82, 86.
20. McGinley, *Staging the Blues*, 42.
21. Gussow, "Blues Talk 2—blues conditions," 14:04–14:07.
22. West, "Hope on a Tightrope."
23. Ellison, *Shadow and Act*, 257.
24. Baker, *Blues, Ideology, and Afro-American Literature*, 3, 4.
25. Gussow, *Seems Like Murder Here*, 4; Cone, "The Blues," 236; Comentale, *Sweet Air*, 45.
26. Spencer, *Blues and Evil*, xxv.
27. Wald, *Escaping the Delta*, 84. Wald's statistics come from Cobb, *Most Southern Place*, 114.
28. Oakley, *Devil's Music*, 45.
29. Gussow, *Seems Like Murder Here*, 2–3.

30. Agamben, *State of Exception*, 3, 4.
31. Edwards, *The World Don't Owe Me Nothing*, 48.
32. A. Davis, *Blues Legacies*, 33.
33. Gussow, *Seems Like Murder Here*, 18. Gussow is quoting Dollard, *Caste and Class*.
34. Perkins and Stephens, *Strange Fruit*, 3 (quoted in Mitchell, *Living with Lynching*, 2).
35. Mitchell, *Living with Lynching*, 2.
36. Locke, "Drama of Negro Life," 124; Locke, "Art or Propaganda?," 312.
37. A. Davis, *Blues Legacies*, 24.
38. Gussow, *Seems Like Murder Here*, 3–4.
39. Lawson, *Jim Crow's Counter Culture*, 2.
40. A. Davis, *Blues Legacies*, 8.
41. Gates, *Signifying Monkey*, 51, 52, 75.
42. Hartman, *Scenes of Subjection*; A. Davis, *Blues Legacies*, 26.
43. Gussow, *Seems Like Murder Here*, 3.
44. McGinley, *Staging the Blues*, 44.
45. Honig, *Antigone, Interrupted*, 19.
46. Edwards, *The World Don't Owe Me Nothing*, 47–49.
47. Cavarero, *For More Than One Voice*, 3.
48. For a discussion of the field holler as a genre, see Tracy, *Langston Hughes and the Blues*, 70–71.
49. Lomax, *Land Where Blues Began*, 275–76.
50. Cavarero, *For More Than One Voice*, 169.
51. S. Williams, "Blues Roots of Contemporary Afro-American Poetry," 446.
52. Jones, *Blues People*, 82; Lawson, *Jim Crow's Counterculture*, 10.
53. Cavarero, *For More Than One Voice*, 5.
54. Butler, *Precarious Life*, xii; Butler, *Giving an Account of Oneself*, 33.
55. Butler, *Precarious Life*, 44.
56. Jones, *Blues People*, 26.
57. S. Williams, "Blues Roots of Contemporary Afro-American Poetry," 448.
58. Pearson, *Jook Right On*, xvii.
59. Hale, *Griots and Griottes*, 19, 57, 23.
60. West, "Hope on a Tightrope."
61. Comentale, *Sweet Air*, 53.
62. Boynton, "Cornel West," 117.
63. Comentale, *Sweet Air*, 57.
64. Pearson, *Jook Right On*, xx; Salaam, *What Is Life?*, 16.
65. Hughes, "Songs Called The Blues," 392.
66. Ellison, *Shadow and Act*, 256.
67. Honig, *Antigone, Interrupted*, 19, 28.
68. White, *Ethos of the Late-Modern Citizen*, 25.

69. Cavarero, *For More Than One Voice*, 240.
70. Tracy, "Defining the Blues," 12.
71. Garon, *Blues & the Poetic Spirit*, 168.
72. Shannon, *Dramatic Vision*, 75.

2. "I Am the Blues"

1. Wilson, "How to Write a Play."
2. Elam, *"Ma Rainey's Black Bottom,"* 80; Plum, "Blues, History, and the Dramaturgy of August Wilson," 564; Shannon, *Dramatic Vision*, 6; Gener, "Salvation in the City of Bones," 24; Harrison, "August Wilson's Blues Poetics," 292.
3. See also Elam, *Past as Present*. Elam does claim that Wilson "functions as bluesman," but his use of *functions* is instructive of his argument. Elam insists that Wilson's bluesman identity manifests itself in the "rhythms and musical inflection" of his plays (33). For Elam, Wilson functions as bluesman most fully when he is borrowing, replicating, or showing an influence of the work of blues musicians.
4. Salaam, *What Is Life?*, 7.
5. Moyers, "August Wilson," 63.
6. Salaam, *What Is Life?*, 7.
7. Gates, "Chitlin Circuit," 134.
8. Moyers, "August Wilson," 72.
9. Moyers, "August Wilson," 72.
10. Watlington, "Hurdling Fences," 83.
11. Livingston, "Cool August," 39.
12. Deavere-Smith, Wilson, and Brustein, "On Cultural Power," 25:04–25:08, 25:47–25:56.
13. Butler, *Gender Trouble*, 34, 45.
14. Feingold, "August Wilson's Bottomless Blackness," 13.
15. Shannon, "Audience and Africanisms," 152.
16. Livingston, "Cool August," 47.
17. Livingston, "Cool August," 44.
18. Moyers, "August Wilson," 67. Wilson does add, "Now, in all fairness to him, I hadn't done any work in his class, and all of a sudden, I turn in this paper."
19. Shannon, *Dramatic Vision*, 18.
20. Lyons, "Interview with August Wilson," 206.
21. Moyers, "August Wilson," 63.
22. Wilson, "Preface," ix.
23. Moyers, "August Wilson," 63–64.
24. Shannon, "August Wilson Explains," 121–22; Shannon, *Dramatic Vision*, 234.
25. Watlington, "Hurdling Fences," 84.
26. Moyers, "August Wilson," 63.

27. Moyers, "August Wilson," 63.
28. The most famous polemic response is Brustein, "Subsidized Separatism," which includes a response from Wilson. For thoughtful analyses of the speech and its claims, see particularly the essays in *African American Review* 31:4 (Winter 1997) and in D. Williams and Shannon, *August Wilson and Black Aesthetics.*
29. Wilson, *Ground,* 14. Further citations to this work are in the text.
30. Asked several years after the speech if he would make any changes had he the opportunity, Wilson replied, "I would leave the colorblind casting alone. . . . that became the lightning rod that everyone focused on as if that was the only thing I was saying. I think it muddled the speech" (D. Williams and Shannon, *August Wilson and Black Aesthetics,* 199).
31. Deavere-Smith, Wilson, and Brustein, "On Cultural Power," 18:10–18:42, 27:58–28:04.
32. Elam, *Past as Present,* 216; Joseph, "Alliances across Margins," 595.
33. Elam, *Past as Present,* 223. See also Harrison, "Crisis of Black Theater Identity." In defense of Wilson against what he calls "Brustein's condescending incredulity," Harrison says, "Maximizing our cultural heritage in the formation of an Afrocentric theatre style does not suggest separatism. It seeks an alternative to a tradition that does not allow the full breath of our African spirit to breathe" (576–77).
34. Henderson interview.
35. Wilson, "Preface," x.
36. Lyons and Plimpton, "August Wilson," 69–70.
37. Elam, *Past as Present,* 17.
38. Bogumil, *Understanding August Wilson,* 18–19.
39. Kreidler quoted in Bogumil, *Understanding August Wilson,* 16. Wilson famously and frequently included Baraka and Bearden with Borges and blues as his "four Bs" of influence. Occasionally he added more: "To those four Bs I could add two more, Bullins and Baldwin" (Lyons and Plimpton, "August Wilson," 74).
40. Portions of this discussion on *How I Learned* were previously published in Maley, "How I Learned What I Learned."
41. Wilson, *August Wilson's How I Learned,* 7. Further citations to this work are in the text.
42. Ellison, *Shadow and Act,* 78.
43. Sheppard, "August Wilson," 108; Wilson, "How to Write a Play."
44. Wilson, "Preface," ix–x.
45. Wilson, "Preface," xi.
46. Rosen, "August Wilson," 199. Wilson credits the "I am the blues line" to Willie Dixon. Few musicians had an impact on the development of blues music greater than Dixon's.
47. Rosen, "August Wilson," 197.
48. Sheppard, "August Wilson," 111.

3. August Wilson's Blues

1. Wilson, *Ma Rainey*, 66.
2. Shannon, *Dramatic Vision*; Elam, "*Ma Rainey's Black Bottom*"; Tracy, "Holyistic Blues."
3. Shannon, "The Good Christian's Come and Gone," 133.
4. Temple, *Aunt Ester's Children Redeemed*, 25.
5. Shannon, *Dramatic Vision*, 76; Tracy, "Holyistic Blues," 52.
6. Plum, "Blues, History," 564, 562.
7. Elam, *Past as Present*, 3. See also Shannon, "Framing African American Cultural Identity." Shannon makes a similar point about the malleability of history in Wilson's work, arguing that his plays frequently contain "a liminal zone that is the focal point of much conflict. This zone represents a site of convergence where past, present, and future constructions of African American cultural identity collide and intersect; some elements survive intact; some are eradicated; and some morph into barely recognizable alternatives. Tensions arise in such zones when the motion of history or cultural amnesia moves headlong in one direction and does not favor turning back to assess past events or to learn from past mistakes" (34).
8. Elam, *Past as Present*, 29.
9. Elam, *Past as Present*, 40.
10. Salaam, *What Is Life?*, 10.
11. Elam, *Past as Present*, xix, 55.
12. See D. Williams and Shannon, *August Wilson and Black Aesthetics*: "My signature play would be *Joe Turner's Come and Gone*. Most of the ideas of the other plays are contained in that one play" (198).
13. Colbert, *African American Theatrical Body*, 195.
14. Temple, *Aunt Ester's Children Redeemed*, 17.
15. Wilson, *Joe Turner*, 6. Further citations are in the text.
16. Rashad, foreword, xxx.
17. Pereira, *August Wilson and the African-American Odyssey*, 56.
18. Colbert, *African American Theatrical Body*, 221.
19. Grant, "'Their baggage a long line,'" 111.
20. Bogumil, *Understanding August Wilson*, 60. See also an earlier version of Bogumil's *Joe Turner* chapter in her "Tomorrow Never Comes."
21. Hale, *Griots and Griottes*, 19, 57.
22. Palmer, *Deep Blues*, 27.
23. Hale, *Griots and Griottes*, 23.
24. Hale, *Griots and Griottes*, 19.
25. Toop, *Rap Attack*, 32. This is the traditional view of a griot, which is the model evident in Wilson's plays. There exist contemporary critiques of the griot, however. See Sajnani, "Troubling the Trope." Sajnani argues that currently some view griots as "parasitic and manipulative" with a propensity for profiteering (160).

26. Hale, *Griots and Griottes*, 20, 24.
27. Colbert, *African American Theatrical Body*, 198–99.
28. Bogumil, *Understanding August Wilson*, 70.
29. See hooks, *Ain't I a Woman?*
30. Shannon, "The Good Christian's Come and Gone," 127.
31. Elam, *Past as Present*, 88.
32. Wittgenstein, *Philosophical Investigations*, 27.
33. Shannon, *Dramatic Vision*, 79.
34. Wilson, *Ma Rainey*, 12. Further citations are in the text.
35. Wilson, *Fences*, 61.
36. See also Morrison's foreword. Morrison calls the condition of the play "like living in a war zone where alertness is all, where fear is simply one element of breathable air" and argues that "the relief, when the turmoil surrounding the ghost and the piano is put to rest, is an extreme, if not permanent, experience of the triumph of bravery over fear. The struggle between memory and foresight, regret and promise operates within a world of terror. In that context, the battles are truly mighty; the victories as rough as they are noble" (xiii).
37. See also Smith, "Questions of Source in African Cinema." Smith points out that "griots enjoy a unique position in society as they are allowed and expected, to criticize those in power. . . . It is the griots' power, and their audacity when speaking in public, that demands respect" (29). Smith makes clear that the griot develops a reputation through performance, and not necessarily through effectiveness.
38. Shannon, "Framing African American Cultural Identity," 37.
39. Shannon, "Framing African American Cultural Identity," 36.
40. Shannon, "Turn Your Lamp Down Low!," 130.
41. Wilson, *Two Trains*, 88.
42. Wilson, *Two Trains*, 89–90.
43. Wilson, *Gem*, 24.
44. Temple, *Aunt Ester's Children Redeemed*, 4.
45. Wilson, *Gem*, 42–44.
46. Wilson, *Gem*, 79.
47. Bogumil, *Understanding August Wilson*, 136.
48. See also Colbert, "If We Must Die." Colbert points out another bleak harbinger in *King Hedley II*: "As a former blues woman, Ruby refusing to sing further solidifies the wasteland that is the setting of Wilson's play for the 1980s. If song functions in Wilson's work as a device that promotes social change, Ruby's unwillingness to sing points to a level of nihilism" (104–5).
49. Wilson, *Radio Golf*, 21.
50. Temple, *Aunt Ester's Children Redeemed*, 118.
51. Crawford, "B^b Burden," 33.

52. See also Mills, "Walking Blues." Mills characterizes the griot as "wise man" and the warrior as "mystifier" in the trickster tradition, suggesting that "the relations between the wise man and the mystifier are repeated from one play to the next, with Wilson seeming to work towards uniting them. . . . At first, their union is unimaginable (Levee kills Toledo); then it becomes a possibility (Troy refuses to listen to Bono and has Gabriel arrested, but does not kill them); and finally becomes a reality (Loomis, Boy Willie and Sterling follow the advice of Bynum, Doaker and Aunt Ester)" (33).
53. Wilson, *Ma Rainey*, 54.
54. Wilson, *Ma Rainey*, 18.
55. Timpane, "Filling the Time," 76. See also Gussow, *Beyond the Crossroads*. Gussow suggests that in his relationship with Mr. Sturdyvant, Levee has fallen prey to "Mr. Devil," a common antagonist in the blues tradition, pointing out how Sturdyvant "shamelessly toys with the black trumpeter, Levee, encouraging his hopes of becoming a well-remunerated song composer before dashing them at the play's conclusion" (139).
56. Clark, "Healing the Scars of Masculinity," 202–3.
57. Elam, *Past as Present*, 127–28.
58. Harrison, "August Wilson's Blues Poetics," 301–2.
59. Pereira, *August Wilson and the African-American Odyssey*, 3.
60. Pereira, *August Wilson and the African-American Odyssey*, 98.
61. Wilson, *Seven Guitars*, 78.
62. Arnold, "*Seven Guitars*," 220–22.
63. Kushner, foreword, xxii.
64. Murphy, "Tragedy of *Seven Guitars*," 133.
65. Savran, "August Wilson," 33.
66. Wilson, *Fences*, 40. Further citations are in the text.
67. Pereira, *August Wilson and the African-American Odyssey*, 38.
68. See also Bogumil, *Understanding August Wilson*. Bogumil suggest that "*Fences* involves a conflict among the characters' desire to break through boundaries, redefine themselves, and discover self-fulfillment versus the fences and boundaries erected by society and individuals that limit, hinder, define, or exclude" (54–55). For warrior Troy, those fences and boundaries are both internalized and social, but other characters who seek to redefine themselves struggle to do so through and against Troy.
69. Wilson, *King Hedley*, 61.
70. Wilson, *King Hedley*, 59.
71. Wilson, *Piano Lesson*, 41.
72. Wilson, *Jitney*, 43–44.
73. Wilson, *Seven Guitars*, 18.
74. Wilson, *Seven Guitars*, 88.

75. Shannon, "The Ground on Which I Stand," 151.
76. Elam, *Past as Present*, 110.
77. Wilson, *Piano Lesson*, 68.
78. Wilson, *Piano Lesson*, 33.
79. Wilson, *Piano Lesson*, 68.
80. Wilson, *Gem*, 18.
81. Wilson, *Two Trains*, 9.
82. Wilson, *Two Trains*, 32.
83. Wilson, *Two Trains*, 43.
84. Elam, *Past as Present*, 108.
85. Elam, *Past as Present*, 92.
86. D. Davis, "'Mouths on Fire,'" 165. See also Bogumil, who argues in *Understanding August Wilson* that "each woman [in *Joe Turner*] is psychologically complex. All three are black female migrants in search of their own songs, a sense of spiritual and emotional stability in their lives. Each woman's interaction with the Joe Turners, those disfranchised African American males, elicits a change to some extent within each one of them, resulting in a song of self that each woman must discover for herself" (73). Certainly Wilson's women search for their song, but the identity of each of the women in *Joe Turner*, and most women throughout the *Cycle*, is defined primarily in relief of a man or masculinity.
87. Wilson, *Fences*, 74.
88. See also Reed, foreword. Reed argues that "if August Wilson's plays have a conservative line, it was not to appeal to those critics who misread him, but a reflection of the attitudes of a large segment of the African American community. Wilson's conservativism was *his*, that of Booker T. Washington, Elijah Muhammad, Malcolm X and Marcus Garvey, all of whom preached self-help and individual responsibility, and all of whom did business with white people; not *theirs*, which often took the form of vicious and nasty comments about the underclass" (xiii).
89. Parks, "Light in August," 24.
90. Elam, "August Wilson's Women," 176.
91. Wilson, *Gem*, 43.
92. Wilson, *Radio Golf*, 73.
93. Kushner, foreword, xiii–xiv.
94. Tyndall, "Using Black Rage," 164.
95. Gates, *Signifying Monkey*, 82.
96. Rocha, "American History as 'Loud Talking,'" 117.
97. Rocha, "American History as 'Loud Talking,'" 119, 124.
98. Rocha, "American History as 'Loud Talking,'" 127.

4. "God A'mighty, I Be Lonesomer'n Ever!"

1. Murphy, *Provincetown Players*, 31.
2. Diggins, *Eugene O'Neill's America*, 3–4, 63.
3. Barlow, "O'Neill's Female Characters," 173.
4. Dowling, *Eugene O'Neill*, 205.
5. O'Neill, *Complete Plays 1913–1920*, 1037, 1039.
6. O'Neill, *Complete Plays 1920–1931*, 129.
7. O'Neill, *Complete Plays 1920–1931*, 121.
8. O'Neill, *Complete Plays 1920–1931*, 125.
9. O'Neill, *Complete Plays 1913–1920*, 1036.
10. See also Steen, "Melancholy Bodies." Steen argues that Jones's flight from engagement with the other people occurs simultaneously with his attempt to divide his outer self from his inner, psychological self where the formless fears reside. For Jones, argues Steen, "internal alienation is produced by being chased or 'hounded' by the masks one wears to hide the self from one's own consciousness. *The Emperor Jones* dramatizes precisely this internal conflict" (358–59). Certainly Jones cultivates an outward self foreign to his psychological self, but since he establishes his being so directly in the social sphere, his downfall results more directly from failing to attend to that aspect of his identity.
11. O'Neill, *Complete Plays 1920–1931*, 144, 148.
12. For this and other reasons, Farhoudi and Zolfaghari dub *The Hairy Ape* "O'Neill's most class-conscious play" ("Under the Shade of Ideology," 162).
13. O'Neill, *Complete Plays 1920–1931*, 148.
14. Wilson, *Ma Rainey*, 54; Wilson, *Piano Lesson*, 41.
15. Diggins, *Eugene O'Neill's America*, 97.
16. O'Neill, *Complete Plays 1920–1931*, 349. Both *Desire* and *Mourning* are in this Library of America volume; further citations to both plays are in the text.
17. O'Neill, *Complete Plays 1932–1943*, 570, 572. Further citations to *Iceman* are in the text.
18. O'Neill, *Complete Plays 1932–1943*, 741, 750. Further citations to *Long Day's Journey* are in the text.
19. This is made all that much more difficult for Mary by having to live under a condition that Michael Selmon calls "domestic surveillance," which is "the men's constant scrutiny of Mary, their ongoing search for signs of a relapse with morphine" ("'Like . . . so many small theatres,'" 526).
20. For a discussion of how this avoidance by the men couples with Mary's linguistic performances to create a dangerous façade of stable Tyrone family life, see Maley, "Mary Tyrone's Crisis of Agency."
21. See also Vera, "Observation as System"; and Eisen, "'Writing on the Wall.'" Vera argues compellingly that the paradox of Harry Hope's bar—at once isolating and

community building—greatly complicates Slade's desire for alienation. She says that "the pub is closed in, closing off, preserving idleness. The pub is the theatre of a slow sleep, of persecution, of death. Within this segmented space, the past and future merge in the present: the pub is the concrete manifestation of memory and forgetting" (448). Eisen also underscores the play's paradoxical union of isolation and community: "*The Iceman Cometh* is primarily a drama of consciousness in which a character passes through a crisis of self-understanding only by seeing himself reflected in the thoughts, dilemmas, ideological beliefs, and observable conditions of others" (61).

22. Dowling, *Eugene O'Neill*, 343.
23. Quoted in R. Williams, *Modern Tragedy*, 116.
24. Diggins, *Eugene O'Neill's America*, 9.

5. "Laws of Silence Don't Work"

1. See, e.g., King, "Tennessee Williams." King argues that Williams "owes a debt to Eugene O'Neill, since O'Neill's dramatic achievements elevated the status of all American theatre. And Williams deftly employs expressionistic devices which had been the forte of the early O'Neill. Arthur Miller, born in 1915, was closer in age to Williams (1911) than O'Neill (1888), and like Williams he masterfully combines naturalistic American family settings with bizarre expressionist devices to create plays with universal significance" (629). The field of dramatic criticism is fond of exploring Williams's influence on his predecessors: a special issue of the *South Atlantic Review* (70.4, Fall 2005), and later a book, *The Influence of Tennessee Williams*, both edited by Philip C. Kolin, are dedicated to discussing contemporary playwrights in light of Williams.
2. Shannon, "Sons of the South," 124, 141. King also argues that Williams's "love/hate relationship with the culture he was born into [the South] provides dramatic conflict and excitement to everything he wrote" ("Tennessee Williams," 627).
3. Fisher, "'Angels of Fructification,'" 13. See also Kolin, "Fission." Kolin claims that "Williams opened the stage to the intimacies of self and desire" (52).
4. See Kimmel, *Manhood in America*.
5. See also Bak, "Dying Gaul." Bak offers a compelling analysis of how these same anxieties of masculinity shaped Williams's short story "Three Players of a Summer Game," out of which grew *Cat on a Hot Tin Roof*.
6. Wilson, *Piano Lesson*, 68.
7. Savran, *Communists, Cowboys, and Queers*, 104–5.
8. Shannon, *Dramatic Vision*, 83.
9. There is a tradition of homophobic Williams criticism that either condemns the homoerotic elements of his plays or grasps eagerly onto the playwright's ambiguity in

order to claim that the lack of overt homosexuality in the plays negates its relevance in discussing his work. This homophobia has given rise to a more recent critical tradition that takes homosexuality in the plays as a clear given. See, e.g., Powers, "Lifted Above Tennessee Williams's *Hot Tin Roof*"; and Paller, *Gentlemen Callers*. Powers argues of Brick that "to evade the truth about his sexual identity, which determines the very essence of his life, he drinks," treating homosexuality for Brick as he does throughout his essay, as a *truth* (124). Paller is more direct still: "Let us state clearly, then, that the homosexuality in *The Glass Menagerie* resides in Tom, and that it is not metaphorical or abstract. Tom is gay. . . . Those who can read the signs, whose eyes do not fail them, will see Tom's gayness; those who cannot will not" (39–40). While it would be wrong to deny the queerness of Brick, Tom, and others, analyses like Powers's and Paller's overcorrect, muting the dramaturgical effect of Williams's opacity.

10. Savran, *Communists, Cowboys, and Queers*, 122–23.
11. Bigsby, "Entering *The Glass Menagerie*," 33.
12. Savran makes a fine observation when he suggests that "given the censorship of the 1940s and 1950s, and Williams's more or less conscious internalization of these prohibitions, his plays and films of this period characteristically translate these inexpressible desires into subtext" (*Communists, Cowboys, and Queers*, 126). Fisher makes a similar point, arguing that "Williams wished to attract a broader audience than gays for his work and seems to have believed that a so-called gay play would limit his access to universal acceptance" ("'Angels of Fructification,'" 16).
13. T. Williams, *Plays 1931–1955*, 400; further citations are in the text. For a discussion on the complexity of citing Williams, see Murphy, *Theatre of Tennessee Williams*. Murphy points out that "in the case of Tennessee Williams, the text of a play is a protean thing, and deciding which of the published versions to use can be as vexing for scholars as for directors" (7). The present chapter uses the Library of America volumes for the same reason that Murphy does: "these are the closest reading versions to the original scripts" (7).
14. Winchell, "Come back to the locker room," 707. See also Bibler, "'Tenderness which was Uncommon.'" Bibler offers a useful rejoinder against any claim of full enlightenment on the part of Big Daddy: "Big Daddy's claim to tolerance is wrong headed to the point that it is either naïve or hypocritical. He claims to be the voice of tolerance, yet the black servants persistently interrupt the play to punctuate his and other characters' speeches and actions, forcing the plantation's deployment of race squarely into the frame of representation" (387). Responding to Winchell, Bibler argues that Big Daddy's and Maggie's tolerance "stems from the fact that they are also the most aware of how to exploit the plantation's complex system of racial and patriarchal oppression for personal gain. . . . In other words, it doesn't matter if Brick is homosexual because the plantation hierarchies work to guarantee the primacy of

his masculine identity and his status as the (potential) patriarch, regardless of his sexual identity" (393).
15. Savran, *Communists, Cowboys, and Queers*, 109.
16. Savran, *Communists, Cowboys, and Queers*, 108.
17. Clum, "Sacrificial Stud," 136. Clum asks a valid question when he queries, "Is Val necessarily exclusively heterosexual?" and suggests that "seeing a straight 'stud' as sexually attractive and available was a reality as well as a fantasy in the pre-Stonewall years in which Williams spent his young manhood. Indeed, Val's reluctance and passivity suggest a sexuality ambiguous figure" (139–40). Certainly it is possible that Val's sexual experience and attraction are not limited to women, but what is most important about his character in the play is that Two River County's women develop strong sexual desire for him, and that he claims to want to abandon his promiscuous past.
18. Savran, *Communists, Cowboys, and Queers*, 122–23.
19. King, "Tennessee Williams," 640.
20. Ovid, *Metamorphoses*, 10.81, 11.7.
21. Lahr, *Tennessee Williams*, 33. Some critics stress the psychological and allegorical aspects of the play's autobiographical content. See, e.g., Price, "Cat on a Hot Tin Roof." Price argues that "the principle characters in *Cat on a Hot Tin Roof*—Brick and Maggie—can be interpreted as representations of Tennessee Williams himself" (324).
22. Adler, "Culture, Power, and the (En)gendering of Community," 652.
23. Lahr, *Tennessee Williams*, 521.
24. Lahr, *Tennessee Williams*, 532.
25. Savran, *Communists, Cowboys, and Queers*, 9.
26. Savran, *Communists, Cowboys, and Queers*, 9, 110.
27. Kolin, "Fission," 50.

6. August Wilson's Legacy and Its Limits

1. Hall, *Plays: 1*, 89.
2. Wall, *Worrying the Line*, 6, 11.
3. Hall, *Plays: 1*, 255.
4. For more discussion of McCraney's personal relationship with Wilson, see Rawson, "Tarell McCraney."
5. Adell, introduction, xv.
6. Tate, introduction, xxiv.
7. Hall, *Plays: 1*, 223. Further citations are in the text.
8. Colbert, "Black Leadership at the Crossroads," 263–64.
9. Colbert, "Black Leadership at the Crossroads," 266.

10. Colbert, "Black Leadership at the Crossroads," 272–73.
11. Wall, *Worrying the Line*, 124.
12. Wall, *Worrying the Line*, 16.
13. Gussow, "Blues Talk 4," 37:42–38:19.
14. McCraney, *Choir Boy*, 127.
15. McCraney, *Wig Out!*, 5.
16. McCraney, *Wig Out!*, 43.
17. McCraney *Brother/Sister Plays*, 209; Wilson, *Fences*, 38.
18. McCraney *Brother/Sister Plays*, 23.
19. Wilson, *Ma Rainey*, 72.
20. McCraney *Brother/Sister Plays*, 19. Further citations are in the text.
21. In *Signifying Monkey*, Gates helpfully delineates the deity's various guises: "This curious figure is called Esu-Elegbara in Nigeria and Legba among the Fon in Benin. His New World figurations include Exú in Brazil, Echu-Elegua in Cuba, Papa Legba (pronounced La-Bas) in the pantheon of the loa of Vaudou of Haiti, and Papa La Bas in the loa of Hoodoo in the United States" (5). Victor Leo Walker II argues that "the different spellings and pronunciations of his name throughout the African Diaspora suggest Legba's archetypal trickster status" (introduction, 134).
22. Awolalu, *Yoruba Beliefs*, 10.
23. Ray, *African Religions*, 70. See also Karade, *Handbook of Yoruba Religious Concepts*: "Orisha as a term, is actually the combination of two Yoruba words. *Ori* which is the reflective spark of human consciousness embedded in human essence, and *sha* which is the ultimate potentiality of that consciousness to enter into or assimilate itself into the divine consciousness" (23).
24. For a succinct list of major orisha and their attributes, see Karade, *Handbook of Yoruba Religious Concepts*, 29. For a more thorough discussion, see Scheub, *Dictionary of African Mythology*.
25. Soyinka, "Tolerant Gods," 48. Orisha humanism is clear in the Yoruba creation myth that tells of a cataclysmic event opening an abyss between the orisha and humans. Longing for human company, orisha consistently and desperately tried to cross the chasm to no avail until Ogun finally built a passageway to unite the spiritual and material worlds. See also Soyinka, *Myth, Literature and the African World*.
26. Spencer, *Blues and Evil*, 11–12, 33.
27. See Colbert, *African American Theatrical Body*. Of this invitation, Colbert says, "The master lyricist, Elegba spits game (a vernacular term for courting) so fluidly one almost mistakes the aggressive sexual advance for a gentle romantic suggestion" (268).
28. Oba's name comes from the orisha Obatala, whom Soyinka calls "the pure unsullied one," and "God of creation . . . essence of the serene arts" (*Myth, Literature and the African World* 140, 140n1). Unlike the Abrahamic creator, Obatala does not sit atop

the Yoruba pantheon. Olodumare is the supreme deity who breathes life into the human forms crafted by Obatala. That Marcus's mother is Oba signals him as specially and carefully crafted, perhaps still awaiting the invigorating breath of life.

29. Wetmore, "Children of Yemayá," 87.
30. Colbert, *African American Theatrical Body*, 266–67.
31. The first two times Elegba sings this refrain are identical, but the opening line in the third version is "Come down peace *now*" (125). Elegba worries the line in classic blues style.
32. Colbert, *African American Theatrical Body*, 267.
33. Wetmore, "Children of Yemayá," 85.
34. Wetmore, "Children of Yemayá," 93.
35. Soyinka, "Tolerant Gods," 49.
36. Wetmore, "Children of Yemayá," 91.
37. Colbert, *African American Theatrical Body*, 269, 266.
38. For Soyinka's concept of the fourth stage, what he calls "the vortex of archetypes and home of the tragic spirit," see *Myth, Literature and the African World*, 140–60.
39. Wetmore, "Children of Yemayá," 93.
40. See Vega, "Candomblé and Eshu-Eleggua."
41. Wilson, *Ground*, 11.

Bibliography

Adell, Sandra. Introduction to *Contemporary Plays by African American Women: Ten Complete Works,* edited by Adell, xi–xiv. Urbana: U of Illinois P, 2015.
Adler, Thomas P. "Culture, Power, and the (En)gendering of Community: Tennessee Williams and Politics." *Mississippi Quarterly* 48:4 (Fall 1995): 649–65.
Agamben, Giorgio. *State of Exception.* Translated by Kevin Attell. Chicago: U of Chicago P, 2005.
Arnold, David L. G. "*Seven Guitars:* August Wilson's Economy of Blues." In *August Wilson: A Casebook,* edited by Marilyn Elkins, 199–225. New York: Garland, 2000.
Awolalu, J. Omosade. *Yoruba Beliefs and Sacrificial Rites.* Burnt Mill: Longman, 1979.
Bak, John. "A Dying Gaul: The Signifying Phallus and Tennessee Williams's 'Thee Players of a Summer Game.'" *Mississippi Quarterly* 58:1/2 (Winter 2004/5): 41–73.
Baker, Houston A., Jr. *Blues, Ideology, and Afro-American Literature: A Vernacular Theory.* Chicago: U of Chicago P, 1984.
Barlow, Judith E. "O'Neill's Female Characters." In *The Cambridge Companion to Eugene O'Neill,* edited by Michael Manheim. Cambridge: Cambridge UP, 1998.
Bibler, Michael P. "'A Tenderness which was Uncommon': Homosexuality, Narrative, and the Southern Plantation in Tennessee Williams's *Cat on a Hot Tin Roof.*" *Mississippi Quarterly* 55:3 (Summer 2002): 381–400.
Bigsby, C. W. E. "Entering *The Glass Menagerie.*" In *The Cambridge Companion to Tennessee Williams,* edited by Matthew C. Roudané, 29–44. New York: Cambridge UP, 1997.

Bogumil, Mary L. "Tomorrow Never Comes: Songs of Cultural Identity in August Wilson's *Joe Turner's Come and Gone.*" *Theatre Journal* 46:4 (December 1994): 463–67.

———. *Understanding August Wilson*. Rev. ed. Columbia: U of South Carolina P, 2011.

Boynton, Robert S. "Cornel West." *Rolling Stone*, 15 November 2007, 116–17.

Brustein, Robert. "Subsidized Separatism." *American Theatre* 13.8 (October 1996): 26–27, 100–107.

Butler, Judith. *Gender Trouble*. New York: Routledge, 1990.

———. *Giving an Account of Oneself*. New York: Fordham UP, 2005.

———. *Precarious Life: The Powers of Morning and Violence*. London: Verso, 2006.

Cavarero, Adriana. *For More Than One Voice: Toward a Philosophy of Vocal Expression*. Translated by Paul A. Kottman. Stanford: Stanford UP, 2005.

Clark, Keith. "Healing the Scars of Masculinity: Reflections of Baseball, Gunshots, and War Wounds in August Wilson's *Fences*." In *Contemporary Black Men's Fiction and Drama*, edited by Clark, 200–221. Urbana: U of Illinois P, 2001.

Clum, John M. "The Sacrificial Stud and the Fugitive Female in *Suddenly Last Summer, Orpheus Descending,* and *Sweet Bird of Youth*." In *The Cambridge Companion to Tennessee Williams*, edited by Matthew C. Roudané, 128–46. New York: Cambridge UP, 1997.

Cobb, James C. *The Most Southern Place on Earth: The Mississippi Delta and the Roots of Regional Identity*. New York: Oxford UP, 1992.

Colbert, Soyica Diggs. *The African American Theatrical Body: Reception, Performance, and the Stage*. Cambridge: Cambridge UP, 2011.

———. "Black Leadership at the Crossroads: Unfixing Martin Luther King Jr. in Katori Hall's *The Mountaintop*." *South Atlantic Quarterly* 112:2 (Spring 2013): 261–83.

———. "If We Must Die: Violence as History Lesson in *Seven Guitars* and *King Hedley II*." In *August Wilson: Completing the Twentieth-Century Cycle*, edited by Alan Nadel, 97–109. Iowa City: U of Iowa P, 2010.

Comentale, Edward P. *Sweet Air: Modernism, Regionalism, and American Popular Song*. Urbana: U of Illinois P, 2013.

Cone, James H. "The Blues: A Secular Spiritual." In *Write Me a Few of Your Lines: A Blues Reader*, edited by Steven C. Tracy. Amherst: U of Massachusetts P, 1999.

Crawford, Eileen. "The B^b Burden: The Invisibility of *Ma Rainey's Black Bottom*." In *August Wilson: A Casebook*, edited by Marilyn Elkins, 31–48. New York: Garland, 2000.

Davis, Angela Y. *Blues Legacies and Black Feminism*. New York: Vintage Books, 1998.

Davis, Doris. "'Mouths on Fire': August Wilson's Blueswomen." *MELUS* 35:4 (Winter 2010): 165–85.

Deavere-Smith, Anna, August Wilson, and Robert Brustein. "On Cultural Power." An NPR broadcast of the debate between playwright August Wilson and critic Robert Brustein. Town Hall, New York City, 27 January 1997. https://www.npr.org/templates/story/story.php?storyId=1109529.

Diggins, John Patrick. *Eugene O'Neill's America: Desire Under Democracy.* Chicago: U of Chicago P, 2007.
Dollard, John. *Caste and Class in a Southern Town.* Garden City, NY: Doubleday, 1957.
Dowling, Robert M. *Eugene O'Neill: A Life in Four Acts.* New Haven: Yale UP, 2014.
Edwards, David Honeyboy. *The World Don't Owe Me Nothing: The Life and Times of Delta Bluesman Honeyboy Edwards.* Chicago: Chicago Review Press, 1997.
Eisen, Kurt. "'The Writing on the Wall': Novelization and the Critique of History in *The Iceman Cometh.*" *Modern Drama* 34:1 (Spring 1991): 59–73.
Elam, Harry J., Jr. "August Wilson's Women." In *May All Your Fences Have Gates: Essays on the Drama of August Wilson,* edited by Alan Nadel, 165–82. Iowa City: U of Iowa P, 1994.
———. "*Ma Rainey's Black Bottom*: Singing Wilson's Blues." *American Drama* 5:2 (1996): 76–99.
———. *The Past as Present in the Drama of August Wilson.* Ann Arbor: U of Michigan P, 1996.
Ellison, Ralph. *Shadow and Act.* New York: Random House, 1953.
Farhoudi, Houriyeh, and Yaser Zolfaghari. "Under the Shade of Ideology: A Marxist Study of Eugene O'Neill's *The Hairy Ape.*" *Eugene O'Neill Review* 35:2 (2014): 161–76.
Feingold, Michael. "August Wilson's Bottomless Blackness." In *Conversations with August Wilson,* edited by Jackson R. Bryer and Mary C. Hartig, 12–18. Jackson: UP of Mississippi, 2006.
Fisher, James. "'The Angels of Fructification': Tennessee Williams, Tony Kushner, and Images of Homosexuality on the American Stage." *Mississippi Quarterly* 49:1 (Winter 1995/96): 13–32.
Gadamer, Hans-Georg. *Truth and Method.* Translated by Joel Weinsheimer and Donald G. Marshall. 2nd rev. ed. London: Continuum, 2004.
Garon, Paul. *Blues & the Poetic Spirit.* New York: Da Capo Press, 1978.
Gates, Henry Louis, Jr. "The Chitlin Circuit." In *African American Performance and Theater History: A Critical Reader,* edited by Harry J. Elam Jr. and David Krasner, 132–48. New York: Oxford UP, 2001.
———. *The Signifying Monkey: A Theory of African-American Literary Criticism.* New York: Oxford UP, 1988.
Gener, Randy. "Salvation in the City of Bones: Ma Rainey and Aunt Ester Sing Their Own Songs in August Wilson's Grand *Cycle* of Blues Dramas." *American Theatre* 20.5 (May/June 2003): 20–24, 64–67.
Grant, Sinikka. "'Their baggage a long line of separation and dispersement': Haunting and Trans-generational Trauma in *Joe Turner's Come and Gone.*" *College Literature* 36.2 (Spring 2009): 96–116.
Gussow, Adam. *Beyond the Crossroads: The Devil and the Blues Tradition.* Chapel Hill: U of North Carolina P, 2017.

———. "Blues Talk 2—blues conditions." Online video clip. YouTube, 2 January 2013. Web. 19 April 2013.

———. "Blues Talk 4—blues expressiveness and the blues ethos." Online video clip. YouTube, 9 January 2013. Web. 30 April 2016.

———. *Seems Like Murder Here: Southern Violence and the Blues Tradition.* Chicago: U of Chicago P, 2002.

Hale, Thomas A. *Griots and Griottes: Masters of Words and Music.* Bloomington: Indiana UP, 1998.

Hall, Katori. *Plays: 1.* London: Methuen Drama, 2012.

Harrison, Paul Carter. "August Wilson's Blues Poetics." In August Wilson, *Three Plays,* 291–317. Pittsburgh: U of Pittsburgh P, 1991.

———. "The Crisis of Black Theater Identity." *African American Review* 31:4 (Winter 1997): 567–78.

Hartman, Saidiya. *Scenes of Subjection: Terror, Slavery, and Self-Making in Nineteenth-Century America.* New York: Oxford UP, 1997.

Henderson, Stephen McKinley. Interview by author, 5 November 2013.

Honig, Bonnie. *Antigone, Interrupted.* New York: Cambridge UP, 2013.

hooks, bell. *Ain't I a Woman?: Black Women and Feminism.* New York: Routledge, 2015.

Hughes, Langston. "Songs Called The Blues." In *Write Me a Few of Your Lines: A Blues Reader,* edited by Steven C. Tracy. Amherst: U of Massachusetts P, 1999.

Jones, LeRoi (Amiri Baraka). *Blues People: Negro Music in White America.* New York: Harper Perennial, 2002.

Joseph, May. "Alliances across the Margins." *African American Review* 31:4 (Winter 1997): 595–99.

Karade, Baba Ifa. *A Handbook of Yoruba Religious Concepts.* San Francisco: Weiser Books, 1994.

Kimmel, Michael. *Manhood in America: A Cultural History.* 3rd ed. New York: Oxford UP, 2012.

King, Kimball. "Tennessee Williams: A Southern Writer." *Mississippi Quarterly* 48:4 (Fall 1995): 627–47.

Kolin, Philip C. "The Fission of Tennessee Williams's Plays into Adrienne Kennedy's." *South Atlantic Review* 70:4 (Fall 2005): 43–72.

———, ed. *The Influence of Tennessee Williams: Essays on Fifteen American Playwrights.* Jefferson, NC: McFarland, 2008.

Kubik, Gerhard. *Africa and the Blues.* Jackson: U of Mississippi P, 1999.

Kushner, Tony. Foreword to August Wilson, *Seven Guitars.* New York: Theatre Communications Group, 2007.

Lahr, John. *Tennessee Williams: Mad Pilgrimage of the Flesh, A Biography.* New York: W. W. Norton, 2014.

Lawson, R. A. *Jim Crow's Counterculture: The Blues and Black Southerners, 1890–1945*. Baton Rouge: Louisiana State UP, 2010.

Livingston, Dinah. "Cool August: Mr. Wilson's Red-Hot Blues." In *Conversations with August Wilson,* edited by Jackson R. Bryer and Mary C. Hartig, 38–60. Jackson: UP of Mississippi, 2006.

Locke, Alain. "Art or Propaganda?" In *Voices of the Harlem Renaissance,* edited by Nathan Irvin Huggins. New York: Oxford UP, 1995.

———. "The Drama of Negro Life." In *The Works of Alain Locke,* edited by Charles Molesworth. New York: Oxford UP, 2012.

Lomax, Alan. *The Land Where Blues Began.* New York: New Press, 1993.

Lyons, Bonnie. "An Interview with August Wilson." In *Conversations with August Wilson,* edited by Jackson R. Bryer and Mary C. Hartig, 204–22. Jackson: UP of Mississippi, 2006.

Lyons, Bonnie, and George Plimpton. "August Wilson, The Art of Theater No. 14." *Paris Review* 153 (Winter 1999): 67–94.

Maley, Patrick. "August Wilson Takes New York." *HowlRound Theatre Commons,* 19 November 2013. howlround.com/august-wilson-takes-new-york.

———. "How I Learned What I Learned." *Exeunt Theatre Magazine,* 5 December 2013. http://exeuntmagazine.com/reviews/how-i-learned-what-i-learned.

———. "Mary Tyrone's Crisis of Agency: *Long Day's Journey Into Night,* Ordinary Language, and the Tragic Humanism of American Drama." *Eugene O'Neill Review* 35:1 (2014): 41–60.

McClinton, Marion. "Foreword: They Might Have Been Giants, They Certainly Were Kings." In August Wilson, *King Hedley II.* New York: Theatre Communications Group, 2007.

McCraney, Tarell Alvin. *The Brother/Sister Plays.* New York: Theatre Communications Group, 2010.

———. *Choir Boy.* New York: Theatre Communications Group, 2015.

———. *Wig Out!* London: Faber and Faber, 2008.

McGinley, Paige A. *Staging the Blues: From Tent Shows to Tourism.* Durham: Duke UP, 2014.

Miller, Karl Hagstrom. *Segregating Sound: Inventing Folk and Pop Music in the Age of Jim Crow.* Durham: Duke UP, 2010.

Mills, Alice. "The Walking Blues: An Anthropological Approach to the Theater of August Wilson." *Black Scholar* 25:2 (1995): 30–35.

Mitchell, Koritha. *Living with Lynching: African American Lynching Plays, Performance, and Citizenship, 1890–1930.* Urbana: U of Illinois P, 2012.

Morrison, Toni. Foreword to August Wilson, *The Piano Lesson.* New York: Theatre Communications Group, 2007.

Moyers, Bill. "August Wilson: Playwright." In *Conversations with August Wilson,* edited by Jackson R. Bryer and Mary C. Hartig, 61–80. Jackson: UP of Mississippi, 2006.

Murphy, Brenda. *The Provincetown Players and the Culture of Modernity*. New York: Cambridge UP, 2005.

———. *The Theatre of Tennessee Williams*. London: Bloomsbury, 2014.

———. "The Tragedy of *Seven Guitars*." In *The Cambridge Companion to August Wilson*, edited by Christopher Bigsby, 124–34. Cambridge: Cambridge UP, 2007.

Murray, Albert. *Stomping the Blues*. Boston: Da Capo Press, 1989.

Oakley, Giles. *The Devil's Music: A History of the Blues*. Boston: Da Capo Press, 1997.

O'Neill, Eugene. *Complete Plays 1913–1920*. New York: Library of America, 1988.

———. *Complete Plays 1920–1931*. New York: Library of America, 1988.

———. *Complete Plays 1932–1943*. New York: Library of America, 1988.

Ovid. *Metamorphoses*. Translated by David Raeburn. New York: Penguin, 2004.

Paller, Michael. *Gentlemen Callers: Tennessee Williams, Homosexuality, and Mid-Twentieth-Century American Drama*. New York: Palgrave Macmillan, 2005.

Palmer, Robert. *Deep Blues*. New York: Penguin Books, 1982.

Parks, Suzan-Lori. "The Light in August: An Interview by Suzan-Lori Parks." *American Theatre* 22:9 (2005): 22–25, 74–78.

Pearson, Barry Lee. *Jook Right On: Blues Stories and Blues Storytellers*. Knoxville: U of Tennessee P, 2005.

Pereira, Kim. *August Wilson and the African-American Odyssey*. Urbana: U of Illinois P, 1995.

Perkins, Kathy A., and Judith L. Stephens, eds. *Strange Fruit: Plays on Lynching by American Women*. Bloomington: Indiana UP, 1998.

Plum, Jay. "Blues, History, and the Dramaturgy of August Wilson." *African American Review* 27:4 (Winter 1993): 561–67.

Powers, W. Douglas. "Lifted above Tennessee Williams's *Hot Tin Roof*: Tony Kushner's *Angels in America* as Midrash." *South Atlantic Review* 70:4 (Fall 2005): 119–38.

Price, Marian. "*Cat on a Hot Tin Roof*: The Uneasy Marriage of Success and Idealism." *Modern Drama* 38:3 (Fall 1995): 324–35.

Rashad, Phylicia. Foreword to August Wilson, *Gem of the Ocean*. New York: Theatre Communications Group, 2007.

Rawson, Christopher. "Tarell McCraney, Once an Assistant to August Wilson, Is a Playwright to Watch." *Pittsburgh Post-Gazette*, 13 November 2008. Web. 12 June 2016.

Ray, Benjamin C. *African Religions: Symbol, Ritual, and Community*. Englewood Cliffs, NJ: Prentice-Hall, 1976.

Reed, Ishmael. Foreword to August Wilson, *Jitney*. New York: Theatre Communications Group, 2007.

Rocha, Mark William. "American History as 'Loud Talking' in *Two Trains Running*." In *May All Your Fences Have Gates: Essays on the Drama of August Wilson*, edited by Alan Nadel, 116–32. Iowa City: U of Iowa P, 1994.

Rosen, Carol. "August Wilson: Bard of the Blues." In *Conversations with August Wilson*, edited by Jackson R. Bryer and Mary C. Hartig, 188–203. Jackson: UP of Mississippi, 2006.

Sajnani, Damon. "Troubling the Trope of 'Rapper as Modern Griot.'" *Journal of Pan African Studies* 6:3 (September 2013): 156–80.

Salaam, Kalamu ya. *What Is Life? Reclaiming the Black Blues Self.* Chicago: Third World Press, 1994.

Savran, David. "August Wilson." In *Conversations with August Wilson,* edited by Jackson R. Bryer and Mary C. Hartig, 19–37. Jackson: UP of Mississippi, 2006.

———. *Communists, Cowboys, and Queers: The Politics of Masculinity in the Work of Arthur Miller and Tennessee Williams.* Minneapolis: U of Minnesota P, 1992.

Scheub, Harold. *A Dictionary of African Mythology: The Mythmaker as Storyteller.* Oxford: Oxford UP, 2000.

Selmon, Michael. "'Like . . . so many small theatres': The Panoptic and the Theatric in *Long Day's Journey into Night.*" *Modern Drama* 40:4 (Winter 1997): 526–39.

Shannon, Sandra G. "Audience and Africanisms in August Wilson's Dramaturgy: A Case Study." In *African American Performance and Theater History: A Critical Reader,* edited by Harry J. Elam Jr. and David Krasner. New York: Oxford UP, 2001.

———. "August Wilson Explains His Dramatic Vision: An Interview." In *Conversations with August Wilson,* edited by Jackson R. Bryer and Mary C. Hartig, 118–54. Jackson: UP of Mississippi, 2006.

———. *The Dramatic Vision of August Wilson.* Washington, DC: Howard UP, 1995.

———. "Framing African American Cultural Identity: The Bookends Plays in August Wilson's 10-Play *Cycle.*" *College Literature* 36.2 (Spring 2009): 26–39.

———. "The Good Christian's Come and Gone: The Shifting Role of Christianity in August Wilson's Plays." *MELUS* 16:3 (Autumn 1989): 127–42.

———. "The Ground on Which I Stand: August Wilson's Perspective on African American Women." In *May All Your Fences Have Gates: Essays on the Drama of August Wilson,* edited by Alan Nadel, 150–64. Iowa City: U of Iowa P, 1994.

———. "Sons of the South: An Examination of the Interstices in the Works of August Wilson and Tennessee Williams." In *The Influence of Tennessee Williams: Essays on Fifteen American Playwrights,* edited by Philip C. Kolin, 122–46. Jefferson, NC: McFarland, 2008.

———. "Turn Your Lamp Down Low! Aunt Ester Dies in *King Hedley II.* Now What?" In *August Wilson: Completing the Twentieth-Century Cycle,* edited by Alan Nadel, 123–33. Iowa City: U of Iowa P, 2010.

Shannon, Sandra G., and Dana A. Williams. "A Conversation with August Wilson." In *August Wilson and Black Aesthetics,* edited by Shannon and Williams. New York: Palgrave, 2004.

Sheppard, Vera. "August Wilson: An Interview." In *Conversations with August Wilson,* edited by Jackson R. Bryer and Mary C. Hartig, 101–17. Jackson: UP of Mississippi, 2006.

Smith, Kate Bolger. "Questions of Source in African Cinema: The Heritage of the Griot in Dani Kouyaté's Films." *Journal of African Media Studies* 2:1 (2010): 25–38.

Soyinka, Wole. *Myth, Literature and the African World.* Cambridge: Cambridge UP, 1976.

———. "The Tolerant Gods." In *Orisha Devotion as World Religion,* edited by Jacob K. Olupona and Terry Rey, 31–50. Madison: U of Wisconsin P, 2008.

Spencer, Jon Michael. *Blues and Evil.* Knoxville: U of Tennessee P, 1993.

Steen, Shannon. "Melancholy Bodies: Racial Subjectivity and Whiteness in O'Neill's *The Emperor Jones.*" *Theatre Journal* 52:3 (October 2000): 339–59.

Tate, Claudia. Introduction to *Black Women Writers at Work,* edited by Tate, xv–xxvi. New York: Continuum, 1983.

Temple, Riley Keene. *Aunt Ester's Children Redeemed: Journeys to Freedom in August Wilson's Ten Plays of Twentieth-Century Black America.* Eugene: Cascade Books, 2017.

Timpane, John. "Filling the Time: Reading History in the Drama of August Wilson." In *May All Your Fences Have Gates: Essays on the Drama of August Wilson,* edited by Alan Nadel, 67–85. Iowa City: U of Iowa P, 1994.

Toop, David. *The Rap Attack: African Jive to New York Hip Hop.* Boston: South End 1984.

Tracy, Steven C. "Defining the Blues—Useful/Interesting/Provocative Definitions." In *Write Me a Few of Your Lines: A Blues Reader,* edited by Tracy. Amherst: U of Massachusetts P, 1999.

———. "The Holyistic Blues of *Seven Guitars.*" In *August Wilson: Completing the Twentieth-Century Cycle,* edited by Alan Nadel, 50–79. Iowa City: U of Iowa P, 2010.

———. *Langston Hughes and the Blues.* Urbana: U of Illinois P, 2001.

Tyndall, C. Patrick. "Using Black Rage to Elucidate African and African American Identity in August Wilson's *Joe Turner's Come and Gone* (1911)." In *August Wilson and Black Aesthetics,* edited by Dana A. Williams and Sandra G. Shannon. New York: Palgrave, 2004.

Vega, Morta Moreno. "The Candomblé and Eshu-Eleggua in Brazilian and Cuban Yoruba-Based Ritual." In *Black Theatre: Ritual Performance in the African Diaspora,* edited by Paul Carter Harrison, Victor Leo Walker II, and Gus Edwards. Philadelphia: Temple UP, 2002.

Vera, Yvonne. "Observation as System in Eugene O'Neill's *The Iceman Cometh.*" *Modern Drama* 39:3 (Fall 1996): 448–56.

Wald, Elijah. *Escaping the Delta: Robert Johnson and the Invention of the Blues.* New York: Amistad, 2004.

Walker, Victor Leo, II. Introduction to *Black Theatre: Ritual Performance in the African Diaspora,* edited by Paul Carter Harrison, Victor Leo Walker II, and Gus Edwards, 131–39. Philadelphia: Temple UP, 2002.

Wall, Cheryl A. *Worrying the Line: Black Women Writers, Lineage, and Literary Tradition.* Chapel Hill: U of North Carolina P, 2005.

Watlington, Dennis. "Hurdling Fences." In *Conversations with August Wilson,* edited by Jackson R. Bryer and Mary C. Hartig, 81–89. Jackson: UP of Mississippi, 2006.

West, Cornel. "Hope on a Tightrope." Lecture given at Indiana University, Bloomington, 23 February 2009.
Wetmore, Kevin J., Jr. "Children of Yemayá and the American Eshu: West African Myth in African-American Theatre." In *Dramatic Revisions of Myths, Fairy Tales, and Legends: Essays on Recent Plays*, edited by Verna A. Foster. Jefferson, NC: McFarland, 2012.
White, Stephen K. *The Ethos of the Late-Modern Citizen*. Cambridge, MA: Harvard UP, 2009.
Williams, Dana A., and Sandra G. Shannon, eds. *August Wilson and Black Aesthetics*. New York: Palgrave, 2004.
Williams, Raymond. *Modern Tragedy*. Stanford: Stanford UP, 1966.
Williams, Sherley A. "The Blues Roots of Contemporary Afro-American Poetry." In *Write Me a Few of Your Lines: A Blues Reader*, edited by Steven C. Tracy. Amherst: U of Massachusetts P, 1999.
Williams, Tennessee. *Plays 1931–1955*. New York: Library of America, 2000.
Wilson, August. *August Wilson's How I Learned What I Learned (And How What I Learned Has Led Me to Places I've Wanted to Go. That I have Sometimes Gone Unwillingly is the Crucible in Which Many a Work of Art Has Been Fired.)*. Co-conceived by Todd Kreidler. New York: Samuel French: 2018.
———. *Gem of the Ocean*. New York: Theatre Communications Group, 2007.
———. "The Ground on Which I Stand." New York: Theatre Communications Group, 2001.
———. "How to Write a Play like August Wilson." *New York Times*, 10 March 1991, H5.
———. *Fences*. New York: Theatre Communications Group, 2007.
———. *Jitney*. New York: Theatre Communications Group, 2007.
———. *Joe Turner's Come and Gone*. New York: Theatre Communications Group, 2007.
———. *King Hedley II*. New York: Theatre Communications Group, 2007.
———. *Ma Rainey's Black Bottom*. New York: Theatre Communications Group, 2007.
———. *The Piano Lesson*. New York: Theatre Communications Group, 2007.
———. Preface to *Three Plays*. Pittsburgh: U of Pittsburgh P, 1991.
———. *Radio Golf*. New York: Theatre Communications Group, 2007.
———. *Seven Guitars*. New York: Theatre Communications Group, 2007.
———. *Three Plays*. Pittsburgh: U of Pittsburgh P, 1991.
———. *Two Trains Running*. New York: Theatre Communications Group, 2007.
Winchell, Mark Royden. "Come back to the locker room ag'in, Brick honey!" *Mississippi Quarterly* 48:4 (Fall 1995): 701–12.
Wittgenstein, Ludwig. *Philosophical Investigations*. German text, with a revised English translation, translated by G. E. M. Anscombe. 3rd ed. Malden, MA: Blackwell Publishing, 2001.
Woods, Clyde. *Development Arrested: Race, Power, and the Blues in the Mississippi Delta*. New York: Verso, 1996.

Index

Abili, Obi, 4
Adell, Sandra, 173
Adler, Thomas P., 166
Aeschylus, 7, 10
Africa/Africans: as black American ancestry, 28, 53, 58, 62, 66, 106, 207n33; in Hall, 170; in McCraney, 173, 191–92, 195, 198; in relation to blues, 35, 42, 204n6; in Wilson, 1, 3, 91, 102. *See also* griot; Middle Passage; religion/religiosity
Agamben, Giorgio, 25
American Century Cycle, 5, 8, 12–14, 21, 41, 63–108, 113–14, 117, 128, 130–31, 158, 168, 172–73, 180, 188, 199, 202, 211n86, 211n88; in relation to other Wilson work, 43–44, 56–57, 60–62; performance series, 1–2, 9, 203n2
ancestry: in Africa, 28, 74; as community, 3, 4, 34, 36; in McCraney, 195; in O'Neill, 128; in Wilson, 12, 57–58, 63, 85–92, 100, 167

antiphony (call-and-response): as blues technique, 12, 34–37, 39–40, 60; as dramaturgical method, 6, 13–14, 51, 67–68, 81, 106–8, 201–2; in Hall, 177, 182; in McCraney, 173, 187–90, 192–95, 198–200; as mode of identity crafting, 5, 34–40, 43–44, 47, 49–50, 52, 53; in O'Neill, 111, 114, 117–18, 122–23, 127–31, 137, 138; in Parks, 170; in Williams, 13, 146, 148–51, 155–56, 158, 160, 162–64, 167; in Wilson, 13, 56–57, 59, 70–71, 76–77, 80, 84–85, 88, 89–90, 92, 93, 96–97, 99, 100, 104, 105, 177. *See also* blues; performance
Arnold, David L. G., 93
Awolalu, J. Omosade, 191

Bak, John, 213n5
Baker, Annie, 10
Baker, Houston A., Jr., 10, 23

Baldwin, James, 207n39
Baraka, Amiri: on blues, 7, 19, 22, 32, 34, 35; as influence on Wilson, 57, 74, 141, 142, 207n39
Barlow, Judith E., 117
Bearden, Romare, 18, 57, 207n39
Bechet, Sidney, 34
Bibler, Michael P., 214n14
Bigsby, C. W. E., 147
Bloom, Harold, 7
blues: aesthetic, 12, 18, 43–44, 51, 53, 58, 60–62, 65–67, 81, 178; community, 27–28, 30–31, 34, 36–39, 40–41, 52, 68, 71–73, 76, 77–78, 80, 82–88, 89–90, 92–94, 97, 98–99, 100, 102, 106–7, 111–18, 120–21, 137, 138–39, 144–45, 150, 160–61, 167–68, 170–71, 173, 200; dramaturgy, 4–8, 12, 55–57, 60–61, 63–108, 144, 149, 167, 175, 186, 200, 201–2; ethos, 5, 12, 18, 32, 39, 42–62, 64, 67, 97, 113–14, 178; history and development, 20–22; humor, 12, 31, 38–39, 40, 58; music, 4, 7, 11–12, 18, 20–22, 27–37, 33, 35–40, 42–43, 50–51, 60, 64–66, 81, 94, 103, 163–64, 179, 207n46, 209n48; Wilson's influence of, 17–19, 39, 42, 49–51, 65, 206n3. *See also* antiphony; performance
Bogumil, Mary L., 57, 71, 75, 88, 210n68, 211n86
Borges, Jorge Luis, 207n39
Brooklyn Academy of Music, 9
Brustein, Robert, 46, 54, 207n28, 207n33
Bullins, Ed, 141, 207n39
Butler, Judith, 25, 35, 46

call-and-response. *See* antiphony
Carby, Hazel, 103, 172
Cavarero, Adriana, 33–34, 39
Chekhov, Anton, 54
Clark, Keith, 90–91
Clum, John M., 158, 215n17
Cobb, James C., 20
Colbert, Soyica Diggs: on Baraka, 74; on Hall, 175–76; on influence, 9; on McCraney, 193–95, 197, 216n27; on Wilson, 68, 69, 74, 209n48
Comentale, Edward P., 19–20, 23, 37–38
Cone, James H., 23, 36
Crawford, Eileen, 89
Cruse, Harold, 54

Davis, Angela Y., 19, 25, 27, 29, 103
Davis, Doris, 102
Deleuze, Gilles, 10
Dixon, Willie, 207n46
Dollard, John, 205n33
Dowling, Robert M., 118, 139
drama, American, 2–4, 6–11, 12, 13–14, 55, 111, 115, 117, 139, 141–43, 145–46, 151
Du Bois, W. E. B, 7, 26

Edwards, David Honeyboy, 25, 32
Eisen, Kurt, 212n21
Elam, Harry J., Jr.: on "The Ground on Which I Stand," 54; on *How I Learned What I Learned*, 56; on masculinity in Wilson, 91; on Wilson and blues, 42, 64, 65–66, 206n3; on Wilson and history, 8; on Wilson's female characters, 79, 99, 102, 103
Ellison, Ralph, 23, 38, 58; *Invisible Man*, 49

Farhoudi, Houriyeh, 212n12
female identity, 46; in Hall, 13, 170, 171–72, 173–86; in McCraney, 194–95; in O'Neill, 116–17, 127–30, 135–37; in Wilson, 78–80, 98–106

Fences, 56, 80, 203n1; Bono as blues griot in, 84, 90; fatherhood in, 2, 120; McCraney's reference to, 188; in relation to *Death of a Salesman*, 10–11; romantic imperative in, 100; Rose Maxson as blueswoman in, 67, 81, 102–4, 186; Troy Maxson as warrior in, 2, 5, 77, 81, 89–97, 111, 128, 210n52, 210n68
Fisher, James, 142, 214n12

Gadamer, Hans-Georg, 8–9
Garon, Paul, 40
Garvey, Marcus, 211n88
Gates, Henry Louis, Jr., 29, 45, 47, 54, 107, 216n21
Gem of the Ocean, 89; Aunt Ester in, 2, 85–88, 102; Caesar Wilks in, 1, 114, 123; Citizen Barlow's journey of identity in, 5, 86–87, 112, 121, 131, 137, 161, 167; City of Bones scene in, 3, 63–67, 141, 188, 196, 198; in relation to *Emperor Jones, The*, 3–4; romantic imperative in, 100, 101, 104–5; Solly Two Kings in, 120
Gener, Randy, 42
Glaspell, Susan, 9
God: in Hall, 175–76, 177; in McCraney, 198; in O'Neill, 113, 124–26, 127, 131; in Wilson, 86, 143. *See also* religion/religiosity
Grant, Sinikka, 70
Greene Space, The, 1–2, 9
griot, 36, 73–74 208n25, 209n37; in Wilson (blues griot), 73–78, 81–88, 89, 90, 92, 93, 95, 104, 106, 144, 210n52
"Ground on Which I Stand, The," 12, 44, 52–56, 207n30
Guattari, Félix, 10
Gussow, Adam, 20, 22–23, 24–26, 28, 29, 30, 180, 210n55
Guthrie, Woody, 163

Hale, Thomas A., 36, 73–74
Hall, Katori, 6, 13, 169–86, 188, 201–2; *Children of Killers*, 170; *Hoodoo Love*, 172, 174–75, 178–81, 182, 184–86; *Hurt Village*, 172, 174–75, 181–86; *The Mountaintop*, 174–79, 182, 184–86; *Our Lady of Kibeho*, 170; *Saturday Night/Sunday Morning*, 170
Hansberry, Lorraine, 9, 141; *A Raisin in the Sun*, 9
Harrison, Paul Carter, 5, 20, 42, 91, 207n33
Hartman, Saidiya, 29
Henderson, Stephen McKinley, 1, 55
heteronormativity: in American history, 143; in McCraney, 189, 196, 200; in Ovid, 164–65; in Williams, 143, 145–46, 146–47, 151, 155–60, 163–68; in Wilson, 101–103, 188
Hill District. *See* Pittsburgh
history: and aesthetic influence, 6–7, 12; Wilson's use of, 8, 55, 57–58, 64–67, 68, 106, 208n7. *See also* griot
Holbert, Luther, 24–25
Holiday, Billie, 22
Honig, Bonnie, 32, 38–39
"Hoochie-Coochie Man," 30–31
Hooker, John Lee, 28
hooks, bell, 78
House, Son, 18, 27–31, 33, 34, 35, 37–38, 61
How I Learned What I Learned, 12, 44, 56–61, 199
Hughes, Langston, 18, 38, 40, 49, 106
humanism: blues as, 11–12, 23–24, 27–28, 31–39, 40–41, 50–51, 200; in Hall, 185; in McCraney, 195–96; in orisha, 191, 216n25; theater as, 14, 26, 52–56, 62, 107, 169, 202; in Williams, 150; in Wilson, 64–65, 68, 77, 81, 84, 87–88, 99–101
Hurston, Zora Neal, 18, 106, 186

influence: aesthetic, 6–11; of Williams on successors, 213n1; on Wilson, 43, 207n39; of Wilson on audiences, 6–11, 12–14; of Wilson on successors, 5–6, 13, 169–73, 188, 198–200, 201–2
Irish Repertory Theatre, 3–4

Jim Crow: as dehumanization, 11, 24–26, 40; history and development, 19–20, 204n9; performance as resistance to, 11–12, 20–24, 26–28, 32–33, 40–41, 200
Jitney, 66; Booster as warrior in, 89, 96–97; Booster's journey of identity in, 111; fatherhood in, 2, 97; pre-*Cycle* version of, 80, 203n1; Rena in, 104
Joe Turner's Come and Gone: Bynum as blues griot in, 70–75, 85, 87, 90, 106, 210n52; Herald Loomis as warrior in, 75–78, 88–92, 96, 143, 179; Herald Loomis's journey of identity in, 97, 161; Herald Loomis's vision in, 63–67, 72–73, 188, 196, 198; Mattie Campbell as blueswoman in, 78–80, 128, 186; romantic imperative in, 98, 99, 100, 103–5, 211n86; space in, 149, 170; as Wilson's signature play, 67–83, 208n12
Johnson, Robert, 18
Jones, LeRoi. *See* Baraka, Amiri
Jongintaba, Yahya. *See* Spencer, Jon Michael
Joseph, May, 54

Karade, Baba Ifa, 216nn23–24
Kazan, Elia, 145
King Hedley II, 1–2, 66, 88; fatherhood in, 2; King Hedley II as warrior in, 65, 77, 89, 92, 96, 112; romantic imperative in, 101, 103, 104; Ruby as blueswoman in, 209n48; Stool Pigeon in, 2, 88, 89
King, Kimball, 164

King, Martin Luther, Jr., 175
Kolin, Philip C., 168, 213n1, 213n3
Kreidler, Todd, 56, 57
Kubik, Gerhard, 204n6
Kushner, Tony, 93, 105

Lahr, John, 166
Lawson, R. A., 20, 23, 28, 34, 204n9
Lead Belly. *See* Ledbetter, Huddie
Ledbetter, Huddie (Lead Belly), 21, 22, 163
Leon, Kenny, 9
Levine, Lawrence, 36
Livingston, Dinah, 46
Locke, Alain, 26
Lomax, Alan, 21, 33–34
lynching, 11, 22, 28, 29, 32; as dehumanization, 23–26
lynching plays, 26–27, 41

Ma Rainey's Black Bottom, 42, 63–64, 80; homoeroticism in, 102–3, 188; Levee as warrior in, 2, 64, 67, 77, 81, 89, 90, 91, 92, 93, 95–96, 97, 111, 114, 124, 144, 210n52; Ma Rainey as blueswoman in, 98; romantic imperative in, 102–3; Sturdyvant as Devil in, 210n55; Toledo as blues griot in, 64, 65, 73, 81, 82–84, 85, 87, 88, 90, 106. *See also* Rainey, Ma
Malcolm X, 86, 211n88
Mamet, David, 54
Marlowe, Christopher, 7
masculinity: in American culture, 113, 143; in Hall, 179–80; in McCraney, 196, 198, 200; in Williams, 6, 13, 141–68, 213n5, 214–15n14; in Wilson, 78–79, 90–92, 188, 211n86
McClinton, Marion, 7
McCraney, Tarell Alvin, 6, 13, 169–73, 187–202; *Brother/Sister Plays, The*, 13, 170–71, 188–90, 192, 194, 196, 198,

199–201; *Brothers Size, The,* 188, 189, 191, 192, 195, 196, 199, 200; *Choir Boy,* 187–88, 189, 198; *Head of Passes,* 171, 188, 198; *In the Red and Brown Water,* 189–90, 191, 192–93, 194–95, 196–97, 199, 200; *Marcus: Or the Secret of the Sweet,* 189, 190, 193, 195–96, 197, 199, 200; *Wig Out!,* 187–88, 189, 198, 200
McGhee, Brownie, 22
McGinley, Paige A., 21, 22, 30
McNally, Terrence, 54
Middle Passage, 3, 63, 74, 173, 196, 198
Miller, Arthur, 10–11, 55, 141, 213n1
Miller, Karl Hagstrom, 21
Mills, Alice, 210n52
Mississippi Delta, 19–20, 24–26, 32–33, 107, 204n9
Mitchell, Koritha, 26
Morisseau, Dominique, 169–70
Morocco, Cy, 59
Morrison, Toni, 174, 180, 209n36
Moyers, Bill, 45, 47
Muhammad, Elijah, 58, 211n88
Murphy, Brenda, 93, 113, 214n13
Murray, Albert, 17, 23

Nietzsche, Friedrich, 113, 127

Oakley, Giles, 24, 25, 28
Oliver, King, 163
O'Neill, Eugene, 3–4, 6–9, 11, 12–13, 111–40, 141, 166, 176, 213n1; *Beyond the Horizon,* 112; *Desire Under the Elms,* 115, 116, 124–31, 132, 137, 176; *The Emperor Jones,* 3–4, 111, 114, 115–16, 117–24, 126, 128, 130, 132, 137, 212n10; *The Hairy Ape,* 115–16, 117–24, 126, 128, 130, 132, 137, 176, 212n12; *The Iceman Cometh,* 9, 11, 111, 115, 116–17, 131–37, 138, 212–13n21; *Long Day's Journey into Night,* 115,

116–17, 131–37, 212nn19–20; *Mourning Becomes Electra,* 111, 115, 116, 124–31, 132, 137; *Strange Interlude,* 139
O'Reilly, Ciarán, 4
Ovid, 164–65

Paller, Michael, 213–14n9
Palmer, Robert, 73
Parchman Farm, 33, 67
Parks, Suzan-Lori, 10, 141, 170
Pereira, Kim, 69, 91, 95
performance: of identity, 18, 23–24, 28–41, 43–44, 186, 209n37; —, "The Ground on Which I Stand" as, 12, 44, 52–56; —, in Hall, 172, 174–77, 180, 183–84, 186; —, *How I Learned What I Learned* as, 12, 44, 56–61; —, in McCraney, 173, 187, 192–201; —, in O'Neill, 123, 126, 128, 136, 138; —, in Williams, 142–50, 154–55, 158, 162–66; —, in Wilson, 67, 68, 69–74, 76, 81, 85–88, 99, 102; —, Wilson's interviews as, 12, 44, 56–61; of music, 11–12, 27–28, 28–31, 33–39, 40–41; of theater, 1–4, 9–11, 12–14, 26, 56–61, 106–8, 166–68
Perkins, Kathy A., 26
Piano Lesson, The, 56, 67, 98; Berniece as blueswoman in, 81, 99–100, 102, 103; Boy Willie as warrior in, 77, 81, 89, 96, 123, 124; Boy Willie's journey of identity in, 97, 114; Doaker as blues griot in, 81, 84, 87, 210n52; productions of, 9; romantic imperative in, 99–100, 103, 104, 105, 143; space in, 149; Wining Boy in, 117
Pittsburgh, 13, 47, 50, 57, 59, 87–88, 92–93, 170, 171
Plum, Jay, 42, 65–66
Powers, W. Douglas, 213–14n9
Price, Marian, 215n21

Princeton University, 112
Provincetown Players, 4, 112, 113, 139

queer identity: in McCraney, 13, 171–73, 187–201; in Williams, 13, 143–46, 146–50, 151, 154–58, 165, 168, 213–14n9, 214n12, 215n17; in Wilson, 101, 102–3

race/racial identity, 7, 10–11, 13–14, 19, 111–40, 202; in O'Neill (whiteness), 12–13, 111–40; in Williams, 214n14; of Wilson, 45–56, 58, 61–62
Radio Golf, 1, 2, 80; Elder Joseph Barlow as blues griot in, 73, 85, 88; Harmond Wilks's journey of identity in, 64, 67, 88, 97, 112, 116, 131, 137, 167; Mame Wilks as blueswoman in, 104–5, 186; romantic imperative in, 103; Roosevelt Hicks in, 114, 144
Rainey, Ma (historical performer), 21, 42, 103, 179
rap music, 181–83
Rashad, Phylicia, 69
Rawson, Christopher, 215n4
Ray, Benjamin C., 191
Reconstruction, 11, 19–20, 45
Reed, Ishmael, 211n88
religion/religiosity: church, 36–37; in Hall, 175; in McCraney, 173, 190–96, 197, 200–201, 216–17n28; in O'Neill, 125–27; in Wilson, 1, 75; Yoruba, 28, 91, 216n21, 216nn23–25. *See also* God
Richards, Lloyd, 9, 57
Rocha, Mark William, 107

Sajnani, Damon, 208n25
Salaam, Kalamu ya, 18, 19, 20, 32, 38, 43, 45, 66
Santiago-Hudson, Ruben, 1, 9

Savran, David, 144–45, 157, 159–60, 166–67, 168, 214n12
Scheub, Harold, 216n24
Selmon, Michael, 212n19
Seven Guitars, 1–2, 63–64, 65, 114; Floyd Barton as warrior in, 77, 89, 92–94, 96, 97, 112, 115, 123; romantic imperative in, 98–101, 103, 104; space in, 170; Vera as blueswoman in, 81
Shakespeare, William, 7, 185
Shannon, Sandra G: on Aunt Ester, 85; on *Ma Rainey's Black Bottom*, 65, 82; on Williams and Wilson, 141–42; on Wilson and African American identity, 7, 144, 208n7; on Wilson and blues, 18, 41, 42, 64, 65; on Wilson's biography, 47, 49; on Wilson's female characters, 78–79, 98
Signifyin(g), 28–34, 37, 40, 44–51, 107–8, 194
Smith, Bessie, 28, 43, 61, 163, 179, 186; influence on Wilson, 4, 18, 21, 50
Smith, Kate Bolger, 209n37
social identity crafting (defined), 5–8, 11–14, 19, 23–24, 26–28, 30–41, 142
Sophocles, 7, 10, 39
Soyinka, Wole, 191, 195–96, 197, 216n25, 216n28, 217n38
space: in Hall, 13, 170; in McCraney, 13, 170–71; in Morisseau, 169; in O'Neill, 121, 134, 212–13n21; in Williams, 144, 149; in Wilson, 5, 149, 170
Spencer, Jon Michael (Yahya Jongintaba), 23, 36, 191–92
spirituality. *See* religion/religiosity
Steen, Shannon, 212n10
Stephens, Judith L., 26

Tangle Eye, 33–34
Tate, Claudia, 174

Temple, Riley Keene, 64, 68, 86, 88
Tharpe, Sister Rosetta, 22
Thompson, John Douglas, 4
Timpane, John, 90
Toop, David, 208n25
Tracy, Steven C., 64, 65, 205n48
tragedy, 10, 217n38; in Hall, 174–75, 184; in O'Neill, 12, 114–18, 121, 126, 131–32, 137–39; in Wilson, 84, 89, 93–94
Two Trains Running, 11; Aunt Ester as blues griot in, 2, 85–87; Holloway as blues griot in, 2, 81, 84–85, 210n52; Risa as blueswoman in, 101, 103, 128, 186; romantic imperative in, 99, 100–105; space in, 149, 170; Sterling Johnson as warrior in, 77, 89; Sterling Johnson's journey of identity in, 111, 114
Tyndall, C. Patrick, 106

Vega, Morta Moreno, 217n40
Vera, Yvonne, 212–13n21
voice, 33–35, 39

Wald, Elijah, 21–22, 24
Walker, Alice, 180
Walker, Victor Leo, II, 216n21
"Walkin' Blues," 27–28, 29–31, 33
Wall, Cheryl A., 171–72, 179, 180
Waller, Fats, 163
warrior, Wilsonian, 75–78, 80, 81, 88–97, 98, 100, 105, 106, 210n52, 210n68; comparisons to O'Neill's characters, 111, 115–16, 123, 139; comparisons to Williams's characters, 142, 144, 146, 155
Washington, Booker T., 84, 211n88
Waters, Muddy, 18, 30–31, 106, 112, 113
Watlington, Dennis, 46
West, Cornel, 22, 36–37, 61

Wetmore, Kevin J., Jr., 193–96, 198–99
White, Stephen K., 39
Williams, Chawley, 59
Williams, Dana A., 207n28, 208n12
Williams, Raymond, 213n23
Williams, Sherley A., 34–35
Williams, Tennessee, 6–8, 11, 13, 141–68, 172, 189, 213n1, 213n3, 213n5, 214nn12–13; *Cat on a Hot Tin Roof,* 144, 145, 150–58, 159, 163, 164, 165, 166, 213–14n9, 214–15n14, 215n21; *The Glass Menagerie,* 144, 145, 146–51, 156, 157–58, 159, 160, 164, 165, 166, 167, 213–14n9; *Orpheus Descending,* 145, 158–66, 168, 215n17; *A Streetcar Named Desire,* 144, 145, 160, 165, 167; "Three Players of a Summer Game," 213n2
Wilson, August: importance to American drama, 2–14, 111, 117, 142, 145–46, 169; influence of blues, 17–19, 39, 42, 49–51, 65, 206n3; interviews, 12, 44–51, 59, 60; racial identity, 45–56, 58, 61–62. See also *American Century Cycle; Fences; Gem of the Ocean;* "Ground on Which I Stand, The"; *Jitney; Joe Turner's Come and Gone; How I Learned What I Learned; King Hedley II; Ma Rainey's Black Bottom; Piano Lesson, The; Radio Golf; Seven Guitars; Two Trains Running*
Wilson, Daisy, 47–48
Winchell, Mark Royden, 156, 214n14
Wittgenstein, Ludwig, 81
Woods, Clyde, 20

Yoruba. *See under* religion/religiosity

Zolfaghari, Yaser, 212n12

www.ingramcontent.com/pod-product-compliance
Lightning Source LLC
Chambersburg PA
CBHW021139230426
43667CB00005B/189